EXPLORING
THE
UNEXPLAINED

EXPLORING
THE
UNEXPLAINED

A Practical Guide to the Peculiar People,
Places, and Things in the Bible

Trent Butler

THOMAS NELSON
Since 1798

NASHVILLE   DALLAS   MEXICO CITY   RIO DE JANEIRO

Published in Nashville, Tennessee, by Thomas Nelson. Thomas Nelson is a registered trademark of Thomas Nelson, Inc.

Thomas Nelson, Inc., titles may be purchased in bulk for educational, business, fund-raising, or sales promotional use. For information, please e-mail SpecialMarkets@ThomasNelson.com.

Unless otherwise noted, Scripture quotations are taken from THE NEW KING JAMES VERSION. © 1982 by Thomas Nelson, Inc. Used by permission. All rights reserved.

ISBN: 978-1-4016-7521-9

Printed in the United States of America

12 13 14 15 16 QG 6 5 4 3 2 1

Contents

Introduction

A peculiar book lies before you. This book isn't peculiar because it is about the Bible, but much of what the Bible says can be peculiar to our modern ears. Here we will explore and elaborate upon some of the more unusal aspects of the Bible's people, places, events, things, and stories. Its peculiar people range from a 969-year-old man, still alive and kicking, to a young lad who ran away from Roman soldiers without any clothes on. Its peculiar places include a city turned to salt and a foreign capital whose people repent and follow God after hearing a five-word sermon. Its peculiar events span from a father ready to sacrifice his son on an altar, to a young man falling to his death after a sermon puts him to sleep. There are also peculiar things in the Bible, like a giant's armor on a young kid or, most important and peculiar of all, a blood-stained cross serving as the torture and death instrument for an innocent man. Some stories seem strange to modern readers, like Deuteronomy's call to annihilate whole nations or Jesus' call for disciples to take up a cross and follow Him. This book will explore these issues, and many like them.

What makes something peculiar, especially something in the Bible? There are several ways:

1. It can be odd or noticeably different, like Noah's ark.

2. It can be strange or not fitting normal expectations, such as manna in the wilderness.

3. It can be weird or out of sync with daily life, such as the giant Anakim or Nephilim.

4. It can simply be unusual or rare, like the man with six fingers on each hand and six toes on each foot.

5. It may be irregular, as the observance of Passover in the second month of the year instead of on the first month.

6. It may be uncharacteristic, like Jesus the Jew deciding to go through Samaria rather than bypassing it.

7. It can be unique, such as Jesus the true God/man.

Peculiar Uses for a Peculiar Dictionary

You go to a dictionary to find the meaning of a word or its spelling, but this dictionary offers much more. It skips over the people, places, and things you already know about, and focuses on the things that you might not understand and sometimes avoid. This peculiar dictionary invites you to develop new and interesting ways to put it to good use. Here are a few suggestions:

1. Look up a biblical person, place, or thing whose meaning or location in Scripture you cannot recall.

2. Read all the significant passages about the term you are investigating.

3. Learn how to spell unusual names and words.

4. Play a game with family or friends. Let one person be the biblical "sage." The sage will open the dictionary to a page at random and ask a specific player or team to define, spell, and locate in Scripture a term on that page.

5. Play a game with family or friends. Let a chosen sage open the dictionary, select a word, and announce its meaning without giving the players the actual word. Give the Book and Chapter in the Bible where the term is found, and challenge the others to guess the word. The sage may find it necessary to provide clues such as identifying the term as a person, place, or thing, give approximate location in the chapter, such as a verse that comes before the term or after the term, or give the beginning word of the verse.

6. Assign a page of the dictionary to each individual, pair of people, or team. Give them time to read the page and select the term whose "issue" they are most interested in discussing. Let each individual or group lead the participants in a discussion of the issue raised and how that issue applies to their specific location and culture today.

Happy dictionarying, you quite peculiar people! (See Ex. 19:5; Deut. 14:2; 26:18; Ps. 135:4; Titus 2:14; 1 Peter 2:9 KJV.)

A

Aaron *Person* Lev. 10:1–7

Aaron was the priest who could not mourn his sons, who spoke for Moses, and who formed a golden calf. The brother of Moses and Miriam and the first high priest, he joined Moses in the sin of unbelief that kept them from entering the Holy Land (Num. 20:7–13).

Issue: How can a godly person do marvelous things for God, and yet still commit flagrant sins?

Aaron's Rod *Thing* Ex. 7–8; 17; Num. 16; 20:7–11

Aaron's rod was a shepherd's staff that became a snake, produced water, and blossomed. God used Aaron's rod or staff to perform miracles in Egypt and in the wilderness.

Issue: What earthly objects can God use for His purposes? What power do magic wands and wizards' rods have?

Abaddon *Place* Job 26:6; 28:22; 31:12; Ps. 88:11; Prov. 15:11; 27:20; Rev. 9:11

Abaddon literally means "Destruction." It is the home of the dead and personified as the angel of the bottomless pit. It is used in parallel with Sheol and Death. Abaddon is known and controlled by God.

Issue: What is your destiny after death?

Abana *Place* 2 Kings 5:12

Abana was a beautiful Syrian river flowing through Damascus where Naaman wanted to be cleansed. God sent him instead to the muddy Jordan. See also Pharpar.

Issue: Why does God often choose a particular place to work even when it seems inferior to another place?

Abba   *Person*   Mark 14:36; Rom. 8:15; Gal. 4:6

Abba is the Aramaic word for "father" that Jesus used when talking to God. It shows the intimacy of the relationship between Father and Son. Believers can know that intimacy and use that term in speaking with God.

Issue: How intimate and trusting are you with God in your prayer life? Do you keep certain things buried in your heart that you do not share with your Heavenly Father?

Abdon   *Person*   Judg. 12:13–15

Abdon was a wealthy judge of Israel who had forty sons, thirty nephews, and seventy donkeys. He judged Israel for eight years.

Issue: Is wealth a requirement for leadership?

Abednego   *Person*   Dan. 1:7; 2:48–3:30

Abednego is the Babylonian name for the Hebrew youth Azariah, who was thrown into and survived the deadly flames of the king's fiery furnace. He worshipped God even though it meant disobeying the king. He became one of the political leaders of the Babylonian Empire because he obeyed God.

Issue: Are you willing to trust God when people threaten to kill you?

Abel's Sacrifice   *Thing*   Gen. 4; Heb. 11:4

God accepted the fattest of Abel's flock as a sacrifice while rejecting his brother Cain's plant or fruit offering. God's displeasure is with Cain and his attitude, not with the nature of the sacrifice. Cain did not do what was right.

Issue: How do you know if God is pleased with you and your service for Him?

Abiathar *Person* 1 Sam. 22–23

Abiathar was the high priest who escaped King Saul with an ephod, their means of communicating with God. Israel's first king had Doeg the Edomite kill the priests and take each one's ephod. Abiathar preserved an ephod and turned it over to David, Saul's chief opponent. Once David's high priest and chief counselor, Abiathar supported Adonijah to succeed David, so Solomon deposed him to live in Anathoth.

Issue: Abiathar served Saul, then David, then Adonijah. When should you change your allegiance from one party to another? What do past loyalties gain you in the present circumstances?

Abigail *Person* 1 Sam. 23:9; 25; 30

Abigail was the wife of the foolish Nabal. When he refused sustenance for David and his fleeing troops, she quickly provided an excess of food. After Nabal's death, she married David, who later rescued her from the Amalekites.

Issue: When is a woman justified in associating with and assisting a male friend when her husband refuses to help as he should?

Abihu *Person* Ex. 6:23; 24:9–10; 28:1; Lev. 10

Aaron's second son, Abihu saw God during Israel's covenant ceremony on Mount Sinai and was ordained with his brothers as priests. Seeking to imitate the power and authority Moses and Aaron had demonstrated in bringing God's glory to appear before the people, they offered strange, unauthorized fire to God and were killed for it.

Issue: Can you worship God in the ways He has described and approved of, or will you invent your own strange ways that God does not accept? How do you determine what types of worship God accepts? Do you, at times, try to gain authority and praise through the ways you lead worship?

Abimelech   *Person*   Judg. 9

Abimelech killed sixty-nine of his half-brothers to become the leader of Israel. His name means "My father is king" but his father Gideon refused the offer of kingship. Abimelech hired a lawless mob for an army rather than summoning an Israelite army and was denounced by his own half brother. Abimelech was defeated when a woman dropped a millstone on his head. He had his armor-bearer run him through rather than suffering an ignoble death by a woman.

Issue: Do you operate and seek power from within or without the traditional power structure? How far are you willing to go to get power for yourself when you are not in line to occupy positions of power?

Abinadab   *Person*   1 Sam. 7; 2 Sam. 6

The ark of the covenant stayed at Abinadab's house twenty years. His son was named priest for the ark and helped to take it to Jerusalem. Apparently, Abinadab was a well-respected priest and community leader of the Gibeonites and their major worship place at Kiriath-jearim. Such a description is built on scholarly reconstructions more than on strict biblical statements.

Issue: What qualifications does a person have to have to serve in God's sanctuary?

Abiram   *Person*   Num. 16; 26

Abiram was swallowed by the earth when he sought priestly authority and function in rebellion against Moses and Aaron.

Issue: God's offices are God-appointed, not self-appointed. How does this affect political power?

Abishag   *Person*   1 Kings 1–2

Abishag served as a bed-warmer for the dying King David. Solomon's brother Adonijah was executed when he asked for her hand in marriage.

Issue: Do political marriages often lead to doubt, distrust, and death?

Ablutions   *Thing*   Ex. 29:4; 30:19–21; Lev. 8:6; 11–15; Mark 7:3–4; Heb. 6:2; 9:10

Ablutions were special baths to remove ritual impurities. People were required to take such baths to become eligible to participate in worship. The ritual of Christian baptism has supplanted ablutions for making people clean.

Issue: What rituals or rites does a person have to participate in to please and approach God?

Abomination   *Thing*   Dan. 9:27; 11:31; 12:11; Matt. 24:15; Mark 13:14

The Bible denounces several things as abominations hated by God. The sacrificing of a pig on an altar to Zeus in the Temple of Jerusalem by Syrian ruler Antiochus IV Epiphanes is an example. It was part of his program to force Jews to adopt Hellenistic (Greek) culture and practices. This example was reinterpreted by later writers as the destruction of Jerusalem by Roman General Titus. It has also been interpreted eschatologically.

Issue: What is the most hideous religious practice you can imagine? How would you react if someone forced you to engage in this practice?

Absalom   *Person*   2 Sam. 15–18

Absalom was a son of David whose hair got caught in a tree as he led rebellion against his father. He claimed David did not punish his brother Ammon when he raped their sister Tamar and that David did not maintain a justice system for the people. Joab, commander of David's army, killed Absalom while he dangled by his hair in the tree.

Issue: How does one correct a system that has gone wrong?

Abyss   *Place*   Luke 8:31; Rom. 10:7; Rev. 9:11; 17:8; 20

Abyss means "without a bottom"; it is used in the Bible as a dark dwelling place of the dead ruled by Abaddon, or the place where Satan is bound and the satanic forces live.

Issue: Where do you think a person goes after death? What will happen to you when you die?

Acacia Wood   *Thing*   Ex. 25–38

Timber ants find acacia wood too bitter to eat. It is also too dense for water or other liquids to penetrate so acacia trees do not decay. Because of this, acacia wood was used to build the tabernacle.

Issue: What type of building materials should one use in a building for God?

Accent   *Thing*   Judg. 12:5–6; Matt. 26:73

An accent is a peculiarity of a person's speech pattern that connects the speaker with a particular geographical region. For example, Ephraimites could not pronounce Shibboleth, and Peter's accent reflected his upbringing in Galilee.

Issue: Whom do you recognize by their accent? How do you respond to an accent?

Aceldama   *Thing*   Matt. 27:7; Acts 1:19

Aceldama is the biblical name for the field that Judas bought with his thirty shekels of silver and where he hung himself.

Issue: Is suicide ever justified?

Achan   *Person*   Josh. 7

Achan's disobedience caused his family to be stoned to death. He took spoils from the battle of Jericho and hid them in his tent, a crime that led God to bring defeat on Joshua's army at Ai. Achan's case illustrates the use of the lot (casting lots) to determine God's will.

Issue: Why kill a sinner's family? How is it fair for one man's sin to lead to the execution of his entire family?

Achish *Person*   1 Sam. 21; 27–31

Achish is the Philistine ruler before whom David acted like a madman in order to escape. Later David joined Achish's army, but other Philistine leaders would not let David join them in battle against Saul and Jonathan.

Issue: How do you prevent a prospective employee from deceiving you and manipulating you?

Achzib *Place*   Josh. 15:44; Mic. 1:14

Achzib is the town whose name means Place of Deceitfulness.

Issue: How does an entire town earn the name of deceitfulness?

Acrostic *Thing*   Pss. 9–10; 25; 34; 111–12; 119; 145; Prov. 31:10–31; Lam. 1–4

An acrostic is a literary device in which the lines of each section begin with a letter of the alphabet in sequence (Eng. a, b, c; Heb. aleph, beth, gimmel). See especially Ps. 119.

Issue: Christian witness in oral or written form should reflect the best possible use of literary devices to make the gospel presentation sharp and interesting. What are some other literary devices you can use?

Adam *Person*   Gen. 1:26–27; 2:15–16; 4:1, 25; 5:3–4; Luke 3:38; 1 Cor. 15:45; 2 Cor. 11:3; 1 Tim. 2:11–15

Adam was the first man. God took Adam's rib and used it to create Eve. Enticed into eating the fruit of the Tree of Knowledge by a talking serpent, they disobeyed God and were cursed. The curse resulted in their being afraid of God, pain in childbirth, hierarchal family life, and the land requiring hard work to remove weeds and produce fruit. Ultimately, their lack of trust brought death to humankind. Their sin, seen as "original sin" in Christian theology, affects every human being.

Issue: How does this origin of the human race through the creation of one couple relate to scientific theory?

Admah   *Place*   Gen. 10:19; 14; 19:29; Deut. 29:23; Hos. 11:8

Admah was a city destroyed with Sodom and Gomorrah. God's love kept Him from destroying Israel.

Issue: How are God's love and God's wrath related?

Adoni-bezek   *Person*   Judg. 1:5–7

Adoni-bezek was a king who cut off the thumbs and big toes of seventy kings. Israel, in turn, cut off his thumbs and big toes.

Issue: Why cut his thumbs off? Do people suffer precise retribution for their sins?

Adonijah   *Person*   2 Sam. 3:4; 1 Kings 1–2

David's fourth son, Adonijah, tried to assume the throne against David and then Solomon. Following this, Nathan established David's line of God-chosen succession that took the place of tradition-mandated first-born succession.

Issue: Does church or societal leadership go to the person God chooses? How can you tell?

Adoniram   *Person*   1 Kings 4:6; 5:14; 12:18

Adoniram was stoned to death for managing Rehoboam's forced labor gangs, an act that led Israel to ultimately rebel against Judah.

Issue: Would you continue in a job that causes you to treat other people unjustly or cruelly?

Adoni-zedek   *Person*   Josh. 10:1–26

Adoni-zedek was a king of Jerusalem who led the southern coalition against Joshua in revenge for Israel supporting the Gibeonites.

Issue: What role does shame or revenge play in your decisions and actions?

Adoption   *Thing*   Rom. 8–9; Gal. 4:5

The transference of a sinner into a child and heir of God when he puts his faith in the Father is called adoption. It is a state of being in which the believer lives through Christ's death and resurrection and has equal rights and responsibilities with other members of God's family.

Issue: How do you enter the family of God? When did you do so?

Adultery   *Thing*   Ex. 20:14; Hos. 4:11–14; Matt. 15:19; John 8; 1 Cor. 6:9; Gal. 5:19

Adultery involves breaking marriage vows in order to have an intimate relationship with someone other than one's marriage partner. Jesus identified it as a thought in the heart, not just the physical act.

Issue: Why should a person limit sexual activity to his or her spouse?

Advocate   *Thing*   John 14:16, 26; 15:26; 16:7; 1 John 2:1

An advocate is one who prays for believers when they sin. Jesus ascended to heaven to advocate on the behalf of believers. The Greek term is *parakletos*.

Issue: What is Jesus doing on behalf of believers today?

Aeneas   *Person*   Acts 9:33–34

Aeneas was bedridden for eight years until he met Peter, who healed him.

Issue: What is the relationship between healing and evangelism?

Agabus   *Person*   Acts 11:27–29; 21:10–11

The prophet Agabus's bad news led the church to start a new ministry. He warned of a coming famine, and the church began hunger relief work.

Issue: What is the church's response to a direct Word from God?

Agape   *Thing*   John 3:16; 1 Cor. 13

Agape is Greek for selfless love. It is the self-giving lifestyle to which God calls us.

Issue: What is the central devotion point of your life?

Age to Come   *Thing*   Matt. 12:32; Mark 10:30; Luke 18:30; Eph. 1:21; 2:7; 1 Tim. 6:19; Heb. 6:5

The age to come is the true "new age," when eternal identities are revealed and the imperfections of this age disappear.

Issue: How and when does God reward His people and fulfill all His promises? In what way will you be part of the new age to come?

Agur   *Person*   Prov. 30

Agur authored a set of proverbs that eventually became part of Solomon's book of Proverbs.

Issue: Describe your understanding of inspiration and authority of Scripture as revealed in the case of Agur.

Ahab   *Person*   1 Kings 16–22

Ahab married Jezebel, the Phoenician princess, and let Baal worship become Israel's religion, making him the worst of the northern kings.

Issue: When should outside political affairs dominate one's choice of a spouse? How much power should the spouse exercise?

Ahaz   *Person*   Isa. 7

King Ahaz refused Isaiah's offer to stand firm in faith and so did not stand at all. He "piously" refused to ask God for any sign at all.

Issue: Do you place your trust in a divine ally or in human allies?

Ahijah *Person* 1 Kings 11; 14; 15:29

Ahijah was a Shiloh prophet who tore his clothes in twelve pieces, which signaled the beginning of the northern kingdom's independence and ended the reign of the first northern dynasty.

Issue: How does God's Word bring hope to God's people but destruction to those who do not obey?

Ahimaaz *Person* 2 Sam. 15:27; 17

Ahimaaz was a spy for David in Absalom's court.

Issue: When are God's people justified in spying and keeping secrets?

Ahinoam *Person* 1 Sam. 25:43; 30:1–20; 2 Sam. 2

David's first son was born to Ahinoam.

Issue: What significance does a woman get from bearing children? What is the biblical teaching on having multiple wives?

Ahithophel *Person* 2 Sam. 15–17

Ahithophel served as David's counselor and gave counseling that was known as equal to God's Word. His name means "brother of folly." He joined Absalom's revolt against David and later committed suicide.

Issue: How do you determine whose counsel to believe?

Ai *Place* Josh. 7–8

Ai is a city whose name means "the ruin." Joshua was first defeated here due to Achan's selfish sin. He later captured the ruins.

Issue: How big and powerful does an enemy have to be for an army to celebrate victory over the "city"?

Aijalon *Place* Josh. 10:12

Aijalon was the city where the moon stood still at Joshua's bidding.

Issue: How can you believe in a miracle involving the planets and moons and stars in light of scientific explanations of the nature of the solar system?

Akhenaton *Person* Ancient History

Akhenaton was the only Egyptian pharaoh to worship just one god—the god Aton. His wife was Nefertiti and his son-in-law is better known as King Tut. He moved the Egyptian capital to Tell El-Amarna.

Issue: In what ways do you think religions of their neighbors influenced Israel?

Alexander the Great *Person* Ancient History

Alexander the Great established the Greek culture that became the background for the last of the Old Testament writings and canonization, as well as for the New Testment period. He was the Greek king of Macedonia who conquered the basic known world from Greece to India.

Issue: How do you judge greatness? Where does Alexander rank in comparison to the Bible's minor heroes such as Enoch, Sarah, or Naphtali?

Alexandria *Place* Ancient History

Alexandria was an Egyptian city housing the world's most famous library with over 500,000 volumes. It was here that the Old Testament was translated into Greek resulting in the Septuagint.

Issue: What is the relationship between Christianity and culture?

Alien *Person* Ex. 23:9; Lev. 17:15; Deut. 10:19; 14:21; 24:17–20; 26:12; 27:19

Aliens are immigrant foreigners living in Israel for whom the Bible contains special laws. God has a special love for aliens.

Issue: How should people of God treat foreign immigrants?

Amalekite　*Person*　Gen. 36:12; Ex. 17:8–16; Num. 14:39–45; 24:20; Deut. 25:17–19; Judg. 3; 6–7; 1 Sam. 14–15; 30

Amalekites are the first people to attack Israel in the wilderness. This early enemy of Israel was defeated by David.

Issue: How does God expect New Testament believers to deal with people who strongly oppose them and become their enemies?

Amanuensis　*Person*　Rom. 16:22; Col. 4:18; 1 Peter 5:12

Amanuensis is the term for a person hired to write letters for another. Paul often made use of an Amanuensis.

Issue: How does the fact of Paul and other biblical writers using other people to actually write their letters or other biblical materials influence your understanding of biblical authority?

Amasai　*Person*　1 Chron. 12:18

Members of David's elite army corps were called Amasai.

Issue: How does God's Spirit relate to the military? Who are the Thirty?

Amaziah　*Person*　Amos 7

Amaziah was the priest who expelled Amos from the temple at Bethel.

Issue: How can you use Amos's claim to not be a prophet, or a son of a prophet, or Amaziah's claim to be the nation's leading priest as you define the religious offices of the Old Testament?

Amen　*Thing*　Num. 5:22; Deut. 27:15–26; 1 Chron. 16:36; Neh. 8:6; Ps. 106:48; Jer. 11:5; 28:6; Rom. 1:25; 6:27; 11:36; 15:33; 1 Cor. 16:24; Gal. 1:5; 6:18; Eph. 3:21; Phil. 4:20

Amen is transliterated from Hebrew to affirm an oath or curse, accept a message, or personalize another's prayer or statement in worship.

Issue: What unifies a worship community?

| **Amen, I say to you** | *Thing* | Matt. 5:18; 16:28; Mark 8:12; 1:23; Luke 4:24; 21:32; John 1:51; 5:19 |

Jesus used the words "Amen, I say to you" to introduce important statements.

Issue: On what basis do you accept Jesus as truthful and as the ultimate authority of life?

| **Amos** | *Person* | Amos 1 |

Amos was the southern farmer God sent north to prophesy against Israel.

Issue: Should political differences prevent ministry evangelism? What would you do to avoid conflicts at this point?

| **Amraphel** | *Person* | Gen. 14 |

The king of Shinar (Babylon), Amraphel, led the coalition of kings that defeated the group run by Sodom and Gomorrah. Their capture of Lot led Abraham to become involved.

Issue: Who are these unheard-of kings, and from where do they come?

| **Ananias** | *Person* | Acts 4–5 |

Ananias and his wife Sapphira were killed by God for lying to the church about the amount he tithed.

Issue: What have you done to impress people and show them you are as religious and good as they are? In what ways does the love of money prevent you from obeying God?

| **Ananias** | *Person* | Acts 9 |

Ananias miraculously enabled Paul to see and receive the Holy Spirit after Paul's Damascus Road experience.

Issue: What are God's ways of choosing and equipping ministers? Have youth in your church dedicated themselves to professional ministry recently?

Ananias *Person* Acts 23–24

The high priest Ananias led the Jewish authorities who presented the case against Paul before governor Felix.

Issue: When should religious authorities go to secular courts to settle differences?

Anathema *Thing* Lev. 27:28; Deut. 20:10–18; Luke 21:5; Rom. 9:3; 1 Cor. 16:22; Gal. 1:8–9

Anathema can mean many things. It can be dedicating spoils of war to God by destroying them, a gift given to God, or an object under curse.

Issue: Is the willingness to give everything to God complete obedience to God?

Anathoth *Place* Josh. 21:18; 1 Kings 2:26–27; Jer. 1:1; 11:21–23; 32:6–15

Solomon banished the High Priest Abiathar and his priestly line to Anathoth, forbidding them to exercise normal priestly ministry. A member of this priestly line, Jeremiah lived in Anathoth and purchased land there as a symbolic act.

Issue: What is the state's power over religion? How should religious institutions respond?

Ancestor/Dead, Worship of *Thing* Ezek. 43:7–9

Ancestor worship is the practice of giving worship and sacrifices in honor of the dead, usually family ancestors, or even seeking an ongoing relationship with dead ancestors.

Issue: What is the continuing situation with believers after death? What responsibilities do the living have for the dead?

| **Angel** | *Thing* | Gen. 18; Judg. 13; 1 Sam. 1:11; 1 Chron. 12:22; Ps. 148:2–5; Luke 1:13, 30; 2; Acts 7:53; Gal. 3:19; Col. 1:16; Rev. 1:1; 5:11; 7:11; 10:1; 19:1–3 |

In Greek and Hebrew the word *angel* refers to a messenger. Messengers can appear as humans but represent God. Messengers may be over-whelmingly awesome, be winged creatures, or be indistinguishable from ordinary people.

Issue: What roles do angels play in God's plan for His world? Have you ever encountered an angel? Would you expect to encounter one?

| **Anna** | *Person* | Luke 2:36 |

An eighty-four-year-old widowed prophetess, Anna, lived at the temple expecting to see the child Messiah as God had promised her. She is one of the early witnesses to the messianic nature of Jesus.

Issue: How long and under what conditions will you wait for God to fulfill His promise to you? How do you recognize His promises?

| **Annas** | *Person* | Luke 3:2; John 18:13; Acts 4:6 |

Annas, the high priest who exercised influence in Jesus' trials, was later deposed.

Issue: When does a church leader stop exercising personal influence on the congregation in favor of the next generation?

| **Annunciation** | *Thing* | Luke 1:26–38 |

Gabriel's angelic announcement to the Virgin Mary of her coming preg-nancy and deliverance is known as the Annunciation.

Issue: How do you see the possibility and importance of the immaculate conception?

Anointed One *Person*   1 Sam. 24:6; Ps. 89:38; Isa. 45:1; Acts 10:38

An anointed one has had sacred oil poured on his or her head to set him or her aside for God's use. More specifically, the king of God's people and the coming King, the Messiah, are anointed. (The Hebrew term *messiah* [anointed] is translated into Greek as *Christos* and into English as *Christ*.)

Issue: Has God sent His Messiah to earth, or is He yet to come?

Antediluvians *Person*   Gen. 1–9

The people before the flood, marked by innovation, invention, and astounding life spans, are known as Antediluvians. Long life spans are miniscule in comparison to the kings in the Sumerian king lists. In the Bible, antediluvians represent growth of immorality through Genesis 6:1–4 and the flood. Genealogies are open or incomplete, as seen in the schematic ten member sets and in other open genealogies such as Ezra 7 compared to 1 Chronicles 6.

Issue: How could our ancestors live so much longer than we do?

Anthropomorphism *Thing*

Anthropomorphism is a literary technique attributing body parts to God when He is in the spirit and not in the flesh. It can also mean portraying God as a human:

God's arm: Ex. 6:6; 15:16; Deut. 4:34; Pss. 44:3; 89:13; 98:1; Isa. 66:13; John 12:38.

God's mouth: Deut. 30:20; Ps. 29:3; Isa. 1:20; 40:5, 24.

God's eyes: Deut. 11:12; Ps. 34:15; Prov. 15:3.

God's ears: Pss. 17:1, 6; 31:2; 34:15; 39:12; 55:1; 71:2; 86:1, 6; 88:2; James 5:4.

God's face: Gen. 32:30; Num. 6:25; Ps. 34:16.

God's hands: Ex. 15:17; Job 5:18; Pss. 37:24; 139:10; Isa. 64:8; Matt. 26:64; Luke 1:66; 23:46; John 10:29; Acts 2:33.

God's lips: Prov. 16:27.

God's finger: Luke 11:20.

God's foot: Lam. 1:15.

God's heart: Ezek. 28:2, 6.

Issue: What are the advantages of using human parts to describe God? What are the disadvantages? What other examples can you find?

Antichrist   *Person*   1 John 2:18, 22; 4:3; 2 John 1:7

The antichrist is the person or group representing the ultimate opposition to God and to His Son Jesus. He establishes his dominion by imitating Christ and denying His authority and messiahship. The antichrist may well be the same as Daniel's king from the north (7–11). The term also applied to the Seleuccids and to the Romans (Matt. 24:24; Mark 13:22; compare 2 Cor. 6:15; 2 Thess. 2; Rev. 13:3).

Issue: If the term antichrist appears only in 1 and 2 John, why do present-day believers spend so much time seeking to identify him?

Antipas   *Person*   Matt. 14:3; Luke 3:1; 23:11

Antipas was the tetrarch of Galilee who ordered the beheading of John the Baptist and dealt scornfully with Jesus during Passion Week.

Issue: Who controls the activities and future of God's special ministers? How is that control evidenced?

Apocalyptic   *Thing*   Rev. 1:1

Apocalyptic refers to an unveiling or revelation. It is a manner of communication that seeks to reveal secret knowledge, most often about the end time, through symbols, metaphors, and visions. It can also refer to end-time literature seeking to provide confidence, hope, and direction for living in the age of persecution.

Issue: Regarding Daniel and Revelation, what should you learn and practice about enduring life during tough times?

Apocrypha *Thing* Ancient Texts

The Apocrypha is a term for non-canonical Jewish literature comprised of fifteen books that were not accepted into the Protestant canon or Bible but recognized as authoritative by the Catholic Church and used in worship by Anglican and other churches. It is comprised of First Esdras, First and Second Maccabees, Tobit, Judith, 107 extra verses of Esther, three extra stories in Daniel (Song of the Three Young Men, Story of Susanna, Bel and the Dragon), Wisdom of Solomon, Wisdom of Jesus the son of Sirach (also called Ecclesiasticus), Baruch, Letter of Jeremiah, Prayer of Manasseh, and Second Esdras.

Issue: Why does the Protestant church dispute the authenticity and authority of these books? What theological or practical changes would Protestant churches have to make?

Apollos *Person* Acts 18; 19:1; 1 Cor. 1:12; 3:4–6, 22; 4:6; 16:12; Titus 3:13

Apollos was an excellent preacher baptized by John and looked to as a leader by part of the Corinthian church. He was taught and trained by Priscilla and Aquila.

Issue: How do you recognize and strengthen areas of weakness in your life?

Apostle *Person* Rom. 1:1; 11:13; 1 Cor. 1:1; 9:1–2; 15:9; 2 Cor. 1:1; 12:12; Gal. 1:1, 19; 2:8; Eph. 1:1; Col. 1:1; 1 Tim. 1:1; 2:7; 2 Tim. 1:1, 11; Titus 1:1; Heb. 3:1; 1 Peter 1:1; 2 Peter 1:1

Three groups are called apostle in the New Testament: the twelve who followed Jesus, the people who delivered messages and gifts to other churches, and the people God has sent on specific mission.

Issue: How is your mission for God different or similar to that of the New Testament apostles?

Apostolic Council   *Persons*   Acts 15; Gal. 2

The Apostolic Council was a meeting of the Jerusalem apostles with Paul and Barnabas where it was established that the church would not require Gentile converts to follow Jewish law.

Issue: What must a person do to become a believer in the church? In what areas do some churches argue this point today?

Apostolic Fathers   *Persons*

The first generation of disciples after the original apostles are known as the apostolic fathers. Some of their writings appear in manuscripts and lists of books the church was using as official teaching, but eventually did not become part of official canon: Clement, Ignatius, Polycarp, Barnabas, Hermas, Didache, Diognetus, and Papias.

Issue: On what basis did the church select certain works as canon while denying other works canonical status? Can today's church challenge or change the early church's decisions?

Apple   *Thing*   Josh. 12:17; 15:34, 53; 16:8; 17:7–8; 1 Chron. 2:43; Prov. 25:11; Song 2:3, 5; 7:9; 8:5; Joel 1:12

The apple is a delectable fruit whose presence in biblical times in biblical lands is disputed. Obviously, the apple does not appear in the Garden of Eden, but early Jewish tradition identifies the apple tree with the Tree of the Knowledge of Good and Evil.

The biblical "apple tree" is a sweet-tasting, golden, scented, shade- and food-providing tree. But exactly which species fits the descriptions? Suggestions include fig, date, quince, citrus, apricot, apple, citron. The wild apricot may provide the best fit.

Issue: Does the fact that the type of fruit is unknown make a difference to your faith, or is it a non-issue?

Apple of the Eye   *Thing*   Deut. 32:10; Prov. 7:2; Zech. 2:8

The "apple of the eye" is a metaphor describing the pupil of an eye, and thus, something precious. The Bible uses three different Hebrew words to describe the same idea: the little man of the eye, the daughter of the eye, and the gate of the eye.

Issue: What is as precious to you as the ability to see?

Aquila and Priscilla   *Person*   Acts 18:2, 19, 25; 1 Cor. 16:19; 2 Tim. 4:19

Aquila and Priscilla were tentmakers expelled from Rome by Claudias. They became close friends and fellow workers with Paul, helped to teach Apollos, and joined in writing letters to Corinth.

Issue: In what ways does a common vocation improve your ministry for Christ?

Ar   *Place*   Num. 21:15, 28; Deut. 2:9, 18, 29; Isa. 15:1

Ar was defeated by Israel but God reserved it for Lot's descendants, not Israel's. Ar provided food for Israel as they passed through the territory.

Issue: What happens when you are denied the spoils of victory?

Aramaic   *Thing*   Ezra 4:8–6:18; 7:12–26; Jer. 10:11; Dan. 2:4b–7:28

The Aramaic language appears in the Old Testament alongside Hebrew and Greek. It became the language of international exchange (2 Kings 18:26). Jesus and His disciples probably spoke Aramaic, a Semitic language akin to Hebrew. Aramaic words in the New Testament are: Abba (father) (Mark 14:36), *talitha, qumi* (maiden, arise) (Mark 5:41), and *lama sabachthani* (why have You forsaken Me?) (Mark 15:34).

Issue: Why is the New Testament written in Greek when Jesus and His disciples spoke Aramaic?

Ararat   *Place*   Gen. 8:4

Ararat is the seventeen-thousand-foot high mountain in Turkey where Noah's ark is said to have landed. Also known as Urartu.

Issue: Do you think it is possible to find remnants of Noah's ark? Why or why not?

Araunah   *Person*   2 Sam. 24:15–25

Araunah was a Jebusite (from Jebus or Jerusalem) whose threshing floor David purchased to make a sacrifice on after his ill-advised census. Also called Ornan.

Issue: What do you do when you know you have displeased God?

Areopagus   *Place*   Acts 17:19

Areopagus is a 370-foot high hill above the agora or marketplace in Athens where Paul preached to Greek philosophers.

Issue: How do you reach well-educated, very intelligent people for Christ?

Aretas   *Person*   Mark 6:17–18; 2 Cor. 11:32

Aretas was the king of Damascus who tried to arrest Paul after his conversion. His daughter married Herod Antipas, who later divorced her for Herodias.

Issue: When is it in the divine will to divorce a mate?

Ark of Noah   *Thing*   Gen. 6

Noah's ark, or boat, represented God's limits with the people He had created. The Holy God could endure their sin no longer and had to punish the sinful crowd. God regretted having made people who devoted their mind to evil things. Only Noah proved righteous before God, so divine orders came forth to Noah: build an ark for your family and two of every ritually unclean animal and seven pair of every ritually clean animal. The finished three-deck product measured 450' x 75' x 45'. Noah's ark showed God's grace in preserving a family with whom He could start over and with whom He made a covenant never to destroy the earth again. The beautiful rainbow certifies that covenant, assuring us that God's grace will prevail.

Issue: Do we have to fear such a flood as what carried the ark over the mountains to Mount Ararat?

Ark of the Covenant *Thing* Ex. 26–40; Num. 10:35–36

The ark of the covenant was a box or chest containing the Ten Commandments that was used as a symbol of divine presence and as a guide for Israel through the wilderness and across the Jordan into the Promised Land.

Issue: What are some symbols that help us worship and experience divine presence?

Armageddon *Place* Rev. 16:16

Armageddon is the transliteration of Hebrew *har Megiddo* or Mountain of Megiddo. It is the site of the final, decisive end-times battle between Satan and God.

Issue: What are you doing to prepare for the battle of Armageddon? Can you locate Armageddon on a map?

Arpachshad *Person* Gen. 10:22; Luke 3:36

Arpachshad was an early ancestor of the Hebrew people who was born two years after the flood.

Issue: How far back can you trace your genealogy? Who is the most famous person on your family tree?

Artemis *Thing* Acts 19:28

The Greek moon goddess Artemis protected nature and was patron god of Ephesus. Her temple in Ephesus was one of the seven wonders of the world and promoted the sale of silver statues. Paul spoke out against the worship of Artemis.

Issue: How does true preaching affect false religions?

Asa *Person* 1 Kings 15; 2 Chron. 16:12

Asa was a king of Judah who reigned for forty-one years after he removed his mother from power. He defeated the large army of Cush but was punished with a foot disease when he called on the King of Damascus to deliver him from the northern kingdom.

Issue: How does a believer deal with sickness?

Asaph *Person* 1 Chron. 6:39

Asaph was a temple musician whose descendants followed in his footsteps as temple musicians and who had prophetic gifts (1 Chron. 25; 2 Chron. 20).

Issue: How does one recognize and utilize special gifts from God?

Ascension *Thing* Acts 1:9

The Ascension refers to the return of Jesus in the clouds to His Father after the crucifixion and resurrection.

Issue: What does the Ascension teach us about Jesus?

Asenath *Person* Gen. 41:50–51

Asenath was a daughter of an Egyptian priest who was given to Joseph as wife by the pharaoh. She was the mother of Ephraim and Manasseh.

Issue: What criteria might you set up as you try to assist your young adult child in selecting a wedding mate? What role will you expect to play in this selection process?

Ashpenaz *Person* Dan. 1

Ashpenaz was the administrator for the family of King Nebuchadnezzar of Babylon and for Daniel and his friends. He gave the four Israelites a special diet.

Issue: In what way is your diet associated with your religion?

Ashurbanipal *Person* Ezra 4:10

The last great king of Assyria (668–629 BC), Ashurbanipal settled his foreign captives in Samaria and built a library with twenty thousand clay tablets in Nineveh.

Issue: Do you have a love of learning? How do you show it in your house?

Asiarchs *People* Acts 19:31

Asiarchs were wealthy people from Asia who sponsored games during religious festivals, supported the worship of the emperor, and underwrote events for the public good.

Issue: How do you make your city a better place to live in?

Assassins *People* Acts 21:38

The assassins were Jewish rebels against Rome. They were also known as dagger men or Sicarii because they used small daggers to kill enemies. Paul was accused of being the leader of four thousand Sicarii.

Issue: What justifies rebellion against the government and wartime killing?

Assayer *Person* Jer. 6:27

Jeremiah's God-given task was as an assayer. He determined if Israel measured up to God's gold standard.

Issue: What measuring tool do you use to determine your obedience to God's expectations?

Atonement *Thing* 1 John 2:2; 4:10

Jesus' work on the cross to gain forgiveness of our sin and restore our relationship with God is known as atonement.

Issue: Have you asked Jesus to let His atoning work bring you personal forgiveness for your sins?

Ax *Thing* 2 Kings 6

An ax, a chopping tool made of iron, floated in the water at Elisha's direction.

Issue: What limits do you place on what God can do? How far can He make miracles happen that override, in some way, the "laws of nature"?

Azazel *Thing* Lev. 16

Azazel is the name for the scapegoat involved in carrying away Israel's sin during the Day of Atonement. Some interpreters see Azazel as wilderness into which the goat is sent. That ritual was supplanted by the once-and-for-all sacrifice of Jesus for our sins.

Issue: Have you let Jesus become your scapegoat and carry away your sins forever?

Azariah (Uzziah) *Person* 2 Chron. 26:16–21

Azariah was a king of Judah who tried to offer incense in the temple, an action limited to the priests. God punished him with a great skin disease.

Issue: Why was a king not allowed to offer incense in the temple? Should the church refuse to let anyone participate in worship?

Azariah *Person* 2 Chron. 31:10–13

High priest Azariah declared that the people had given enough and that the priests had plenty to eat.

Issue: What did God show Israel about providing for the priests? Does your church provide sufficiently for your minister(s)?

B

Baalah   *Place*   Josh. 15:9–11; 1 Chron. 13:6

Baalah was the home of the ark of the covenant until David took it to Jerusalem.

Issue: What role do symbols produced by artists play in your worship of God?

Baal-berith   *Thing*   Judg. 8:33; 9:4

Baal-berith, "lord of the covenant," was a god worshiped in Canaan near Shechem where Joshua concluded his covenant with the Israelites (Josh. 24). The Canaanite practice behind this divine name may have contributed to early Israelite worship.

Issue: What practices in your church can you trace back to ancient non-Christian or superstitous practices?

Baale-Judah ("Lords of Judah")   *Place*   2 Sam. 6:2

Baale-Judah is the full name of the place where David found the ark of the covenant and where he decided to take it back to Jerusalem.

Issue: How do you seek God and why? Do you find God, or does He find you?

Baal-Gad   *Place*   Josh. 11:17

The northern limit of Joshua's conquest was the city Baal-Gad.

Issue: Do you reach the limits God sets out for you?

Baal-Hazor   *Place*   2 Sam. 13:23

Baal-Hazor is the town where Absalom had his brother Ammon killed and began his campaign to replace his father David as king.

Issue: What causes adult children to resent and rebel against their parents?

Baalis   *Person*   Jer. 40:14

Baalis was the king of Ammon who dispatched Ismael to kill Gedaliah, the governor of Judah, after Babylon had captured and exiled the population of Judah.

Issue: How can nations disagree over policy or leadership and still maintain the peace?

Baal-Peor   *Thing*   Num. 25:3 (compare Deut. 4:3; Ps. 106:28)

Moabite fertility god Baal-Peor was worshiped by Israel in the wilderness through sexual acts, resulting in God punishing Israel by having twenty-four thousand people killed.

Issue: What is the relationship between religion and sex?

Baal-Perazim   *Place*   2 Sam. 5:20

Baal-Perazim, literally "Baal (lord) of the breeches," was where David first defeated the Philistines.

Issue: How does a believer celebrate victory?

Baal-Shalishah   *Place*   2 Kings 4:42–44

Baal-Shalishah was the home of an unnamed man who brought a first-fruits offering to Elisha, who used them to feed one hundred men.

Issue: Are you willing to give your tithes and offerings and watch what God does with them?

Baal-Tamar   *Place*   Judg. 20:33

Baal-Tamar is the name of the battlefield where Israel went to war with and defeated its own tribe of Benjamin for not showing hospitality to strangers.

Issue: Why do families fight other family members? What issues lead to fights or shouting matches in your family?

Baal-Zebub *Thing* 2 Kings 1:2

King Ahaziah of Israel went to Baal-Zebub, a Philistine god, for healing after he suffered a fall.

Issue: How much faith do you have that God can heal you? Do you follow any superstitions or false prophets in seeking healing? What do you expect to happen when people of the church pray for healing?

Baal-Zephon *Place* Ex. 14:2, 9

Baal-Zephon was the final Egyptian location where Israel camped before God led them across the Red Sea.

Issue: Where did you last experience the powerful presence of God? With whom are you willing to share this experience?

Baasha *Person* 1 Kings 15

Baasha (908–886 BC) killed everyone in the line of Jeroboam I in Israel and started a new dynasty with himself as king.

Issue: What role does God play in biblical violence? How does this affect your understanding and experience with God?

Babbler *Person* Acts 17:18

The term *babbler* originally referred to birds, especially crows, who picked up seeds they had done nothing to produce. Philosophers and writers used *babbler* to designate a person who stole or plagiarized material from others without proper attribution and without knowing enough to use the borrowed piece correctly. Athenian sages applied the term to Paul as one who did not know what he was talking about.

Issue: In what areas do you really have expertise, and in which fields do you only pretend to have some mastery?

Babel *Place* Gen. 11

Descendants of Noah built the tower of Babel so they would not be separated from one another and to compete with God. God felt the danger of the people working in arrogance to create a tower reaching the heavens and foiled their scheme by giving people different languages and spreading them across the world unable to communicate with each other.

Issue: What problems have you encountered because you could not speak someone else's language? Does your pride see only the need for the other person to speak your language?

Baboon *Thing* 1 Kings 10:22

King Hiram of Tyre brought a baboon to Palestine with his massive trading fleet. Baboon has been variously interpreted as peacock (HCSB, NRSV, NASB95, CEB) or monkeys (TEV, REB).

Issue: Do you collect anything other people might call exotic or at least unusual? Why do you keep adding to the collection?

Baca *Place* Ps. 84:6

Baca is a name used in word play. Its sound is closely related to the Hebrew term for crying or weeping and shares sounds with the Hebrew for blessing. The place is named thus to testify that God makes fresh well or spring water out of a time of mourning and weeping.

Issue: What may you ask God for when life becomes a valley of tears?

Balaam *Person* Num. 22:5–31:8; Deut. 23:4–5; Josh. 13:22; 24:9–10; Neh. 13:2; Mic. 6:5; 2 Peter 2:15; Rev. 2:14

Balaam was a Near-Eastern prophet hired by Barak, King of Moab, to curse Israel as they approached Moabite territory. God consistently refused to let Balaam curse Israel, bringing blessings instead. The famous morning star passage of Num. 24:17 finds messianic reference in early Jewish and Christian sources (Rev. 22:16). Balaam appears as a prophet in a plaster inscription discovered at Tell Deir Alla in Jordan dating to the end of the eighth century BC. He is a "seer" for the god El.

Issue: Is Balaam a true prophet or a false prophet? On what do you base your decision?

Balak *Person* Num. 22:2

Balak was the king of Moab who called Balaam, the prophet, to curse Israel.

Issue: Does any person have the right to call down God's curse on another person or group of people?

Bald(ness) *Thing* Lev. 11:22; 13:40–43; 21:5; Isa. 3:24; 15:2; 22:12; Jer. 47:5; Ezek. 7:18; 27:31; 29:18; Amos 8:10

Baldness refers to the state of having no hair, particularly on the head. Israel leaves no record of bald people except those in ritual mourning. The Bible includes rules and rituals related to bald people.

Issue: What do hairstyles signify about people? Do people in your church or your family tend to mock, sneer at, or condemn people for wearing certain types of hairstyles?

Baptism *Thing* Matt. 3:7–16; 21:25; Mark 1:4-9; 10:38–39; 11:30; 16:16; Luke 3:3–21; 7:29–30; 12:50; 20:4; John 1:26–33; 3:22–23; 4:2; Acts 1:5, 22; 2:38, 41; 8:12–38; 9:18; 10:37, 48; 11:16; 13:24; 16:15, 33; 18:8, 25; 19:3–5; 22:16; Rom. 6:3–4; 1 Cor. 1:13–17; 10:2; 12:13; 15:29; Gal. 3:27; Eph. 4:5; Col. 2:12; 1 Peter 3:21

Baptism is a Christian rite of passage where a person is dedicated to Jesus Christ as Lord and Savior and enters the fellowship of the church. Through history, churches have disputed the time of baptism, the method of baptism, and the effect of baptism. Disagreements between denominations include whether a person is sprinkled with water or fully immersed in water, should infants or children be baptized, and does baptism guarantee eternal salvation or must salvation involve continued action?

Issue: Baptism is a most important issue within the Christian community, leaving many open issues. Who should be baptized? At what age? For what purpose? By what methods? With what results or expectations? Does the New Testament give any evidence about how baptism was done?

Baptism by Fire *Thing* Matt. 3:11; Luke 3:15–16

John the Baptist promised that Jesus' ministry would bring a Pentecost baptism of the Holy Spirit (fire) and the final days of judgment and punishment. He contrasted it with his baptism by water for repentance.

Issue: What is baptism by fire? When do people experience it? In what way is it especially connected to Jesus? Is it a continuing part of the church's experience?

Baptism for the Dead *Thing* 1 Cor. 15:29

A probably heretical action in the Corinthian church that attempted to bring the benefit of Christ's salvation to believers unable to be baptized or to those who died without being baptized. Paul condemned the practice.

Issue: Why did the Corinthians (and why do present-day Mormons) baptize the dead?

Barabbas *Person* Mark 15:15

Barabbas was a murderer and political rebel who was jailed by the Romans. The crowds demanded his release from prison rather than Jesus'.

Issue: Did Jesus deserve to be crucified?

Barak *Person* Judg. 4:6–22; 5:1, 12, 15; 1 Sam. 12:11; Heb. 11:32

Barak was an Israelite army leader called by God through the prophet Deborah to lead Israel's war against Sisera and his commander Jabin, the king of Canaan ruling from Hazor. Barak insisted that Deborah must go with him. She said his lack of courage meant the rewards of battle would not go to him but to a woman, a prophesy fulfilled when Jael killed Sisera.

Issue: Should women be directly involved in international warfare? If so, should any limits be placed on their involvement?

Bar-Jesus *Person* Acts 13

Bar-Jesus was a Jewish magician and false prophet whom Paul called a son of the devil. Paul called on God to blind Bar-Jesus so he could continue his conversation with Sergius Paulus, the Roman proconsul on Cyprus. This led to conversion of the important Roman official.

Issue: When is it appropriate to call another person a son of the devil? When should you interrupt a conversation about salvation to steer another person away?

Barsabbas *Person* Acts 1:23

One of the candidates to replace Judas as the twelfth apostle was Barsabbas. Matthias was eventually selected.

Issue: How do you respond when you do not get a position you desire?

Barsabbas (Judas) *Person* Acts 15:22

The Jerusalem church chose Barsabbas (Judas) to go to Antioch and report on the results of the Jerusalem council.

Issue: What role did Paul and Silas's "third man" play in their ministries? Are you willing and available to be the lesser-known leader in church and business projects?

Bartimaeus *Person* Mark 10:46–52

Bartimaeus was the blind beggar whose sight Jesus restored.

Issue: What is the value of every person in society? How can a blind beggar get Jesus' attention?

Barzillai   *Person*   2 Sam. 17:27–29

Barzillai helped supply David with necessities when the king retreated from Absalom.

Issue: How could David survive in the wilderness?

Beautiful Gate   *Thing*   Acts 3:10

The Beautiful Gate was the entranceway into Jerusalem providing access to the Temple. Peter and John healed a lame man there. It is mentioned nowhere else in early literature, so its precise location remains a question.

Issue: What does it mean for your faith when you discover you cannot answer some questions about details in the Bible?

Behemoth   *Thing*   Job 40

God used a behemoth, a large, hippopotamus-like animal, to show Job His incomparable majesty.

Issue: How does God reveal divine majesty to you?

Beka   *Thing*   Ex. 38:26

A beka was a coin worth one half-shekel and was used for the temple tax each Israelite male paid.

Issue: Does the state or the church or both have the right to collect an annual payment from you?

Belial   *Person*   2 Cor. 6:15; compare Deut. 13:13; Nah. 1:5

Belial is a mysterious being whose Hebrew name means useless or worthless. It is referred to as an evil being equated with, or an ally of, Satan.

Issue: What do you think about powerful spiritual enemies? Why?

Beloved Disciple   *Person*   John 20:2; 21:7

The beloved disciple is the disciple with whom Jesus had a special relationship. Found only in John's gospel, the beloved disciple is most often identified as John, the brother of James. John is also one of the Sons of Thunder (Mark 3:17).

Issue: Did Jesus love the beloved disciple more than the other disciples? What is meant by "beloved"?

Belshazzar   *Person*   Dan. 5

Belshazzar was the Babylonian crown prince and co-ruler with his father Nabonidus when Babylon fell to Cyrus of Persia, making it possible for Israel to return from exile. Daniel 5 relates how Belshazzar literally saw the writing on the wall that predicted his defeat and death.

Issue: How would you respond to a divine message predicting your imminent death?

Benedictus   *Thing*   Luke 1:68–79

Benedictus, or "blessed," is the first word of the hymnic prophesy of Zacharias in the Latin translation (the Vulgate). Zacharias was the husband of Elizabeth and the father of John the Baptist.

Issue: How do you ordinarily respond to the sense of God's calling on your life? When and how does doubt enter the picture? Do you feel blessed?

Ben-Hadad   *Person or Title*   1 Kings 15; 20; 2 Kings 6; 8; 13

Ben-Hadad means either the "son of the god Hadad," or it could simply be the personal name for a devotee of storm god Hadad. This dynasty ruled Syria and fought with Israel, sometimes successfully.

Issue: What does it mean to have a Jr. or III after your name? How does this relate to family tradition?

Beor   *Person*   Num. 22:5

Beor was the father of Balaam, the prophet paid to curse Israel. Balaam ultimately found it impossible to curse Israel because God made him bless Israel. He and Balak, king of Moab, were accustomed to having their words obeyed. Finding a situation they could not control with power or money perplexed them.

Issue: What does God control that you cannot buy? What kind of limits does this show you must deal with?

Beracah   *Person and Place*   1 Chron. 12:3; 2 Chron. 20:26

Berachah can mean two things, either David's ambidextrous (both right- and left-handed) soldier whose name means "blessing" or the name of the valley where King Jehoshaphat of Judah (873–848 BC) led his people in thanking God for providing victory in battle against Edom, Moab, and Ammon.

Issue: What special skills do you have that can contribute to the success of God's army—the church—today?

Bernice   *Person*   Acts 25:13

Bernice loved men. Born about AD 28 to Herod Agrippa I, she married an otherwise unknown Marcus and then divorced him to marry her uncle Herod. After bearing Herod two sons, she was widowed in AD 48. She became the "companion" of King Agrippa II and was present when he and Festus called on Paul to defend himself against the charges brought by Jewish leaders. Agrippa and Festus agreed on Paul's innocence. She later married Palemo, king of Cillicia, and apparently had an affair with Titus, the Roman emperor.

Issue: What leads people to have affairs inside of or outside of marriage? Proclaimed innocent, why did Paul not go free?

Besor   *Place*   1 Sam. 30

Besor was a valley or wadi about fifteen miles south of Ziklag where David left two hundred exhausted troops. He then rode after the Amalekites, who had burned Ziklag and captured David's wives. Following the defeat of the Amalekites, David distributed the spoils equally among the two hundred exhausted troops as well as with the four hundred who fought.

Issue: Was David fair in rewarding the troops who did not fight? Is the pay system of your church and/or the company where you work fair?

Beth-aven   *Place*   Hos. 4:15

Beth-aven literally means "House of idolatry." Hosea used it in word play for Beth-el, "House of God."

Issue: How would a prophet describe your place of worship and the activities that transpire there?

Beth-Eden   *Place*   Amos 1:5

Beth-Eden was a Syrian kingdom on the northern end of the Euphrates River, about two hundred miles northeast of Israel, and was cited by Amos along with Damascus for inhumane war practices.

Issue: How can rules of war be enforced in the midst of fierce international warfare?

Beth-Eked   *Place*   2 Kings 10

Beth-Eked was the village between Jezreel and Samaria where the rebellious Jehu had forty-two relatives of King Ahaziah of Judah killed.

Issue: How thorough must a rebel be in killing enemies in an effort to claim leadership of the nation?

Beth-peor   *Place*   Deut. 3:29; 4:46; 34:6; Josh. 13:20

Moses was buried in Beth-peor, the transjordan location of a worship house for Baal-peor, where Israel camped prior to invasion of the Promised Land.

Issue: Why does it often seem to take God a long time to fulfill His promises?

Beth-saida *Place* Matt. 11:21; Mark 6:45; 8:22; Luke 9:10; 10:13; John 1:44; 12:21

Beth-saida was a town on the northeastern tip of the Sea of Galilee. It was the town that Philip, Andrew, and Peter called home.

Issue: Will Jesus include you among the blessed or the cursed when He returns?

Beth-zatha *Place* John 5:2

A pool in Jerusalem has been given several different names in the textual tradition of John: Beth-zatha, Bethsaida, Bethesda, and Beteshdathayim. Jesus cured a man who had tried but had not succeeded in leading the way into the pool for thirty-eight years.

Issue: How does it affect your belief in God when you discover we have different manuscripts with different spellings of the same city? Did the man at the pool have a realistic hope of healing?

Beulah *Thing (Symbolic Name)* Isa. 62:4

Beula, a Hebrew noun meaning "married," applied to exiles who had returned or were returning from Babylon to the promise that they were not forsaken.

Issue: Do believers act in a wrong manner when they complain about God forsaking them?

Bewitch *Thing* Acts 8:9–11; Gal. 3:1

The King James Version of the Bible translates two Greek terms referring to being captivated or amazed as "bewitched." The term is used in relationship to people opposing the gospel with magic.

Issue: How do you distinguish between miraculous power from God and unexpected help from human-invaded mystical, demonic forces?

Bezalel or Bezaleel *Person* Ex. 31:2; 1 Chron. 2:20

Bezalel and his apprentice Aholiab built the tabernacle and all its furnishings and adornments.

Issue: What special skill—artistic or not—has God given you to assist in building His kingdom?

Bezek *Place* Judg. 1:4; 1 Sam. 11:8

Bezek, "lightning," is where Judah and Simeon defeated Adoni-bezek (the lord of Bezek) and cut off his thumbs and big toes. It was also the mustering place for Saul's army.

Issue: What is cruel and unjust punishment?

Bible *Thing* 2 Tim. 3:14–17

The Bible is a book whose production God directed through two millennia to provide His people a trustworthy record of His will. The 2 Timothy reference emphasizes the authority and function of the Hebrew Bible, which the church has transferred to the New Testament as well. The church's experience and testimony, built on the experience and written testimony of Israel, affirms the Bible's self-testimony to be the living Word of God. Protestants, Catholics, and Orthodox define the content and authority of the Bible in different ways. The Bible remains the major source for church teaching and doctrinal statements.

Issue: Describe when and how God has spoken to you through the Bible. Why do you prefer one translation over another? What terms would you use to describe the nature of the Bible in the life of the church?

Bildad *Person* Job

Bildad was Job's friend who defended traditional theology. He tried to show that Job deserved the suffering and loss he was experiencing.

Issue: Does God ever punish an innocent person?

Bilhah   *Person*   Gen. 29–30; 35:22, 25; 46:23–25; 49:3–4

Bilhah was the secondary wife (or concubine) of Jacob and a maid of Rachel. When Rachel proved barren, she gave Bilhah to Jacob. She bore Dan and Naphtali to Jacob. Jacob's oldest son Rueben lay with his stepmother Bilhah, so his father took the blessing of the firstborn from him.

Issue: How should your church minister to couples who cannot produce children or to couples who openly live in adultery?

Binding and Loosing   *Thing*   Matt. 16:19; 18:18

Jesus gave Peter and the disciples a promise of binding and loosing the Word of God using the same language the Jewish rabbis used concerning the correct interpretation of Torah. The disciples can determine proper conduct for believers by studying the Word of God and calling people to accept the good news of the gospel. They have a calling from Jesus to bring the good news of salvation to people.

By preaching the gospel of Jesus, disciples open the door to the kingdom. They do not have a special privilege or extraordinary authority, but they have a responsibility entrusted to them by Jesus Christ to extend His work. Their responsibility involves nothing magical, mysterious, or arbitrary. Those who correctly interpret Scripture and lead people to Jesus do so not with ecclesiastical or official position or authority, but instead with spiritual and primarily personal responsibility to the Master and to the kingdom.

Issue: What authority do you have from Jesus? How do you exercise that authority? To whom have you loosed the kingdom by your witnessing and teaching?

Birsha   *Person*   Gen. 14:2

Birsha was the king of Gomorrah who fought with the coalition against the eastern kings; their defeat brought Abraham into the war to recapture Abraham's nephew Lot.

Issue: What actions do you take on the basis of family ties?

Birthright   *Thing*   Gen. 25; 27; Heb. 12:16

A "birthright" is the right of the first-born son of a family to claim an extra portion of the family inheritance and to become the head of the family at the death of the patriarch. Esau sold his birthright to Jacob for a bowl of stew.

Issue: What position or asset have you ever forfeited without reason and in return for almost nothing?

Bithynia   *Place*   Acts 16:7; 1 Peter 1:1

Paul's destination was Bithynia Place; however, God had other plans, and sent him instead to Macedonia.

Issue: When has God turned you away from one direction in life and onto another life path?

Boanerges   *Persons*   Mark 3:17

Boanerges, or "Sons of Thunder," is the title that Jesus gave to James and John because of their strong, inquisitive personalities.

Issue: Do you have a nickname? How did you get the name, and what does it signify for you?

Book of Jashar   *Thing*   Josh. 10:12–13; 2 Sam. 1:17–27; 1 Kings 8:12–13

The Book of Jashar was a volume of war poetry that no longer exists. It was probably collected during United Monarchy.

Issue: Of what value are references to ancient sources behind the Bible when these sources are no longer preserved?

Book of Life   *Thing*   Phil. 4:3; Rev. 3:5; 13:8; 17:8; 20:12, 15; 21:27

The Book of Life is the heavenly record book listing the names of those God has chosen to gain heavenly reward (compare Luke 10:20; Heb.

12:23). It also serves as a call to faithfulness before God. Those not recorded in the Book of Life will be blotted out and will not go to heaven.

Issue: What do you expect to discover in your heavenly reward? Are you sure you will receive one?

Book of the Acts of Solomon   *Thing*   1 Kings 11:41

The author of 1 Kings cited the book of the Acts of Solomon to document his historical materials. It no longer exists.

Issue: What evidence do we have that the Old Testament contains true historical materials? What kind of witness is there for us in a volume that no longer exists?

Book of the Covenant   *Thing*   Ex. 24:7

The Book of the Covenant is the book from which Moses read on Mount Sinai during the covenant-making ceremony with Israel. It contained at least Ex. 20:23–23:33.

Issue: Are you in a covenant relationship with God? What is the nature of your covenant relationship?

Book of the Law   *Thing*   2 Kings 22:8

The "Book of the Law" refers to a copy of God's law that was found during a cleansing of the temple under Josiah. It appears to be carefully tied to the laws of Deuteronomy.

Issue: How do you relate to God's moral and ritual laws? Do you tend to pick and choose as to which ones you obey and which you ignore?

Book of the Wars of the Lord   *Thing*   Num. 21:14–15

The Book of the Wars of the Lord is a mysterious book mentioned in Numbers that described the early wars God fought for Israel. No copy of the text exists today.

Issue: What do we learn about the Prince of Peace from a book with a title like The Wars of Yahweh?

Bottomless Pit *Place* Rev. 9:1–2, 11; 11:7; 17:8; 20:1

"Bottomless Pit" is a synonym for hell or Sheol. It is the home of evil, death, and destruction.

Issue: What leads you to believe or not believe in a literal hell? How do you describe hell?

Bronze Serpent; Serpant of Brass *Thing* Num. 21:9;
2 Kings 18:4

Moses made a bronze serpent during the wilderness wanderings when God punished Israel with poisonous snakes. Looking at the bronze serpent saved a person from the danger of real snakes. People called the bronze snake Nehushtan and sacrificed to it, so King Hezekiah had to have it broken to pieces and removed from the temple.

Issue: How does an item used in legitimate worship and service of God become evil? Can you think of an illustration?

Bul *Thing* 1 Kings 6:38

The eighth month on Jewish calendar, Bul (October-November), is when Israel celebrated the harvest and the completion of the temple.

Issue: What importance do special days on the Christian calendar carry? Which is your favorite? Why?

Bulwark *Thing* Ps. 8:2; Isa. 26:1; 1 Tim. 3:15

A bulwark is a defensive wall that was built to protect a city from a siege. It is used in the Bible as a symbol of God's protection for His people.

Issue: When and how have you experienced God's protection?

Burning Bush *Thing* Ex. 3:2; Acts 7:30

The burning bush was God's instrument in gaining Moses' attention so He could call Moses to deliver his people from Egypt. Moses had fled from Egypt after killing an Eyptian guard who was wounding a Hebrew slave. Moses fled to Midian. Tending the sheep of his father-in-law, he noticed a bush that burned but did not disappear. There God revealed the holy name to Moses and called him back to Egypt to deliver his people.

Issue: God controls all of nature and can use each of its parts to reveal Himself to His people. Have you had a special experience with God that you should share with others?

C

Cabul   *Place*   1 Kings 9:13

Cabul was the region of cities in Galilee that Solomon gave to Hiram of Tyre for the materials and workers to build the temple. These were cities Hiram designated as Cabul, or good for nothing.

Issue: What value do you expect to receive from other people, and what value do gifts you give represent to the recipient?

Caesarea Philippi   *Place*   Matt. 16:13–20; Mark 8:27–30; Luke 9:18–22

Caesarea Philippi was a city and its environs about twenty-five miles (forty km) north of the Sea of Galilee at the foot of Mount Hermon, near the Syrian border. The city was originally named for Pan, the god of nature. Here Jesus queried the disciples as to His identity and found they did not want a suffering, dying messiah. Transfiguration may have occurred here.

Issue: How do you identify Jesus for people who do not know Him? Is a call to suffer for Him in that definition?

Caesar's Household   *People*   Phil. 1:13; 4:22

Caesar's household consisted of persons born into the Roman emperor's (that is, Caesar's) family, bought for his service, or employed in his court.

Apparently some from this large group accepted Christ and asked Paul to send their greetings to people in Philippi.

Issue: How do you witness to and win people of high political influence or people who are employed in a situation that fights against the gospel?

Caiaphas *Person* Matt. 26:3, 57; Luke 3:2; John 11:49; 18:13–14, 24, 28; Acts 4:6

Caiaphas was the Jewish high priest who led the demand for Jesus' crucifixion. His father-in-law was Annas.

Issue: How did Caiaphas's plan fit in with God's?

Cain *Person* Gen. 4:1–25; Heb. 11:4; 1 John 3:12; Jude 11

Cain was the first child born to Adam and Eve and the first murderer. He murdered his brother, Abel, in anger when God accepted Abel's offering but rejected Cain's. God exiled him as a nomad but refused to let any person punish him.

Issue: In what way did the younger brother, Abel, prove superior to the older one?

Calah *Place* Gen. 10

Calah was an Assyrian city on the Tigris River approximately twenty miles south of Nineveh. It was built by the Antediluvian Nimrod and was the site of Ashurnasirpal II's capital (883–859 BC).

Issue: What significance does it have that an Assyrian city was first founded by a primordial man?

Calcol *Person* 1 Kings 4:31; 1 Chron. 2:6

Calcon was a wise man who was compared in wisdom to Solomon.

Issue: What part does human wisdom play in God's eternal plans?

Caleb   *Person*   Num. 13; Josh. 14–15

Caleb, whose name means "dog," was a spy who encouraged Moses and his people to enter the promised land. Only he and Joshua of his generation crossed into the promised land and participated in the Holy Land conquest.

Issue: In what ways does God use senior adults?

Calendar   *Thing*   Ex. 13:4; 23:15; 34:18; 1 Kings 6:1, 37–38; 8:2

The Hebrew Calendar is twelve months of the year whose name and beginning point shifted during Israel's history. Months are often called by number rather than name. The final list of months include:

Nisan (March-April);

Iyyar (April-May);

Sivan (May-June);

Tammuz (June-July);

Ab (July-August);

Elul (August-September);

Tishri (September-October);

Marcheshvan (October-November);

Chislev (November-December);

Tebeth (December-January);

Shebat (January-February);

Adar (February-March)

Issue: In what way does worship of God and life's emergencies create your calendar?

Calneh (or) Calno   *Place*   Isa. 10:9; Amos 6:2

Calneh was a Syrian city three hundred miles north of Israel that Tiglath-pileser III of Assyria captured in 738 BC, the year Menahem, king of Israel, paid tribute to Assyria. Prophets interpreted the battle as a foreshadowing of Israel's ultimate defeat in 722 BC and the basis of Assyrian grand views of invincibility.

Issue: What does military victory or defeat signify for a country in the long run?

Calves, Golden   *Things*   Ex. 32:4–5; compare 1 Kings 12:28; Ps. 106:19–20

Calf-shaped, gold overlay figures were used to represent a pedestal for God to ride on and were found on the ark of the covenant. Worship of Egypt's and Canaan's El and Baal also included young bulls representing the strong and fertile. Moses' absence on Sinai led Aaron to collect jewelry and create a golden calf, while King Jeroboam I created two such calves, one for Dan and one for Bethel, in order to divert northerners from going to Jerusalem to worship. God wanted the ark of the covenant as His only pedestal, relegating calves to Baal and its false worship.

Issue: In what ways do God's people worship the right God in the wrong way?

Cananaean   *Person*   Matt. (or Canaanite) 10:4; Mark 3:18

Simon the Cananaean, also called the Zealot, was one of the twelve disciples. "Cananaean" was a political term used for a group of Jewish zealots.

Issue: Do people have to place a tagline after your name to distinguish you from other people with the same name? How do you react to this secondary name?

Cana of Galilee   *Place*   John 2:1, 11; 4:46; 21:2

Cana of Galilee was the small town in Galilee whose name meant "the nest." There Jesus performed His first miracle of turning water into wine. Jesus was in Cana when He agreed to go with a nobleman to Capernaum to heal the man's son. Cana was also the home of the disciple Nathaniel.

Issue: What does Jesus' first miracle have to say to present-day discussions about the use and abuse of alcoholic beverages?

Candace   *Person*   Acts 8:27

Candace was the title of the Ethiopian or Sudanese Queen or Queen Mother. Philip led her chariot-riding treasurer to Christ.

Issue: Do you know how to use your Scripture to show a person how to believe in Jesus Christ as their personal Savior? When did you last use this skill?

Canon   *Thing*   See 2 Peter 1:16–21

The canon is the collected Scriptures that make up the Bible, which the church studies as God's Word of self-revelation. The books of the Apocrypha are recognized as "Deuterocanonical" but authoritative by Catholics. Protestants relegate these books to a non-authoritative status even when they were included in the earliest Christian manuscripts. Deuterocanonical works are shown below.

Title	Language	Type	Approximate Date	Information
The Epistle of Jeremiah	Hebrew	Letter	300 BC	Based on Jeremiah 10:1–16; fragment in Dead Sea Scrolls
Tobit	Aramaic with sources such as Ahiqar and "Grateful Dead"	Romantic novella set in Nineveh	180 BC	God helps the obedient; demon slays girl's seven husbands
Judith	Hebrew	Historical novella	150 BC to 100 AD	Heroine Judith defeats and beheads Holofernes, the Assyrian general; call to oppose evil and obey Torah; Judith prays to God to help her to lie.
3 Ezra (1 Esdras or III Esdras)	Hebrew	Theological history	150 to 100 BC	Rewrites 2 Chron. 35:1–36:23, Ezra, and Neh. 7:38–8:12; promotes Ezra as "High priest"; centers on temple and Zerubabel; Orthodox, but not Catholics, recognize.

Title	Language	Type	Approximate Date	Information
6 Additions to Esther in its Greek form	Part Hebrew, part Greek	Midrash	From 167 to 70 BC; perhaps at different times	1. Mordecai's dream, 2. Artaxerxes' ordering the Jews to be exterminated, 3. prayers by Mordecai and Esther, 4. Esther's successful audience before King Artaxerxes, 5. the king's second letter praising the Jews, and 6. the interpretation of Mordecai's dream. Added color, defended Judaism, and supplied God's name and theological interpretations
Additions to Daniel				
The Prayer of Azariah	Hebrew	Midrash to Daniel	Between 165 and ca. 100 BC	Turns attention away from the wicked king to Jews facing martyrdom and to one just God
Susanna	Greek or possibly Hebrew	Tale used as Midrash to Daniel	Between 165 and ca. 100 BC	Desirable and virtuous woman refuses sex to two elders and is rescued by Daniel
Bel and the Dragon	Hebrew	Midrash to Daniel	Between 165 and ca. 100 BC	Daniel proves priests, not the idol Bel, eat sacrificed food; second story shows Daniel destroys an idol and is saved by Habakkuk angels.
1 Baruch	Hebrew and Greek	Prophecy	Composite from first or second centuries BC	Jerusalem was destroyed because of 3 parts: 1:1–3:8; 3:9–4:4; 4:5–5:9; confesses Israel's sins and pleads for God's forgiveness; poetic celebration of wisdom; description of how Jerusalem's lament was heard.

TITLE	LANGUAGE	TYPE	APPROXIMATE DATE	INFORMATION
Sirach	Hebrew (Hebrew manuscript found at Masada near Dead Sea Scrolls)	Wisdom apology for Judaism with a critique of Greek culture	180 BC	Reverence for Temple, Torah, and one just and merciful God
The Wisdom of Solomon	Greek	Exhortation	First century BC or AD	Jewish wisdom traditions using Greek and Egyptian ideas
1 Maccabees	Hebrew	Celebrative history	100 BC	Celebrates Maccabees to John Hyrcanus (175 to 134 BC); major source for second-century Palestine history.
2 Maccabees		Anti-Hasmonean, theologically oriented historical epitome of Jason of Cyrene's five-volume work	100 BC	Emphasis on resurrection of body, efficaciousness of martyrdom, and the revelatory dimension of miracles. Two letters may have been composed in Greek.

Caperberry   *Thing*   Eccl. 12:5

The caperberry is a fruit (*Capparis spinosa*) believed to increase sexual desire and ability. The term is often translated as desire.

Issue: In what ways should the church provide different sexual knowledge and understanding for different age groups?

Caphtor   *Place*   Deut. 2:23; Jer. 47:4; Amos 9:7; (compare Gen. 10:14)

Caphtor is the original home of the Philistines in modern Crete.

Issue: How do you treat foreigners who come to live in your country?

Cappadocia   *Place*   Acts 2:9; 1 Peter 1:1

Cappadocia was a region in present-day central Turkey. Some Jews from Cappadocia were in Jerusalem at Pentecost and started a church upon returning home.

Issue: When you are traveling far from home, do you maintain your worship of and witness to Jesus?

Carmel   *Place*   Josh. 15:55; 1 Sam. 15:12; 25

Carmel is the town where Nabal showed disrespect for David. The action eventually led to Nabal's death and David's marriage to Abigail, his widow.

Issue: In what ways do we show disrespect to people in church, in business, and in social life?

Carmel   *Place*   Josh. 19:26; 1 Kings 18:19–20; 2 Kings 2:25; 4:25; Song 7:5

Carmel is also the name of a 1,750-foot mountain near the Mediterranean Sea between Acco and Dor. There, Elijah argued with prophets of Baal.

Issue: If the population overwhelmingly opposed Christianity, how would you behave in public? What have you done to go against the stream in standing for Christ?

Carpus *Person* 2 Tim. 4:13

Paul left his cloak with Carpus, "fruit," from Troas.

Issue: What friends are close enough to you that you would entrust them with important personal property?

Carshena *Person* Est. 1:14

Carshena was the Persian counselor who helped King Ahasuerus deal with Vashti, his wife, when she refused his order to show off her beauty before his guests and subjects.

Issue: How much do you value your self-respect? Whose orders are you willing to disobey to preserve your self-respect?

Cassia *Thing* Ex. 30:24; Ps. 45:8; Ezek. 27:19

The cassia tree is related to cinnamon and used to add aroma to anointing oil.

Issue: What do you learn from Scripture about the use of sweet-smelling substances? Why were they so important in biblical times?

Castor and Pollux *Things* Acts 28:11

The constellation Gemini is seen as the Greek gods Castor and Pollux, twin sons of Zeus and Leda, a good omen when seen in bad weather. Navigators placed it as an identifying omen on the prow of a ship and viewed it as a good luck charm.

Issue: What types of superstition or magic do you practice? Why?

Cenchrea (Cenchreae)   *Place*   Acts 18:18; Rom. 16:1

Cenchrea was a port city for Corinth and served as Paul's barbershop, where he cut his hair in fulfillment of a vow. Phoebe was a member of the church there.

Issue: Phoebe was a *diakonon*, which may be translated servant or deacon. Which translation would you see as correct? Why?

Chebar   *Place*   Ezek. 1:1; 3:15; 10:15; 43:3

The river in Babylon where God gave Ezekiel his fantastic visions was called the Chebar.

Issue: Has God ever revealed something special to you in visions? Has He revealed things in other ways? How do you explain this experience to other people?

Chedor-Laomer   *Person*   Gen. 14

Chedor-Laomer was the king of Elam who led the coalition against Sodom and Gomorrah that eventually captured Lot. He and the coalition were defeated by Abraham.

Issue: Why was Abraham so concerned to protect Lot?

Chemosh   *Thing*   Num. 21:29; Judg. 11:24; 1 Kings 11:7, 33; 2 Kings 23:13; Jer. 48:7, 13, 46

Moab's god, Chemosh, tempted Israel at several points in their history. Jeremiah foretold his destruction.

Issue: What foreign goods or practices are exotic enough that you want them more than you want to be true to God?

Chenaniah   *Person*   1 Chron. 15

Chief Levite musician under David, Chenaniah helped return the ark of the covenant to Jerusalem.

Issue: Why did David have to retrieve the ark? What role did the ark play in Israelite life?

Chephirah *Place* Josh. 9:17; 18:26; Ezra 2:25

Chephirah, or "queen of the lions," was a town four miles west of Gibeon. Joshua saved it from the attacking southern coalition.

Issue: Why would Joshua rescue native Canaanites? Do you ever help ungodly people? Why?

Cherethites (Cherethim) *People* 1 Sam. 30:14; 2 Sam. 8:18; Ezek. 25:16; Zeph. 2:5

Cherethites were closely related to Philistines and could often be found working as paid soldiers.

Issue: How and why would you use soldiers related to the enemy as your own bodyguard?

Cherith *Place* 1 Kings 17:3

Elijah found water and protection at Cherith, a brook east of the Jordan and south of Jericho, after prophesying a two-year drought.

Issue: Have you experienced protection from God?

Chileab *Person* 2 Sam. 3:3

David's second son, Chileab, disappears from history.

Issue: How does it affect a family when one member disappears and cannot be located by any means? Do you know a family who has experienced such a loss?

Chilion *Person* Ruth 1:2

Chilion, the son of Elimelech and Naomi, moved to Moab, married the Moabite Orpah, and then died.

Issue: How does one feel when losing a child? How is this feeling multiplied when it occurs in a foreign land?

Chinnereth   *Place*   Num. 34:11; Deut. 3:17; Josh. 13:27

Chinnereth is the Hebrew Bible name for the Sea of Galilee, which was also known as the Sea of Tiberius and Lake Gennesaret.

Issue: How do places get several different names? Do you know of places today with more than one name?

Chios   *Place*   Acts 20:15

Chios, five miles off the coast of Asia Minor, was the island home of the Greek poet Homer. Paul landed there on his third missionary journey.

Issue: What famous person lives nearest to you? Do you ever visit that person's home? Why?

Chloe   *Person*   1 Cor. 1:11

Chloe's household informed Paul of dissension in the church at Corinth.

Issue: Is it truly Christian to tell on another Christian? Does telling of dissension increase or decrease it?

Chorazin   *Place*   Matt. 11:21; Luke 10:13

Chorazin was a Galilean farming town two miles north of Capernaum that Jesus rebuked for not recognizing Him.

Issue: How does economic prosperity blind people to God's activity?

Claudia   *Person*   2 Tim. 4:21

Claudia was the last person on Paul's list of greetings in his second letter to Timothy.

Issue: What does Paul accomplish by listing people who send greetings? What do greetings accomplish when you are last on the list?

Clement   *Person*   Phil. 4:3

Paul's partner in gospel ministry, Clement, was apparently a member of the church in Philippi.

Issue: How many people in ministry get little, if any, recognition? What person has ministered to you in important ways but received no recognition?

Cleopas *Person* Luke 24

Cleopas walked with the resurrected Jesus toward Emmaus without recognizing Him.

Issue: What was different about Jesus after He was resurrected that people did not recognize Him? How did the breaking of bread open their eyes to Jesus? When have you sensed the presence of the risen Christ in your life? What led you to recognize His presence?

Clopas *Person* John 19:25

Clopas was a relative, possibly the husband, of one of the Marys at the cross, though the Greek New Testament is not clear as to the exact relationship. He was apparently the one who contributed financially to Jesus' ministry.

Issue: How is Clopas related to Mary? How is he related to Jesus? Is financial support all one needs to give to Jesus?

Cloud, Pillar of *Thing* Ex. 13:21–22; 14:19; 33:9–10; Num. 12:5; 14:14; Deut. 31:15

God sent a pillar of clouds to lead Moses and the Israelites through the wilderness.

Issue: How do you recognize God's leadership for you and your family? Does His path at times conflict with your plans?

Cockcrowing *Thing* Matt. 26:34, 74–75; Mark 13:35; 14:30, 68, 72; Luke 22:34, 60–61; John 13:38; 18:27

The Roman time system had four watches (6 a.m. to 9 p.m.; 9 p.m. until midnight; midnight to 3 a.m.; 3 to 6 a.m.). The cockcrowing was the third watch. The Jewish system had only three watches (see Luke 12:38).

Issue: Does God have a warning system for you? Do you repeat your sins even when you know better? Why?

Cohort *People* Acts 27:1

A Roman military unit comprising up to one thousand soldiers was called a cohort. It was one-tenth of a Roman legion.

Issue: Why would the Roman government deploy its finest military unit to guard Paul? What is the proper relationship between the church and the military?

Comforter (Helper) *God* John 14:16, 26; 15:26; 16:7

Jesus promised to send a comforter to the disciples to help, comfort, and adjudicate for them in His absence.

Issue: What experiences have you had in gaining comfort and help from God's promised Holy Spirit?

Concubine *Person* Gen. 22:24; 25:6; Deut. 17:17; Judg. 18–19; 2 Sam. 5:13; 1 Kings 11:3

A concubine, or secondary wife, went without inheritance rights and often without a dowry. The man who could afford a concubine was usually wealthy and influential.

Issue: Was it wrong for men to have concubines? Why? How do you define concubines? Are they good or bad for society?

Corban *Thing* Mark 7:11

The Jewish practice of Corban involved reserving a gift for God so that it could be used for no other purpose. Jesus condemned the misuse of this practice when people designated resources for God so that they would not have to use them to take care of needy family members.

Issue: What religious practices are misused today to get personal gain rather than honor God? What about churches and property taxes or contributions to get tax deductions?

Cornelius   *Person*   Acts 10

Cornelius was a Roman military officer (a centurion) who worshiped the Jewish God and assisted the Jewish people. Both he and Peter had visions leading to the first Gentile conversions.

Issue: Why do people sometimes restrict membership in a group to one color, economic class, or gender? How does prejudice against others develop?

Cornerstone   *Thing*   Job 38:6; Ps. 118:22; Isa. 28:16; Zech. 10:4; Matt. 21:42; Mark 12:10; Luke 20:17; Acts 4:11; 1 Peter 2:6–7

The strong building stone set in a corner and connecting and strengthening two walls is known as a cornerstone. This image was used metaphorically to explain the key position of rulers and kings. It was later applied to Jesus as the One with the key role in salvation.

Issue: How does a cornerstone work in architecture? What does this language imply about Jesus?

Cos   *Place*   Acts 21:1

Cos was the island between Miletus and Rhodes where Paul stopped briefly on the way home from his third missionary journey. Hippocrates started a famous medical school there.

Issue: What kind of healing did Hippocrates offer? Compare this to what Jesus offers.

Council, Heavenly   *God*   1 Kings 22:20; Job 1:6; 2:1; 15:8; Pss. 29:1; 82:1–8; 89:5–8; Isa. 6; Jer. 23:18, 22; Zech. 3:1–2

The heavenly council is the gathering of God with the heavenly host for worship and for discussion of the activities and assignments of the council members, which, at times, can involve prophets.

Issue: What roles do the heavenly host and the prophets play in the "meetings" of God's council?

Council of Jerusalem   *People*   Acts 15

At the Council of Jerusalem, church leaders gathered to hear Paul's report of successful ministry among the Gentiles and to determine requirements for Gentiles to become Christians. They decided Gentiles can be Christians without fully observing Jewish ritual laws.

Issue: What basic elements must a person experience and practice to become and be a Christian believer?

Covenant   *Thing*   Ex. 19–24, 33–34; Josh. 24

A covenant is the relationship between God and His people based on promises by each partner. It is similar to political treaties in that it shows God claiming His people and promising to protect them while they in turn pledge loyalty and obedience to Him. Noah and Abraham made covenants with God prior to the Mosaic covenant (Gen. 9; 15). God's new covenant or testament writes God's will on the human heart and brings salvation through the cross and the resurrection of Jesus Christ.

Issue: Is covenant with God a relationship you earn? In what way do you show loyalty to God in thanks for His promised salvation?

Covering the Head   *Thing*   1 Cor. 11

Paul discussed the matter of covering one's head with the church at Corinth because of the Jewish practice of women wearing a veil to cover their heads any time they left their house. Some Corinthian women claimed freedom from this practice. Paul insisted on observance of the practice for the sake of witnessing to others outside the church and for those inside the church who were disturbed by the exercise of such freedom. To continue the practice today would bring about the opposite effect. Christian women wearing hair covering today would draw attention to themselves as unusual, strange people nonbelievers would not respect. Today, this practice might cause dissension in the church.

Issue: In what ways do you limit your personal freedom in consideration of the feelings of others and to keep unity in the church?

Cozbi   *Person*   Num. 25:15

Zimri brought Cozbi, a Midianite woman, into his tent, bringing a plague to the wilderness camp until Phinehas the priest killed the pair.

Issue: Are you practicing overt sin whose evil no one questions? What will be the ultimate result of such practice?

Crescens   *Person*   2 Tim. 4:10

Paul's ministry partner Crescens was in Galatia when Paul wrote 2 Timothy.

Issue: Whom do you have as a ministry partner? What kind of ministry do you participate in? Does it lead you out of town?

Crispus   *Person*   Acts 18:8; 1 Cor. 1:14

Crispus was a Jewish synagogue leader in Corinth who became a believer. He was one of the few people that Paul personally baptized.

Issue: What is the meaning and purpose of baptism for you?

Crown of Thorns   *Thing*   Matt. 27:29; Mark 15:18; John 19:3

The Romans placed a crown of thorns on Jesus' head to mock "King Jesus" during His trial.

Issue: How do our thoughts, words, actions, and relationships mock Jesus and cause Him pain?

Cushan-Rishathaim   *Person*   Judg. 3:8

Cushan-Rishathaim was a Syrian king who was given a symbolic name meaning "dark one of double evil." God used him to punish Israel until God sent Othniel to deliver Israel.

Issue: How does a person acquire such a sinister name? Do you know of people to whom the name might apply? Would anyone attach such a name to you? Why?

Cyrene   *Thing*   Matt. 27:32; Mark 15:21; Luke 23:26; Acts 2:10; 11:20; 13:1

Cyrene was the North African home of Simon, the man ordered to carry Jesus' cross. It was the capital city of the Roman district of Cyrenaica including Libya and Crete. Some of its citizens participated in Pentecost and in witnessing to the Antioch church about Gentile conversions. Lucius of Cyrene was a Christian prophet in Antioch. Cyrene was famous for medical school, a classical academy, and a school of philosophers (the "Cyrenaics") who pioneered what came to be known as Epicureanism.

Issue: Jesus used a cross as a symbol of a disciple's life. Stephen showed what following the cross meant. Are you ready to live crossward rather than selfward?

Cyrenius (Quirinius)   *Person*   Luke 2:2

Publius Sulpicius Quirinius was the governor of Syria, appointed by Rome, from 6 to 9 AD and possibly for a previous stint near 6 BC at the time of Jesus' birth. Luke 2:2 places Jesus' birth at the time of Herod's death and of Quirinius' governorship. Many scholars find Luke's date for Jesus' birth difficult to interpret because there is evidence that Herod died in 4 BC, which does not match the date when Quirinius was governor of Syria. Nonbiblical sources place either Saturninus (9–7 BC) or Varus (6–4 BC) as governor of Syria at the time of Christ's birth. After long public service in various posts, Quirinius died in AD 21.

Issue: Does anything about your view of Scripture change if the dates of this governor's reign do not match the exact time of Jesus' birth?

Dagon *Thing* Judg. 16:23; 1 Sam. 5:2–5, 7; 1 Chron. 10:10

Samson pulled down the temple to the Philistine god, Dagon. Dagon's statue toppled before the ark of the covenant. When they entered Palestine, the Philistines adopted Dagon from native Canaanites.

Issue: In your experience, how has God proven Himself to be the only God?

Dalmanutha *Place* Mark 8:10

After feeding the five thousand, Jesus brought His disciples to Dalmanutha, a town apparently on the northwest shore of the Sea of Galilee. Greek manuscripts have several different readings for this name. Compare Matt. 15:39.

Issue: Why did Jesus seek out small, basically insignificant places to be with His disciples after performing major works?

Dalmatia *Place* Rom. 15:19; 2 Tim. 4:10

The southern part of Illyricum, Dalmatia, is north of Greece and across the Adriatic Sea from Italy. Both Paul and Titus ministered there.

Issue: Do you have someone you mentor in church ministry or with whom you work closely on special projects? What happens when that person is not available to minister with you?

Damaris *Person* Acts 17:34

Damaris was a woman who accepted Jesus as her Savior when Paul preached on the Areopagus in Athens.

Issue: In what way was Paul's ministry on the Areopagus successful? How do you witness for Christ with intellectuals?

Damascus *Place*   1 Sam. 22:2; 2 Sam. 8:5–6; 1 Kings 11:23–25; 15:16–23; 2 Kings 5:18; Amos 1:3–5

Damascus is the capital city of Syria and the world's oldest city. It is located sixty miles east of the port city of Sidon. Two major roads, the Via Maris and the King's Highway, intersected there. While a great location for commerce and trade, Damascus also faced a great risk of military invasion.

Issue: What makes a city great? How would you describe the city you live in or near?

Dancing *Thing*   Ex. 15:20–21; Pss. 149:3; 150:4; Eccl. 3:4; Matt. 11:17; 14:6; Mark 6:22; Luke 7:32; 15:25

Dancing is described by eleven different Hebrew terms: twisting or whirling in circles, jumping, leaping, or skipping. It is a part of weddings, victory celebrations, mourning, and worship.

Issue: Why would some churches ban dancing as sinful? Can you describe a situation in which dancing was a vital part of your worship?

Daric *Thing*   Ezra 2:69; Neh. 7:70, 72

The Persian daric, a coin representing four days' wages, was introduced by Daris (522 to 486 BC). It was possibly the first coin Jews used.

Issue: In what ways are coins superior to weights and scales for a country's trade and commerce?

Darius the Mede *Person*   Isa. 13:17–18; 21:2; Jer. 51:1, 27–28; Dan. 5:31; 6:26, 28

Darius the Mede captured Babylon from Belshazzar and had Daniel thrown in the lions' den in an apparent fulfillment of prophecies. We have no outside (non-biblical) evidence of his existence. "Darius" may be the throne name used by the elderly Gubaru (or Gobyrus), governor of Gutium, who seized Babylon for Cyrus and was viceroy over Mesopotamia.

Issue: Why would you take the Bible as a reliable historical source if all our sources apart from the Bible do not mention the person or seem to have other people accomplishing the same task as that described in the Bible?

Darius I *Person* Ezra 4–6; Zech. 1–8

Darius I, a Persian king (521–486 BC), was also known as Darius Hystaspes or the Great. He assumed power after his cousin Cambyses died, but was not recognized by the entire empire. He enlarged the Persian Empire to include territory from India to Greece establishing an administration with twenty satrapies or provinces. He began issuing gold coins (darics); and allowed the Jews to finish building the temple. He was the loser in the Battle of Marathon (490 BC) with the Greeks.

Issue: By what evidence or criteria do you declare a politician great? Can a person who does not believe in God qualify as great?

Darius the Persian *Person* Neh. 12:22

Darius the Persian is a mystery. He may be the same as Darius III Codomannus (336–331 BC) or Darius II Nothus (423–404 BC), son of Artaxerxes I. Others identify him with Darius I, whose defeat by Alexander ended the Persian Empire. His empire, though considered corrupt, conquered the Greek coastline on the Aegean Sea in the Peloponnesian War.

Issue: What does it signify for you that we cannot identify every ruler the Bible names?

Dathan *Person* Num. 16

When Dathan and his brother Abiram rebelled against Moses, God opened the earth and they disappeared, authenticating Moses' authority.

Issue: Who has authority in your church to assume major leadership roles and make decisions? What process do you have to quell individuals or groups who strongly oppose the church's leadership?

Day of Atonement   *Thing*   Lev. 16:16–28; 23:27–28; 25:9; Heb. 8:6; 9:7, 11–26; 13:11–12

The Day of Atonement, the tenth day of seventh month (September-October) is a day of fasting and offering sacrifices to God and to receive atonement for one's sins. Only on this day could the high priest enter the holy of holies in the tabernacle or temple. He offered sacrifices for the sanctuary, the altar, and the sins of the nation. One goat was slain; the other, hearing the people's sins confessed over his head, was sent into the wilderness.

Issue: Human sin separates the holy God from the sinful people. Every person must have help in covering sins so they no longer separate the person and God. God provided Israel a way in the Day of Atonement. He provides everyone a way through belief in the atoning sacrifice of Jesus Christ. Have you accepted Christ's atonement for your sins?

Day's Journey   *Thing*   Gen. 30:36; 31:23; Ex. 3:18; 8:27; Deut. 1:2; Luke 2:44

A day's journey was a Jewish measurement of distance approximating the distance a person or group could travel in one day, typically between twenty and thirty miles but sometimes as little as ten miles. The rabbis eventually created rules on the distance one could travel on the Sabbath day.

Issue: How do you measure distance as you journey from one part of the country to another? How far do you run in a day's workout, travel on family vacation, or move in a typical day at work?

Daysman   *Person*   Job 9:33; 1 Tim. 2:5

A daysman was a mediator or arbitrator seeking an agreement between two parties or imposing a binding judgment on the parties. Job wants "justice" from God but can find no one qualified to arbitrate between himself and the sovereign God.

Issue: Do you ever argue with God, seeking what you consider to be fair and just? What do you seek when you ask God for justice? Do you really want Him to give you what you deserve?

Day (Morning) Star   *Thing*   Isa. 14:12; 2 Peter 1:19

The popular understanding of the term "day star" is that it refers to "Lucifer" and to the fall of Satan, but the biblical context quickly shows it applied to a human, the king of Babylon. The king falls from his throne into the realm of the dead to be covered with worms and maggots.

Issue: What is your greatest achievement as a human being? What is the proudest moment of your life? Have you experienced a great fall from your proud throne of achievement?

Deacon   *Persons*   Matt. 20:26; 22:13; 23:11; Mark 9:35; 10:43; John 2:5, 9; 12:26; Rom. 13:4; 15:8; 16:1; 1 Cor. 3:5; 2 Cor. 3:6; 6:4; 11:15, 23; Gal. 2:17; Eph. 3:7; 6:21; Phil. 1:1; Col. 1:7, 23, 25; 4:7; 1 Tim. 3:8, 12; 4:6

The Greek term *diakonos*, deacon, is translated to mean servant or minister. The term gradually was limited to referencing a person who takes part in a church ministry of service to the church and its needy members.

Issue: Do the Scriptures above set qualifications of age, nationality, economic status, gender, or education for deacons? What makes one eligible to be a deacon? Does the Bible differentiate between the work of a deacon and the office of a deacon? Can the same person be a pastor, a deacon, and an elder?

Dead Sea (Salt Sea)   *Thing*   Gen. 14:3; Num. 34:3, 12; Deut. 3:17; Josh. 3:16; 12:3; 15:2, 5; 18:19

The Dead Sea, or Salt Sea, is a lake at the southern end of the Jordan River with the highest salt content (25 percent) of any body of water on earth. Because of its high salt content, nothing lives in it. At its largest point, it measures fifty miles long and ten miles wide with its surface 1,292 feet below the level of the Mediterranean. It ranges from 1,300 to ten feet in depth, and receives six million tons of water daily from the river Jordan without any outlet.

Issue: A body must give out as well as take in to have life. What do you give?

Deborah   *Person*   Judg. 4–5

The prophet Deborah, whose name means "bee," called Barak to action against the Canaanite army, but then warned him the glory would go to a woman since he did not obey quickly. One of Israel's oldest songs (Judg. 5) is attributed to her.

Issue: Are some roles designated by God for men and some for women? Are you able to take charge when a leader is obviously not fulfilling a God-given role?

Decapolis   *Place*   Matt. 4:25; Mark 5:20; 7:31

The Decapolis was a group of ten Gentile cities—Damascus, Philadelphia (modern Amman), Canatha, Scythopolis (the only one west of Jordan), Pella, Hippos, Gadara, Dion, Raphana, and Gerasa (modern Jerash). Other sources raise the number to 14 or 18. Jesus dared to take His teachings to these Gentile people and cities.

Issue: Are there places in your town or county where your church never reaches out in witness or ministry? Do you have the courage and faith to start ministering there? Does something prohibit you from participating in volunteer missions to certain countries?

Dedan   *Place*   Gen. 10:7; 25:3; 1 Chron. 1:9, 32; Jer. 25:23; 49:8; Ezek. 25:13; 27:20; 38:13

The Arabian village of Dedan at al-Alula, seventy miles southwest of Tema and four hundred miles from Jerusalem, was a station on the caravan road between Tema and Medina known for incense trade. Ezekiel and Jeremiah condemned Dedan for carrying out commerce with Edom. The Arabian tribes like those of Dedan carried on intense rivalries and competitions. When King Nabonidus went there to look for relics, he gave authority to his son Belshazzar.

Issue: Ancient antipathies such as those of Israel's small neighbors—Edom, Moab, and Arabian tribes—affect life for long centuries. Do you have any organizations or persons with whom your family or organization has been arguing or fighting for generations?

| **Deep** *Thing* | Gen. 1:2; 7:11; 8:2; 49:25; Ex. 15:5, 8; Deut. 8:7; 33:13; Job 28:14; 38:16, 30; 41:32; Pss. 33:7; 36:6; 42:7; 71:20; 77:16; 78:15; 104:6; 106:9; 107:26; 135:6; 148:7; Prov. 3:20; 8:24, 27–28; Isa. 51:10; 63:13; Ezek. 26:19; 31:4, 15; Amos 7:4; Jonah 2:5; Hab. 3:10 |

The peculiar Hebrew term *tehom*, or deep, refers to the primordial, dark waters that were present as God created the world and separated the elements, placing each in the proper environment. He rescued His people at the Red Sea and the Jordan by having the people cross through the path of the deeps. Floods represent the deep bursting its bonds for a time period until restrained by God's Spirit or wind (same Hebrew word, *ruakh*). Rough seas with unknown animal inhabitants represent the fearful deep, as does the abode of the dead.

Issue: Life brings fears, threats, dangers, and disasters. They carry us to the brink of despair. How do you respond? Do you trust God as the only person able to lift you out of the deeps?

| **Delilah** *Person* | Judg. 16 |

Delilah finagled Samson's secret and gave him a close shave (Samson was powerless without his hair), allowing the Philistines to capture and make sport of Israel's strong man.

Issue: What value do you place on the unique gifts God has given you? What temptations do you face because you possess such unique gifts?

Demas   *Person*   Col. 4:14; 2 Tim. 4:10; Philem. 24

Demas deserted Paul, choosing the lures of the world rather than the love of the gospel.

Issue: What temptation exercises the strongest pull on you, luring you back to the world's way of living?

Demeter   *Person*   Acts 19:24–41

Demeter was a silversmith in Ephesus whose name means "belonging to Demeter," the Greek goddess of crops. He started a riot when he saw Paul's gospel was winning converts and thus taking away clientele in silver shrines for the goddess Diana.

Issue: Clients or converts? Which group is more important to you? Do you spend most of your time, resources, and energy on your job or on your church?

Demeter   *Person*   3 John 12

This Demeter seems to have been a worshiper of Demeter, a god in the Eleusian mystery religions, before converting. John praised him as one recommended by all in the congregation and by the truth he taught.

Issue: What type of recommendation do people in your church testify to regarding your Christian life?

Demon   *Thing*   Lev. 16–17; Deut. 32:17; 1 Sam. 16:15–16; 18:10; 2 Chron. 11:15; Ps. 106:37; Isa. 34:14

Demons are beings promoting evil in Israel, accepting unclean and outlawed sacrifices, and apparently living in the wilderness. The New Testament builds on intertestamental literature to recognize these evil characters that were taking possession of a person's life to control the person's actions and to cause people to be mute (Matt. 9:32; 12:22; Mark 9:17, 25; Luke 11:14), deaf (Mark 9:25), or blind (Matt. 12:22; John 10:21). Possessed people have convulsions (Mark 1:26; 9:26), superhuman strength

(Mark 5:4), and self-destructive behavior (Matt. 17:15). Jesus repeatedly showed His power over demons.

See Azazel; Lilith.

Issue: How do you describe the powers of evil that threaten the faithful and our world? Have you ever experienced evil powers? How did those experiences affect you?

| Denarius | *Thing* | Matt. 20:2, 9–10, 13; 22:19; Mark 12:15; Luke 20:24; Rev. 6:6 |

The denarius was a Roman coin worth the amount paid to a day laborer for a day's work.

Issue: What is the fair minimum wage for a modern worker? Do you feel your wages are fair? Are the wages you pay your employees less than they deserve? Why?

| Derbe | *Place* | Acts 14:6, 20; 16:1; 20:4 |

Derbe was a city in the region of Lycaonia in the province of Galatia, a large area of Asia Minor. Derbe and Lystra spoke a language different from that spoken in northern Galatia. Driven from Iconium, Paul found gospel success in Derbe. Paul's co-worker, Gaius, hailed from Derbe.

Issue: In what area of Christian ministry have you found the greatest success? Have you had to overcome language differences?

| Descent into Hades | *Thing* | Acts 2:27, 31; Eph. 4:9; 1 Peter 3:19 |

This theme shares certain topics with Near Eastern tales about a god entering the realm of death and returning to bring new seasons, to announce a takeover in the underworld, to rescue relatives from the underworld, to show the power of death, or to limit the power of death. The Bible makes a brief mention of the topic without a clear narrative description. Where quick reference is made, no explanation or result is described (1 Peter 3). The basic thrust of the topic is to glorify Jesus as having done everything necessary for believers to gain salvation and deliverance.

Issue: What comfort do you receive, knowing Jesus has covered all bases and conquered all enemies, providing you complete salvation with no enemies to fear or fight?

Desire of All Nations   *Thing*   Hag. 2:7

The Hebrew phrase, desire of all nations, refers to the treasures or wealth of the rebuilt temple. The Latin Vulgate began the messianic translation of this phrase.

Issue: How do you determine whether a passage is referring to a coming Messiah or to the writer's own period in history? And can it refer to both periods?

Desolation, Abomination of

See Abomination.

Devil

See Satan.

Devoted to Destruction

See Anathema.

Dibri   *Person*   Lev. 24:10–23

Dibri was an Israelite whose name meant "talker" or "gossip." His daughter gave birth to an Egyptian's son who grew up and cursed God's name. The people then stoned him to death.

Issue: What do you think the Bible teaches about interracial marriage? How would you react if your child wanted to marry someone of different race or culture?

Didrachma   *Thing*   Gen. 20:16; 23:16; Ex. 30:13–15; Matt. 17:24

The Greek coin didrachma was worth one-half of a Jewish shekel, the amount of the annual temple tax.

Issue: Should the church or the state have the authority to issue a tax based on religious considerations?

Didymus   *Person*   John 11:16

Didymus, meaning "twin," was the name given to the apostle Thomas.

Issue: Do you know people who have or are twins? What special blessings do twins bring? What about any difficulties and problems?

Dinah   *Person*   Gen. 30:21; 34

Dinah was the daughter of Jacob and Leah who was raped by Shechem. This created a disturbance among her brothers and led to atrocities.

Issue: How do Christian siblings relate to one another; how do brothers protect their sisters?

Dionysius   *Person*   Acts 17:34

Dionysius was an intellectual member of the Areopagus in Athens who responded in faith to Paul's presentation there.

Issue: How does the church today present its message to the intellectual elite of our world? How do you respond to an intellectual challenge against the gospel?

Diotrophes   *Person*   3 John 9

Diotrophes' name means "nurtured by Jove." He rejected John's authority, pushed his own, and threatened the unity of the church.

Issue: How do you deal with someone who splits the church?

Discerning of Spirits   *Thing*   1 Cor. 12:10

Discerning of spirits is the activity and gift of determining which voice in the church comes from God's Spirit and which comes from foreign evil spirits.

Issue: How does your church decide which voices to follow and which to reject?

Dives *Person* Luke 16

The Latin word for rich in Vulgate is *dives*, and it is used with the rich man at Lazarus's gate in Jesus' parable (Luke 16:19). The Bible has nothing to suggest that dives is a proper name.

Issue: Why do some traditions live on in Bible studies even when they have no supporting evidence? What difference does it make if Dives is not a proper name?

Divided Kingdom *Thing* 1 Kings 11:43

The time period after Jeroboam I led the northern tribes in revolt against Rehoboam and the southern kingdom (Judah) until the northern kingdom (Israel) fell to Assyria (922–722 BC) is known as the divided kingdom period.

Issue: What causes people to separate from relatives, believers, governments, organizations, and friends?

Diviner's Oak *Thing* Judg. 9:35–37

The diviner's oak was a tree near Shechem where people sought an oracle or revelation from God. Several terms describe special trees near Shechem and may refer to the same tree. See Gen. 12:6; 35:4; Deut. 11:30; 33:19–20; Josh. 24:25–26.

Issue: What means of divination, if any, are legitimate today? Do you know of superstitious ways of seeking God's will today?

Divorce *Thing* Gen. 1:27; 2:21–25; Deut. 24:1–4; Ezra 10; Mal. 2:14–16; Matt. 5:31–32; 19:3–12; Mark 10:4–12; Rom. 7:1–3; 1 Cor. 7:10–16

Divorce is the breaking or renouncing of the God-witnessed covenant between a wife and a husband. The rabbis argued the conditions under which divorce could be permitted according to Deut. 24. A husband apparently had the right to divorce his wife if he found she had been sexually active before the marriage. Jesus placed rigid limits on divorce, expecting obedience to the covenant equally. Divorce thus becomes a forgivable sin that should be the rare exception, not the rule.

Issue: How and why did divorce become so common in our country? How do you counsel someone contemplating divorce?

Dizahab   *Place*   Deut. 1:1

Dizahab was a place east of the Jordan River whose name meant "place of gold." Moses' last address to Israel, contained in Deuteronomy, was delivered there.

Issue: What last words would you leave with your family if you knew death approached for you?

Doeg   *Person*   1 Sam. 21:7; Ps. 52

Doeg was an Edomite whose name means "full of fear." He reported to King Saul how Abimelech, the priest, had assisted David and followed Saul's orders to kill the eighty-five priests.

Issue: Are you guilty of a sin when you carry out the sinful orders of a superior officer and manager? Explain a modern example.

Dor   *Place*   Josh. 11:2; 12:23; 17:11; 21:32; Judg. 1:27; 1 Sam. 28:7; 1 Kings 4:11; 1 Chron. 7:29; Ps. 83:10

Dor was a city-state below Mount Carmel ruled by Egypt. Around the year 1300 BC, it was defeated by a branch of Sea People related to the Philistines. It later joined the northern coalition that Joshua defeated and became one of Solomon's district capitals.

Issue: Israel was told to completely destroy all the Canaanite cities to the ban (see Herem), killing all living beings. How can a loving God issue such a command?

Dorcas *Person* Acts 9:36

Dorcas was a woman with the Greek name meaning "gazelle" and the Aramaic name Tabitha, which also means "gazelle." Peter raised her from the dead.

Issue: Why do good people get sick and die? How can we best minister to dying people and their friends and relatives?

Dothan *Place* Gen. 37:17; 2 Kings 6:13

Dothan was the town where Joseph's brothers sold him into slavery and where Elisha led the besieging army from Syria back to Samaria and defeat. It lies eleven miles northeast of Samaria and thirteen miles north of Shechem.

Issue: What causes sibling rivalry? Have you experienced mistreatment and seen it later turn to your advantage?

Dresser of Sycamores *Person* Amos 7:14

Amos identified himself as a dresser of sycamores, a professional job that he saw as different from the job of professional prophets. The job involved cutting the top of each piece of fruit from the sycamore tree to hasten ripening and increase flavor.

Issue: How does God use laity to accomplish His purposes? What identity do you give yourself? How do you distinguish a true prophetic word from a false one?

Dropsy *Thing* Luke 14:2

Dropsy was a disease marked by fluid retention and swelling. Jesus healed a man with dropsy on the Sabbath and infuriated the Pharisees.

Issue: What special ways do you and your family mark God's Sabbath day? What do you see as wrong to do on the Sabbath?

Drusilla *Person* Acts 24:24

Drusilla was the wife of Felix, the Roman-appointed governor of Judea, who heard Paul's testimony. The daughter of Herod Agrippa I, she broke off her engagement to Antiochus Ephiphanes of Commagene when he refused to be circumcised and become a Jew. She married King Aziz of Emesa, who did convert. Felix won her away from her husband.

Issue: Marriage scandals and religious disputes too often go hand-in-hand. What are some examples of such misbehavior?

Ebed-melech *Person* Jer. 38:7; 39:15–18

Named Ebed-melech, "servant of the king," this Ethiopian eunuch served Zedekiah, the king of Judah. He rescued Jeremiah from imprisonment in a cistern and was rewarded.

Issue: Why does God let His faithful prophet suffer? Who in the present church serves the King so well?

Ebenezer *Place/Thing* 1 Sam. 4:1; 7:12

Ebenezer is the name of the site of the battle where the ark of the covenant was captured and of the battle where Samuel led Israel's army to victory over the Philistines. Samuel then raised up a memorial stone he named Ebenezer, "stone of help."

Issue: Why was the capture of the ark a disaster for Israel? Do you have any memorials in your home or town that let parents show children what God has done?

Ed   *Thing*   Josh. 22:34

An Ed was an altar eastern tribes built to maintain unity with western tribes who saw it as disobedience to God's command. Phinehas arbitrated an agreement between the two groups, preserving the unity of all Israel.

Issue: How do church leaders maintain and/or arbitrate agreement and unity in the worship community?

Eden   *Place*   Gen. 2:8, 10, 15; 3:23–24; 4:16; Isa. 51:3; Ezek. 28:13; 31:9, 16, 18; 36:35; Joel 2:3

Eden was the region where God planted a paradise and where man and woman committed the first sin.

Issue: What is the connection between the sin in the garden and the sins you commit? Why did Adam and Eve choose to sin?

Edrei   *Place*   Num. 21:33–35; Deut. 1:3–4; 3:1, 10; Josh. 12:4; 13:31

Edrei was the royal city of King Og of Bashan, whom Joshua defeated. It lies midway between Amman, Jordan, and Damascus, Syria.

Issue: How does one determine the legal border between tribes and nations? How long does a nation retain legal control of another country?

Eglah   *Person*   2 Sam. 3:5

David had a wife, Eglah, whose name means "heifer" or "young cow."

Issue: Who are legitimate heirs of David?

Eglon   *Person*   2 Sam. 3:5

Eglon was an obese Moabite king who ruled over Israel for eighteen years before sly Ehud killed him.

Issue: How do you avoid falling victim to a trickster's antics? How does God work to deliver His people from their enemies?

Eglon *Place* Josh. 10:3

Eglon was also the name for a city-state whose king joined the southern coalition against Joshua and his Gibeonite covenant partner.

Issue: When does a group have the right to refuse to follow regulations of a treaty or covenant they have signed with someone else?

Egyptian, The *Person* Acts 21:38

The Egyptian was the leader of a league of four thousand "assassins" who tried to capture Jerusalem in about 54 AD. Procurator Felix easily defeated the rebels. The commander of Antonia Fortress protecting Jerusalem accused Paul of being the Egyptian.

Issue: Why should you count your resources and those of the enemy before you enter battle?

Ehud *Person* Judg. 3:15–4:1

Left-handed Ehud was an Israelite judge who used trickery to kill obese Eglon, king of Moab.

Issue: Is Ehud an example of God's justice or of human violence?

Elah *Place* 1 Sam. 17:2; 21:9

The valley north of Socoh where David defeated Goliath was known as Elah.

Issue: Can God plus one devoted person accomplish whatever God desires, no matter the apparent odds?

Elah *Person* 1 Kings 6:6–14

Elah, the King of Israel from 886–885 BC, was killed in a drunken stupor during a successful rebellion led by his general, Zimri.

Issue: What causes a person to get drunk repeatedly, even at the most crucial moments? Can God use a drunken person to accomplish His divine will?

Elah   *Person*   2 Kings 15:30

One of Elah's sons, Hoshea, revolted successfully and became the last king of Israel (732–723 BC).

Issue: Does violence breed violence? What can a commander or other leader accomplish when controlled by a stronger ruler?

Elasah   *Person*   Jer. 29:3–14

Elasah, the son of Shaphan, was a scribe in King Zedekiah's court. Elasah took the king's and Jeremiah's letters to the Babylonian exiles.

Issue: Can one serve God while employed by the secular state? How?

Elath   *Place*   Deut. 2:8; 1 Kings 9:26; 2 Kings 14:22; 16:6; 2 Chron. 8:17; 26:2

Elath was Solomon's port city on the northern end of the Gulf of Aqaba near Ezion Geber. It was a vital transportation hub for trade with the Arabs, Egyptians, Mesopotamians, and Syrians. It also served as a departing place for Israelites coming from the wilderness to go around Edom.

Issue: Describe the appearance, lifestyle, and importance of a port city. In what way is your lifestyle dependent on ports?

El-berith   *Thing*   Judg. 9:46–49

El-berith, the "god of the covenant," was a Canaanite god whose worship apparently centered around Shechem and who could not defend his territory against Yahweh. See Baal-berith.

Issue: How can true parts of religion be taken up into false worship?

El-bethel   *Place*   Gen. 28:10–19; 35:7

Jacob built an altar at El-bethel, "god of the house of God," where he had experienced God.

Issue: Recall the last vivid experience you have had with God. What do you have to remind yourself of this experience? How can you communicate your experience to your family, to your church, and to future generations?

Eldad *Person* Num. 11:16–29

Eldad and Medad were two of seventy elders. Despite their absence from the congregational meeting, God sent the Spirit on them, causing them to prophesy. Joshua tried to silence them, but Moses prayed that the Spirit phenomenon might come to all God's people.

Issue: Why are good leaders on opposite sides of an issue at times? How does a church solve such a problem?

Eleasar *Person* 1 Sam. 7:1

Eleasar was the son of Abinadab in whose house Israel placed the ark after the Philistines returned it. Eleasar was commissioned to take care of the ark.

Issue: Who takes care of your worship place? Do you recompense them monetarily and with signs of appreciation?

Eleazar *Person* Ex. 6:23; Num. 20:28; 27:22; Josh. 14:1; 24:33; Ezra 7:5

Eleazar, the second high priest of Israel and third son of Aaron, participated in the commissioning of Joshua and the distribution of land among the tribes.

Issue: What does it mean and feel like to have the second highest position in the land? Have you ever experienced being second in command?

Elect Lady *Person* 2 John 1

The book of 2 John was addressed to a person or group known only as "Elect Lady." This may be a kind of code word to address the entire church.

Issue: Have you ever addressed people in a "code language" to prevent others from reading your message quickly? On what occasion(s) would one use code language today?

El-Elohe-Israel   *God*   Gen. 33:20

Jacob used the phrase, *El-Elohe-Israel*, or "El the God of Israel," for the altar he built near Shechem.

Issue: How many names for God do you use in your worship and prayer life? How do you decide which one to use?

El-Elyon   *God*   Gen. 14:18–20

El-Elyon is a term for God made up of a combination of the Canaanite high god El and the popular Elyon (fifty-seven times in the Hebrew Bible). Israel has taken over a Canaanite epithet and claimed it solely for Yahweh, which may have happened by contact with the Jebusites in Jerusalem. Yahweh is absolutely the highest and thus the ruler of all gods.

Issue: God can be addressed through many names. Many of these express the differing functions Yahweh fulfills as the only God. What are your favorite names for God? Or do you think God must have only one name?

Elementary Spirits   *Things*   Gal. 4:3, 9; Col. 2:8, 20

"Elementary Spirits" is a disputed Pauline term expressing devotion to the elements, principles, religious teachings of the universe, or the simplest spiritual beings. Believers should mature beyond being bound or slaves to such childish beliefs to become devoted to Christ as our redeemer.

Issue: What elementary spirits or teachings do you or your family hold on to which are not part of Christ's teachings? What signs do you give that you have matured?

Elhanan *Person* 2 Sam. 21:19; 1 Chron. 20:5

Elhanan receives credit for slaying Goliath in the Hebrew text. The Greek text says that Elhanan killed "the brother of" Goliath.

Issue: How does one determine the correct textual reading? How do you interpret this story in light of the more well-known story of David and Goliath?

Eli *Person* 1 Sam. 3; 4:18

Eli was a priest who mentored Samuel but whose own sons desecrated the priesthood with their selfish demands and behavior. Hearing of the capture of the ark of the covenant, Eli fell and died.

Issue: What lifestyle do you expect from a minister? How does a minister's child face more pressure than other children?

Eliab *Person* 1 Sam. 16:6; 17:13, 28; 2 Chron. 11:18

David's oldest brother Eliab angrily tried to prevent David from fighting Goliath. He was the first of Jesse's sons rejected as God's choice to replace Saul as king. His daughter married King Rehoboam.

Issue: Hebrew Bible often features the younger sibling gaining the rights of an older sibling. What causes such things to happen? How should the older sibling react? How about the younger one?

Eliakim *Person* 2 Kings 18:18, 26, 37; 19:2; Isa. 22:15–25; 36:3, 11, 22; 37:2

Eliakim was the "master of the palace" (comparable to Egyptian vizier), a royal official under Hezekiah, fulfilling Isaiah's prophecy. He headed Hezekiah's embassy to the Assyrian delegation to discuss the Assyrian siege of Jerusalem.

Issue: Some people must be accountable as second-in-charge, taking orders from the chief commander. Have you ever filled such a responsibility? How did you feel? Why?

Eliashib   *Person*   Neh. 3

High priest Eliashib operated in Nehemiah's day. He led in rebuilding the Sheep Gate of the Jerusalem wall. His grandson married the daughter of Sanballat, who opposed Nehemiah.

Issue: How do family members get on the opposite sides of an important national or religious decision? Who is most likely to be able to settle such a family feud?

Eliashib   *Person*   Ezra 10:6

Another Eliashib, or possibly the same as above, was a priest who managed the temple storerooms and provided room for Tobiah, who opposed Nehemiah, and for his own son.

Issue: Should religious ministers become involved in politics? When? Why?

Elkanah   *Person*   2 Chron. 28:7

Elkanah was the minister to King Ahaz of Judah whom Zichri assassinated.

Issue: How loyal are you to the people or company you work for? Do you believe that loyalty is a lost art?

Elkannah   *Person*   1 Sam. 1

Elkannah, the father of Samuel, was a dedicated husband and father who endured Hannah's lamentation over her barren state.

Issue: How does a barren family deal with their situation and discuss it with others?

Elkosh   *Place*   Nah. 1:1

Elkosh was the home of Nahum, the prophet.

Issue: People make a town. Name one or two persons who have added to the fame and recognition of your hometown.

Elnathan   *Person*   Jer. 26:22–23; 36:12–26

The advisor to King Jehoiakim who retrieved the prophet Uriah from Egypt to be punished, Elnathan tried unsuccessfully to prevent the king from burning Jeremiah's scroll.

Issue: Obeying God does not always bring success. When have you seen this teaching come true? What does it say about God?

Eloi, Eloi, Lama Sabachthani   *Thing*   Ps. 22:1; Matt. 27:46; Mark 15:34

Jesus' Aramaic words from the cross were *Eloi, Eloi, lama sabachthani,* meaning "My God, My God, why have you forsaken Me?" Jesus took on humanity's sins for Himself and felt the forsakenness that only sin can bring. Even the feeling of desperate aloneness did not lead Jesus to forsake praying to the Father.

Issue: What does this saying from Jesus' lips convey about the nature of the Trinity and the relationships among Father, Son, and Spirit? Has sin ever made you feel separated from the Father? How did you overcome such a feeling?

El-Olam   *God*   Gen. 21:33

El-Olam is a term used for the eternal El or God Everlasting. It is a divine title that apparently originated in Beersheba and was applied by the patriarchs to Yahweh, the God of Israel.

Issue: Why would anyone worship a god who was not eternal or who had not always been god? Do you know of people or groups today who worship a god who has just come on the scene?

Elon   *Person*   Judg. 12:11–12

Elon was one of the so-called minor judges who led Israel for ten years.

Issue: History forgets so quickly. We know virtually nothing about this judge of Israel. Name someone significant in history but unknown by most people. What does this say about God's leadership in history?

El Shaddai   *God*   Gen. 17:1; 28:3; 35:11; 43:14; 48:3; Ex. 6:3;
Job 8:5; 13:3; 15:25; Ezek. 10:5

El Shaddai was a patriarchal name for God meaning "God of the Mountains," "the Almighty God; El of the Mountains," or "Almighty El." God's name was later revealed to be Yahweh.

Issue: Why would God change His own name in His revelation to Israel? What did Israel learn from the various names God revealed?

Elul   *Thing*   Neh. 6:15

The sixth month of Jewish calendar is Elul. The name was taken over from the Babylonian calendar.

Issue: Exile to a foreign land or long exposure to foreign customs brings changes in one's own culture, even the way people tell and record time. What major cultural change have you experienced?

Elymas   *Person*   Acts 13:6–11

See Bar-Jesus.

Emim (Emites)   *Persons*   Gen. 14:5; Deut. 2:10–11

The Emim were giants who belonged to a coalition that lost a battle to a troop of easterners whom Abraham eventually defeated.

Issue: Forces and faces opposing us seem large and impregnable. What task do you face that you see no way of completing?

Emmaus   *Place*   Luke 24:13

Emmaus was a small village seven miles from Jerusalem to which two disciples walked after Jesus' burial. Jesus joined the pair on the way, but He was unrecognized.

Issue: Recognizing Jesus is not always easy. What might prevent you from recognizing the presence of our Lord?

Enaim (Enam) *Place* Gen. 38:14; Josh. 15:34

Enaim was a small town near Timnah where Judah had sex with Tamar and intended to employ capital punishment until she proved he was the guilty party.

Issue: Sins find you out. Gaining personal pleasure at the expense and suffering of another person brings divine wrath. In which way have you placed your own personal pleasure above the needs and hurts of someone else?

Endor *Place* 1 Sam. 28:7; Ps. 83:10

Endor was the hometown of a witch or medium whom Saul called on to call forth Samuel from the dead. A witch supposedly had special powers to predict the future including reading animal livers, drawing arrows from a collection, reading the stars, and consulting the dead. All such practices of sorcery and divination faced strong condemnation in all parts of the Bible. Saul outlawed the practice before he turned to the witch of Endor out of desperation in his attempts to consult Samuel concerning future battles with the Philistines.

Issue: Necromancy claims power to speak with the spirits of the dead. Under what conditions would you practice necromancy? Why?

En-eglaim *Place* Ezek. 47:10

Ezekiel promised that the spring *En-eglaim*, near the Dead Sea, would become a fresh-water fishing hole. The name means "spring of the two calves."

Issue: Does God control all of nature and perform changes in nature that natural science proclaims impossible?

En-gedi *Place* Josh. 15:62; 1 Sam. 23:29–24:1; 2 Chron. 20:2; Song 1:14; Ezek. 47:10

En-gedi, "the place of the young goat" on the western side of the Dead Sea, thirty-five miles southeast of Jerusalem, has the only natural waterfall in

Israel and enjoys a semitropical climate. Gardeners there produce dates, balsam, and other plants used in making perfume, healing herbs, and other semitropical plants. David hid from Saul there, cutting off part of the king's robe to show his innocence over Saul. *En-gedi* also served as a military launching place.

Issue: Every country needs sections of fertile land where major crops and export items flourish. What happens to an area that does not have such an area? What such a piece of land lies near you to supply specialty items and necessary income?

En-Hakkore *Place* Judg. 15:18–19

The spring En-Hakkore, "the spring of the partridge" or "the spring of the caller," is where Samson used the jawbone of a donkey to drink from after he had used it to kill a thousand Philistines.

Issue: What has God provided for you in an unusual manner? How did you respond?

Enoch *Person* Gen. 5:18; Heb. 11:5; Jude 14

Enoch went to heaven without dying and was the father of Methuselah, the oldest person to ever live. Much later Jewish traditions from the period of the second temple connected Enoch to apocalyptic writings, testaments, heavenly wisdom, and eschatology preparing for the end times. Enochian literature showed a hidden world of God waiting to be revealed as the real world God has for His people.

Issue: Life's goal is eternal life with God. We do not expect to be translated like Enoch, but we can have assurance of life after death through faith in Jesus Christ. Do you have such assurance of eternal life?

Enos(h) *Person* Gen. 4:26; 5:6–11

Enos(h)'s name means "man." He was Adam's grandson. After his birth, people began to worship Yahweh.

Issue: Worship is the heart of the human response to God. When did you begin to worship God? What elements of worship do you find most meaningful?

Epaenetuse *Person* Rom. 16:5

Epaenetuse was the first person in the region of Achaia to accept Christ as Savior.

Issue: Our generation loves to record "firsts." What firsts do you have with Jesus?

Epaphras *Person* Col. 1:7; 4:12; Philem. 23

Epaphras, whose name means "lovely," was a young preacher tutored by Paul. He ministered to churches in Hierapolis, Laodicea, and Colossae.

Issue: Young ministers need tutoring by an experienced pastor as well as seminary education. Are there any young ministerial candidates in your church? What is your church doing to help train these young ministers?

Epaphroditus *Person* Phil. 2:25; 4:18

Epaphroditus, whose name means "favored by Aphrodite," was another young minister Paul trained. While Paul was in prison, Epaphroditus took the gift from the church at Philippi to Paul but became critically ill, so Paul had to send him back home.

Issue: Prison ministry is a key aspect of a church's obedience to Christ, yet one modern churches too often ignore. What are you and your church doing to minister to the needs of prisoners? How are you incorporating them into the life of the church?

Ephes-Dammim *Place* 1 Sam. 17:1

The Philistines mustered their troops at Ephes-Dammim to fight Saul just before David killed Goliath. The town name means "end of bloodshed."

Issue: Geographical names do not always describe the real conditions of the area. Ephes-Dammim actually began bloodshed in many ways. Does the name of your hometown reflect the true conditions there?

Ephphatha   *Thing*   Mark 7:34

Jesus used the Aramaic word, *Ephphatha*, or "be opened," in healing a deaf man who could not speak plainly.

Issue: Do you believe in faith healing today? The New Testament speaks of anointing the sick with oil. Is that the only way God will use people in the church to heal?

Ephraim, Forest of   *Place*   2 Sam. 18:5–8

David's loyal forces fought the army of Absalom, David's rebelling son, in the Forest of Ephraim. Absalom's long hair apparently got caught in a tree, and his mule rode away without him.

Issue: Wisdom of the experienced often overcomes the vigor and numbers of youth. Can you recall a time when experience defeated youth?

Ephraim Gate   *Thing*   2 Kings 14:13; 2 Chron. 25:23; Neh. 8:16

The Ephraim Gate was one of the gates allowing entrance into Jerusalem. King Jehoash destroyed the wall between this gate and the Corner Gate. It was used in post-exilic times as the post for the Feast of Tabernacles.

Issue: Antique relics and places gain different meanings as time marches on. Does your church possess objects dating back near the founding of the church? How are those objects stored? Do you ever use relics for education or for preaching?

Ephrathah (Ephrath)   *Place*   Gen. 35:16, 19; 48:7; Ruth 4:11; 1 Chron. 2:19, 50; 4:4; Ps. 132:6; Mic. 5:2

Ephrathah, "fruitful," was a town near to, or equated with, Bethlehem, where Jacob buried his wife Rachel. The home of Jesse and his son David, it is also the home of the promised Messiah.

Issue: Some places bring out feelings of sadness and joy because of past joy and sorrow experienced there. Do you have a place that overwhelms you with memories of loss, shame, or death and yet also brings smiles from memories of promises, love, joy, and celebration?

| Ephron | *Person* | Gen. 23:8, 10, 13–14, 16–17; 25:9; 49:29–30; 50:13 |

Ephron was a Hittite who sold the cave of Machpelah to Abraham as a burial place for his wife Sarah.

Issue: Dealing with death is one of the most difficult things we do. The last rites have become lost dollars as cultural expectations and burial costs continue to rise. Are you willing to row against the stream and demand less cost in funeral materials? Would such actions dishonor and shame the deceased?

| Epicurean | *Person* | Acts 17:18 |

An Epicurean is an adherent to a philosophy, introduced by Epicurus, that emphasizes true happiness as one's life goal. Paul met such philosophers while preaching in Athens.

Issue: Define happiness and pleasure from your point of view. Is this a definition most people would hold? How can you witness to a person whose search is for worldly pleasures?

| Epilepsy | *Thing* | Matt. 4:24; Mark 9:17–29 |

Epilepsy is a disease of the nervous system that causes convulsions. The ancient world connected it with the moon; the Greeks use a term meaning, "moonstruck" for epilepsy. People brought those who had been "moonstruck" to Jesus so He could heal them.

Issue: Biblical medicinal practices differ substantially from modern ones. How do you correlate biblical practices and modern healing? In what way do you expect God to intervene and act in a desperately sick person's life?

Epiphany   *Thing*   Matt. 2:1–12; Mark 1:9–11

Epiphany is the holiday celebrating the coming of Jesus to earth. The western church observes Ephiphany on January 6 as the coming of the Magi representing Christ's appearance to the Gentiles. The Eastern church celebrates Epiphany as the baptism of Jesus, representing the Son of God becoming human. The period from Christmas to Epiphany is called the "Twelve Days of Christmas."

Issue: What is a "holy day"? How does your church celebrate Epiphany?

Er   *Person*   Gen. 38:3–7

Jacob's grandson and Judah's son was named Er. He was married to Tamar. God killed him for his sinfulness.

Issue: Does God actually punish people on earth for sin and wrongdoing? Do you feel that He has ever punished you?

Erastus   *Person*   Acts 19:22

Paul mentored Erastus, a young believer who went to Macedonia with Timothy to strengthen the churches.

Issue: How does one strengthen a church? In what areas do you feel your church needs strengthening? What are you doing to help strengthen your church?

Erastus   *Person*   Rom. 16:23

Another biblical Erastus was a city official who dealt with finances in Corinth. He joined Paul in greeting the church at Rome.

Issue: How does the church relate to the government? Do you have government officials in your church? What special role do they play in your church?

Erastus *Person* 2 Tim. 4:20

A third Erastus Paul mentioned was a disciple whose ministry for Paul was important enough that Paul felt it necessary to inform Timothy that Erastus was not with him but was in Corinth.

Issue: The ministry of some people is so vital that the church notices when they are absent. When you are absent from church, how is the church affected?

Esarhaddon *Person* 2 Kings 19:36–37; Ezra 4:2; Isa. 19:4; 37:37–38

Esarhaddon, the King of Assyria from 681–669 BC, was known for fierce atrocities.

Issue: Why are some rulers and commanders known only for their fierce and cruel treatment of enemies? Is our side always the innocent one?

Esh-baal (Ishbosheth) *Person* 1 Sam. 14:49; 2 Sam. 2:8–15; 3:7–15; 4:1–12; 1 Chron. 8:33; 9:39

Esh-baal was the son of Saul whose name, "man of Baal," was recorded by Judean scribes as "man of shame." He reigned as king over Israel for two years, depending on the military abilities of Abner. He was killed by David's servants, whom David rewarded by killing them for not honoring the king.

Issue: At times, leaders do not want to return violence or evil on a defeated enemy, but in this case, David's followers think they will gain glory by killing the defeated opponents. When is it proper not to treat our enemies the same way that they treat us?

Ethan *Person* 1 Kings 4:31

Ethan was a wise man who was set up as the norm for wisdom to compare with Solomon's unexcelled wisdom.

Issue: Who is the wisest person you know? What criteria do you use to determine a person's wisdom? Who are the wise people in your church? Do you consider yourself wise?

Ethanim   *Thing*   1 Kings 8:2

Ethanim is the seventh month of Canaanite calendar, later adopted by Israel. The name means "ever flooding," in reference to the fall season when the snow melted and flooded rivers. The alternate calendar made this the first month and called it Tishri.

Issue: In today's economic scene, where small farms seem to disappear, what significance do changing seasons make? Is your life in any way dependent on flooding waters?

Eth-Baal   *Person*   1 Kings 16:31

Eth-Baal was the father of Jezebel, queen of Israel. Jezebel made Baal worship a significant element in Israel's worship life.

Issue: Is some false religion creeping into your church? How do you identify it? How do you destroy it?

Ethiopia (Cush)   *Place*   2 Kings 19:9; Est. 1:1; 8:9; Job 28:19; Pss. 68:31; 87:4; Isa. 11:11; 18:1; 20:3, 5; 37:9; 43:3; 45:14; Jer. 46:9; Ezek. 29:10; 30:4–5; 38:5; Nah. 3:9; Zeph. 3:10; Acts 8:27

Ethiopia is the land south of Egypt below the first cataract of the Nile River; in the Bible, it is often called Cush. The biblical Ethiopia is not equal to modern Ethiopia but to Nubia. In 715, this country captured complete control of Egypt. Tirhakah of Ethiopia supported Hezekiah against King Sennacherib of Assyria in 701 BC. By 664 BC, Assyria had conquered Egypt and the Nubians retreated to their home country.

Issue: Have you ever heard of Nubia? How do we measure the significance of such "minor kingdoms"? How does God measure and use such countries?

Eubulus *Person*   2 Tim. 4:21

Eubulus, who sent greetings to Timothy, was part of Paul's ministry team.

Issue: Paul did not minister alone. He built up a strong team of young ministers whom he could send where they were needed. Does your church have young ministers to support the senior staff? How much responsibility are you willing to give them?

Eunice *Person*   2 Tim. 1:5

Eunice, whose husband was an unconverted Gentile, was Timothy's mother. Paul praised her for the way she raised Timothy.

Issue: Religious differences in a home can cause strong problems, but such problems can be solved. Are some of your relatives or friends joined in such a relationship? What is the best advice you can give them?

Eunuch *Person*   Lev. 21:20; Deut. 23:1; 2 Kings 23:11; Est. 2:3–15; Isa. 56:3, 45; Jer. 38:7; Matt. 19:12; Acts 8:27–39; 1 Cor. 7:32–34

A eunuch, or castrated male, was often assigned to protect and take care of the needs of the members of a king's harem. A eunuch was excluded from Jewish worship, leadership, or participation in the assembly of Israel. Even though eunuchs didn't choose their fate, a person could choose a single life without sexual relationships to devote full energy to God's kingdom and its mission. Such a person becomes a eunuch for the kindgom of heaven.

Issue: Does the church have the right to exclude people with disabilities from serving the church as ministers or worshipers? Does your church have any rules or practices that, in reality, ban people from full participation in the church? Does your church support and encourage single adults to participate fully in church life?

Eunuch, Ethiopian   *Person* Acts 8:27

An Ethiopian eunuch, minister to the Queen (or Candace) of Ethiopia, came to Jerusalem where he encountered Scripture. Philip explained the Scripture to him and led him to Jesus.

Issue: Can you take an Old Testament passage and use it to lead someone to Jesus? When was the last time you did this?

Euodias   *Person*   Phil. 4:2–3

Euodias, a female leader in the church at Philippi, was in a disagreement with Syntyche. Paul sought reconciliation in their relationship. See Syntyche.

Issue: Are individuals in your church, especially in its leadership, causing your church to lose its growth and ministry? What can you do to help bring reconciliation?

Eutychus   *Person*   Acts 20:9–10

Eutychus was a young man whose name means "good fortune." Listening to Paul preach put him to sleep, and he fell from his perch in the third-floor window and died. Paul brought him back to life.

Issue: Preachers need to constantly keep their sermons interesting and abbreviated while congregation members need to do all that is possible to stay awake and involved in the truths of the sermon. Have you ever gone to sleep in church? Why?

Evil-Merodach   *Person*   2 Kings 25:27

Evil-Merodach was a Babylonian king (562–560 BC) who gave Jehoiachin, the exiled king of Judah, a place at the royal table.

Issue: Readers of the ending of Kings are divided as to the meaning of this passage. Was Jehoiachin restored to honor with the possibility of restoration to political power? Or was he simply joined with other captives to keep an eye on what they were doing or to prepare them for ultimate punishment? Have you ever received a change of position from your employer and not been certain as to the employer's intentions? How did you feel and act?

Fable *Thing* Judg. 9:8–15; 2 Kings 14:8–10; 2 Chron. 25:17–19

A fable is a story portraying animals, plants, and other non-human characters that is used to show moral, practical, or religious truths. Judges includes Jotham's fable of the trees seeking a king. The other biblical fable shows a thistle claiming equality with the magnificent cedars of Lebanon.

Issue: Bible narratives must be read carefully to make sure what kind of literature is being used. Must every story in the Bible be a literal recording of an event? Did thistles and trees actually talk?

Fair Havens *Place* Acts 27:8–20

Fair Havens was an insecure harbor on the southern side of Crete where Paul wanted the sailors taking him to Rome to stop for winter; but they refused and, as a result, wrecked the ship.

Issue: Facing danger is a daunting task, providing a time to listen closely to God. As a captain in command of the ship, would you have listened to prisoner Paul or to your own experience with storms? Have you faced storms in life and heard God's voice directing you through the storm? Did you listen?

Fall *Thing* Gen. 2–3; Rom. 1–3

The Fall refers to the actions of the first earthly couple, Adam and Eve, when they did not trust God and instead followed their desire to partake of the fruit of the Tree of Good and Evil. Their sin brought new knowledge and new suffering with new limitations. This suffering and limitation passed on to all humans, so that all will sin and trust their own wishes rather than God's will.

Issue: You are a sinner, separated from God and His love. Jesus died for sinners. Will you accept God's death on the cross as the payment for your sin and accept His gift of eternal life, guaranteed by His resurrection and ascension?

Fear of Isaac   *God*   Gen. 31:42; Ex. 6:3

The "Fear of Isaac" was another name used by the patriarchs for God as they worshiped the "God of our Fathers." Some translators use "Kinsman of Isaac" or "Refuge of Isaac." Israel concentrated on the name Yahweh for God after the revelation to Moses.

Issue: Divine revelation comes in different ways at different times. God is not static. He continues to find ways to communicate who He is to us humans. In what ways have you experienced God's revelation to you?

Feet, (Un)covering of   *Thing*   Deut. 28:57; Ruth 3:7; Isa. 6:2; 7:20; Ezek. 16:25

Hebrew uses expressions with the word *feet* to indicate sexual organs. Angelic seraphim have six wings, two of which they use "to cover the feet." Ruth uncovers "the feet" of Boaz to show him she is ready for marriage.

Issue: Such use of *feet* is called a *euphemism*. What euphemisms do we use today and why?

Felix   *Person*   Acts 23:24–25:14

Felix was the procurator or governor of the Roman province of Judea (AD 52–60). Felix heard Paul's case but refused to rule on it or to accept Paul's invitation to believe in Jesus, instead hoping for a bribe. Tacitus, a Roman historian, and Josephus, a Jewish historian, describe Felix as brutal and incompetent.

Issue: Do we tend to stereotype politicians as incompetent, self-seeking, and mean? Why? Do you know some capable, dedicated politicians?

Festus *Person* Acts 24:27–26:32

Festus was the Roman governor or procurator (AD 60–62) who succeeded Felix. He found no grounds to keep Paul in prison and granted Paul's plea to be judged by Caesar.

Issue: How would you describe the Roman justice system? Is our system any better? How would you change our system?

Fig *Thing* Gen. 3:7; Deut. 8:8; Judg. 9:10–11; 1 Kings 4:25; 2 Kings 18:31; Ps. 105:33; Prov. 27:18; Song 2:13; Isa. 34:4; 36:16; Jer. 5:17; 8:13; Hos. 2:12; 9:10; Joel 1:7, 12; 2:22; Amos 4:9; Mic. 4:4; Nah. 3:12; Hab. 3:17; Hag. 2:19; Zech. 3:10; Matt. 21:19–21; 24:32; Mark 11:13, 20–21; 13:28; Luke 13:6–7; 21:29; John 1:48, 50; James 3:12; Rev. 6:13

Figs provide a staple part of the Near Eastern diet. Each household had at least one fig tree, indicating safety and normality. Inability to sit peacefully under one's own fig tree indicated war, captivity, and defeat. Jesus cursed a fig tree for not bearing fruit, a story that appears in the context of Jesus cleansing the temple. Jesus saw religious Israel as appearing productive on the outside, but it was not producing fruit. The curse on the fig tree equaled a curse on Israel's unproductivity.

Issue: Is your church proud of its prosperity, growth, popularity, and reputation in its community? Is it really facing a divine curse for its lack of spiritual production? How would you measure the spiritual growth of your church?

Figurehead *Thing* Acts 28:11

See Castor and Pollus.

Finger of God *Thing* Ex. 8:19; 31:18; Deut. 9:10; Luke 11:20

"Finger of God" is a metaphorical expression signifying the work of a deity in the lives of His people. The Egyptian magicians recognized the plagues as the work of God's finger. The Ten Commandments came from God's finger, and Jesus cast out demons by the finger of God.

Issue: Does a God who is an invisible spirit have fingers? How do you describe the work of God in human language?

Foreskin   *Thing*   Gen. 17:11–17, 21–18:1; Ex. 4:22–28; Lev. 11:47–12:6; Deut. 10:13–19; Jer. 4:1–7; 9:22–10:2

The foreskin is the piece of skin removed when a man is circumcised. Having no foreskin was a sign of participation in God's covenant with Abraham. The law required a male baby to receive circumcision on the eighth day. Moses began traveling to Egypt to free the Israelites, but he had either not been circumcised or only partially circumcised according to Egyptian practice. In a confusing story in Exodus, God confronted Moses to make sure he became a true Israelite under Abraham's covenant of circumcision.

Circumcision, at that time, would have forced Moses to delay the journey to free Israel until after he healed. His wife Zipporah circumcised their son in place of Moses, and by touching the child's removed foreskin to Moses', she transfered the meaning of circumcision from child to father. The circumcision rite also appears to have qualified a man for marriage, so Zipporah called Moses a bridegroom of blood or of circumcision. Israel learned God wanted the foreskin of the heart circumcised to indicate purity and obedience.

Issue: Rituals are practiced as part of a person's religion. What rituals do you and your church see as necessary to be a member in good standing? Do you always perform these rituals in the right manner, or do you, at times, perform rituals half-heartedly? What is the true connection between ritual and relationship with God?

Fortunatus   *Person*   1 Cor. 16:17

Fortunatus was a convert at Corinth who went to Ephesus to help Paul. Paul may have been sick or in need of word from the church at Corinth.

He may have taken letters to Paul and then taken Paul's letters back to Corinth.

Issue: God's ministers and pastors experience human weakness and need help. How does your church recognize times when your minister(s) need help? How do you help the minister(s)?

Freedmen, Synagogue of | *Thing*   Acts 6:9

The synagogue of the freedmen was a worship place for Greek-speaking Jews in Jerusalem. Its members started the argument that led to Stephen's death. The synagogue was apparently made up of several groups: Cyrenians, Alexandrians, Cilicians, and Asians.

Issue: What percentage of the membership of your church is different from the majority in race, color, mother language, country of origin, or economic status? What has your church done to reach more minority groups or to provide programs that encourage present minority members? Does your church help integrate these people into current programs and activities?

Fringe (Tassels) | *Things*   Num. 15:38–39; Deut. 22:12; Matt. 9:20; 23:5; Luke 8:44

Fringes are the twisted cords on the four ends of an observant Jew's outer garment. They are worn to remind one of the vow to keep the commandments. Jesus apparently obeyed the law and wore the tassels, but He criticized those who displayed them only to call attention to themselves.

Issue: How does one obey God's commands properly without drawing attention to oneself? What relation do Christian believers have to the Old Testament laws? Why don't Christians wear fringes?

Frontlets (Phylacteries) | *Thing*   Ex. 13:1–16; Deut. 6:4–9; 11:13–21; Matt. 23:5

Phylacteries, or frontlets, are boxes containing the Scriptures of Ex. 13: 1–16; Deut. 11:13–21; 16:4–9 that Jews wear strapped to the forehead and left arm. Jesus condemned those who ostentatiously wore large frontlets to draw attention to their righteousness.

Issue: Do you have ways of reminding yourself and your family about the great works of salvation God has done for us? How can this practice become self-glorifying?

G

Gaal   *Person*   Judg. 9:26–41

The name Gaal means "abhorrence" or "dung beetle," and was probably a change by scribes, as it is not a name a mother is likely to give her son. He persuaded the Shechemites to follow him rather than Abimelech, but then was killed in battle.

Issue: Leaders must be able to deliver more than political speeches and promises. Do your local and national leaders live up to their promises? What can the local electorate do to ensure leaders are representatives of popular opinion?

Gabbatha   *Thing*   John 19:13

The Gabbatha was a platform in Jerusalem where Pilate sat to judge Jesus. The transliterated word means "elevation" in Aramaic or "stone pavement" (*lithostrotos*) in Greek. It was probably located in front of Herod's palace.

Issue: The idea of Pilate judging Jesus is an oxymoron because Jesus stands beyond anyone's judgment. Do you know people who deny Jesus and try to point out problems with Jesus? How can you respond to them?

Gabriel *Heavenly Being* Dan. 8:15–27; 9:20–27; Luke 1:8–20, 26–38

The angel Gabriel is the heavenly messenger who brought God's revelation to Daniel and announced the birth of Jesus.

Issue: How surprising were Gabriel's visits and the news Gabriel brought? How has God surprised you?

Gadarene *Person* Matt. 8:28–34 (Gerasene); Mark 5:1–17; Luke 8:26–37

A Gadarene is a resident of Gadara, a city in the Decapolis known for its pigs. In Mark and Luke, we have the story of a man possessed by demonic beings which Jesus cast out into the pigs, who ran over the cliff.

Issue: Can Satan's demons take over and possess a person? What is the result of such demon-possession? Have you met or heard about people who appear to be possessed? How do you respond to them?

Gaius *Person* Acts 19:29

Gaius was a man from Macedonia who became one of Paul's trusted preachers. He was arrested during riots in Ephesus when Demetrius, the silversmith, feared converts to Christianity would cut off the demand for his silver idols.

Issue: Witnessing for Jesus may affect the wealth of humans. Are you willing to witness for Jesus knowing it may lead you to poverty, imprisonment, suffering, and the cross?

Gaius *Person* Acts 20:4

Another biblical Gaius was the companion of Paul from Derbe who met Paul in Troas.

Issue: Only a few people lead, command orders, and exercise control over the movements and ministry of others. Are you willing to let someone else play Paul's public role, while you are relegated to a non-speaking part behind the scenes?

Gaius   *Person*   Rom. 16:23; 1 Cor. 1:14

A third Gaius was the host for Paul in Corinth and one of the few people Paul baptized.

Issue: Hospitality was an important matter for the early church, for its leaders like Paul were constantly traveling and needed places to sleep and eat. How do you provide hospitality for other people, especially Christian believers?

Gaius   *Person*   3 John 1

The fourth biblical Gaius was the beloved of John, to whom he addressed 3 John.

Issue: Christian love binds people together in affection for one another and in service for God. How do you define and demonstrate Christian love? Give examples of ways and times you have shown such love to another person.

Galeed   *Place*   Gen. 32:43–52

Galeed, or "pile for witness," was the place where Jacob and Laban made a covenant with one another delineating the boundary dividing their properties.

Issue: How do Christians settle disputes with one another? What do you need to do to settle a dispute with another believer that has been seething for months and months?

Gallim   *Place*   1 Sam. 18:20–29

Gallim was the home of Paltiel, to whom Saul gave his daughter Michal as a wife, and from whom Ishbaal took her to give her back to David as he commanded.

Issue: Why did David want Michal back? Whose integrity are you willing to sacrifice to enhance your position in politics, business, society, or family?

Gallio *Person*   Acts 18:12–17

Gallio was the Roman proconsul in Corinth who refused to grant the request asking for the Roman government to convict and punish Paul. Gallio brushed the request off as a matter concerning the Jewish religion and not Roman law. Archaeologists have discovered Gallio's judgment seat in Corinth.

Issue: How do you determine whether an issue is a matter for the government or for the religious "system" to handle?

Gallows *Thing*   Est. 2:23; 5:14; 6:4; 7:9–10; 8:7; 9:13, 25

Gallow is a basic word for tree, especially when used as the instrument of capital punishment. In the Persian period of Esther, the normal method of execution was impalement on a stake.

Issue: Do you believe the state should have the right to sentence a convicted criminal to death? Why or why not? What instrument should be used to enforce such a penalty?

Gamaliel *Person*   Acts 5:34; 22:3

The Pharisee Gamaliel was a member of the Sanhedrin and Paul's mentor in Judaism. He steered the Sanhedrin away from the plan to kill the leaders of the church by noting that if their work was of God, then no one could stop it, but if it was not from God, then it would die of its own accord.

Issue: How does God work out His will, even through the most unlikely people? What does this show about God's ability to use you in His kingdom work?

Garments (Festal) *Thing* Gen. 45:22; Judg. 14:12–13, 19; 2 Kings 5:5, 22–23; Isa. 3:22; Zech. 3:4

Garments is another word for a change of clothing or pure, white clothing. Owning multiple sets of clothing indicated wealth and status in the upper class. One set of clothing might be for festivals and weddings, etc.

Issue: What indicates wealth and upper class in your hometown? In the world outside the United States, what does your wardrobe communicate to others? What do your clothes indicate about your stewardship before God?

Garrison *Thing* 1 Sam. 10:5; 13:3–4, 23–14:1; 14:4, 6, 11–12, 15; 2 Sam. 23:14; 1 Chron. 11:16

A garrison is an armed military force used to occupy a conquered land or to defend an international border. The word garrison is often used in the Bible in reference to the Philistines.

Issue: What is the difference between relying on military garrisons and on divine protection? When would you choose one over the other?

Gaspar *Person* Ancient Texts

Gaspar is the traditional name of one of the Magi, or wise men, who visited the baby Jesus. His name appears first in the Armenian Infancy Gospel.

Issue: How did outside sources for New Testament times and for New Testament history and narrative develop? What distinguishes the books we now have in the canon of Scripture from ancient books that were not seen are authoritative Scripture?

Gath-hepher *Place* Josh. 19:13; 2 Kings 14:25

Gath-hepher is the home of the prophet Jonah, three miles northeast of Nazareth.

Issue: How can a small, out-of-the-way village produce an important prophet of God? Do you know of modern heroes of the faith who grew up in your vicinity?

Gauagmela   *Place*

Gauagmela was a city near modern-day Mosul, Iraq, where Alexander the Great's vastly outnumbered army defeated Darius III in 331 BC.

Issue: How does background information not mentioned in the Bible aid us in interpreting the Bible?

Gedaliah   *Person*   2 Kings 25:22–25; Jer. 40:7–41:18; 43:6

After destroying Jerusalem in 587 BC, Nebuchadnezzar appointed Gedaliah, who was Jewish, as the local governor over Judah. Ishmael assassinated Gedaliah two months later and fled to Egypt for asylum. Gedaliah means "Yahweh has done great things."

Issue: What do you expect of a local official who is appointed governor or president by a foreign ruler? Does any modern situation resemble this one?

Gedaliah   *Person*   Jer. 38

A different Gedaliah was a court official under King Zedekiah (597–596 BC) who led the conviction and imprisonment of Jeremiah.

Issue: How do you respond when another person attacks your leader and constantly predicts bad things ahead? Does the person who disagrees with you deserve respect and a sovereign court?

Gehazi   *Person*   2 Kings 4:12–36; 5:20–25; 8:4–5

Gehazi was the greedy servant of Elisha whose name may mean "goggle eyes." He could not fulfill Elisha's commission to restore the Shunammite woman's child to life and instead pushed her away from the prophet. He also claimed a reward from Naaman, the Syrian general, for Elisha's work after the prophet refused it. For this, he incurred the disease Naaman had endured. He did tell the king of all Elisha's good deeds and helped a widow get her property back.

Issue: Can you trust the people you work with? How do you know?

Gemara   *Thing*   Jewish Texts

The Gemara is a rabbinic commentary in Aramaic on the Mishnah, from about AD 400. It emanated from the discussions at the Jewish academies in Babylon and Palestine. The Mishnah plus the Gemara on one biblical passage equals one tractate of the Talmud. Some of the Mishnah's sixty-three tractates have no Gemara.

Issue: Jewish interpretation of Scripture takes us far back in history but shows us only some of the various ways people have used to study Scripture. What ways do you use to study Scripture? What resources or study tools do you use?

Gemariah   *Person*   Jer. 39:3

King Zedekiah's messenger to Babylon, Gemariah, carried Jeremiah's letter to the exiles.

Issue: When do God's people take advantage of opportunities offered by the government?

Gemariah   *Person*   Jer. 36

Another Gemariah was the son of Shaphan, the court scribe. He tried to prevent the king from burning Jeremiah's scroll.

Issue: In what circumstances should a believer oppose government policies or actions?

Gennesaret   *Place*   Matt. 14:34; Mark 6:53; Luke 5:1; compare
1 Macc. 11:67

An alternate name for Sea of Galilee is Gennesaret.

Issue: Why do many biblical areas have two or more names?

Gerah *Thing* Ex. 30:13; Lev. 27:25; Num. 3:47; 18:16; Ezek. 45:12

The smallest measure of weight in the Bible is the gerah. It equals one-twentieth of a shekel. Archaeologists have found gerah weights weighing half a gram.

Issue: What weight systems do you use? Do you know how to calculate meters to feet or grams to ounces?

Gerar *Place* Gen. 10:19; 20:1–2; 26:1–26; 2 Chron. 14:13–14; see 2 Macc. 13:24

Gerar was the home of Abraham. It may mean "drag away." It was a place on the Canaanite border between Beersheba and Gaza where both Abraham and Isaac used wives for political purposes. Twice Abraham gave his wife to an Egyptian or a Philistine ruler to seal treaties of peace. Isaac gave away his wife once. As guarantor of the treaty, the patriarch involved gave his beautiful wife to the foreign king to ensure the foreign leader would not hurt the patriarch by taking his wife by force. All three times God made sure the new relationship was not consummated.

Issue: Why would Abraham and Isaac commit similar sins in regard to their wives? Is it proper to use one's spouse for political purposes?

Gerizim *Place* Deut. 11:29; 27:12; Josh. 8:33; Judg. 9:7; See 2 Macc. 5:23; 6:2

Mount Gerizim and Mount Ebal tower over the city of Shechem. In a covenant ceremony, six tribes of Israel stood on Mount Gerizim and pronounced the covenant blessings on Israel, while the other six tribes stood on Ebal and pronounced covenant curses on Israel. Abimelech gained control of Shechem and then burned it down. Jotham's kingship fable was also delivered in Shechem. The Samaritans built their temple on Shechem in the Greco-Roman period.

Issue: How does your church teach its members which acts bring blessing and which ones bring curse on the community?

Gershom   *Person*   Ex. 2:22; 18:3; Judg. 18:30; 1 Chron. 23:15–16; 26:24

Gershom was the son of Moses. His name is interpreted as meaning "stranger" or "alien." His birth in Midian shows he was a stranger to Egypt and was carrying out the divine will. He was the recipient of circumcision in the rare note of Ex. 4:25.

Issue: How do children gain a feeling of isolation or alienation? How do you treat such children?

Geshem   *Person*   Neh. 2:19; 6:1–6

Geshem, "rain," was the ruler of Kedar who joined Sanballat and Tobiah in opposing the wall of Ezra and Nehemiah. Archaeologists found his name on a silver vessel his son Qainu dedicated to Egyptian goddess Han-Ilat. Even as a Persian vassal, he controlled a large portion of land and exercised much power.

Issue: Relatively unknown people may exercise great power and influence. In your community, who exercises power without demanding public attention?

Geshur   *Place*   2 Sam. 3:3; 13:37–38

Geshur was an Aramean city-state whose name means "bridge." It was the home of David's wife, Maacah, and their son Absalom.

Issue: How can a couple from different cultures make a marriage work for themselves and their children?

Gezer Calendar   *Thing*

A piece of a schoolboy's tablet found at Gezer quotes a rhyme to help remember the months of the year. It is one of the earliest examples of Hebrew writing.

Issue: What does your garbage say about you and your life?

Giah   *Place*   2 Sam. 2:24

Giah, or "bubbling," was where Joab, the general of David's army, met Abner, Saul's general, who had killed Joab's brother, Asahel.

Issue: Do you have places that call you to vengeance?

Giants   *People*   Gen. 6:1–4; Num. 13:33; Deut. 2:11, 20; 3:11, 13; Josh. 12:4; 13:12; 17:15; 1 Sam. 17:23–54; 2 Sam. 21:20

Giants were creatures of extraordinary size who may have connections to the heavenly world (Gen. 6:1–4; Jude 6). See Nephilim.

Issue: God maintains the divine sovereignty over the most fearful creatures of the created order. Do such frightening creatures exist today?

Gin   *Thing*   Job 18:9; Pss. 140:5; 141:9; Isa. 8:14; Amos 3:5

The King James Version translates a trap or a snare as a "gin." The old English term has nothing to do with modern drinks.

Issue: How much archaic (no longer in use) language is the modern Bible reader expected to recognize? What is the function of the King James translation for the modern church?

Gittith   *Thing*   Pss. 8; 81; 84

Gittith is a technical musical term used in the headings of three psalms. It may reflect the tune to which a psalm is played, a ritual part of the service in which the psalm is employed, or an instrument like a Spanish guitar.

Issue: What role does music play in worship of God?

Glede   *Thing*   Deut. 14:13

A glede is an unclean bird of prey, possibly from the hawk family.

Issue: How important is the presence of many words whose exact meaning we do not know for your understanding the Scripture?

Gob *Place* 2 Sam. 21:18–19

Gob was the site of one of David's battles with Philistines. Textual differences may point instead to Gath or Gezer.

Issue: What does it mean theologically that we cannot determine the exact site of a biblical battle?

Goblet *Thing* Song 7:2

A goblet is a drinking vessel without handles.

Issue: What significance do you place in archaeologists being able to match vessels they find with terms for biblical vessels?

God fearer *Person* Acts 10:2, 22; 13:16, 43, 50; 16:14; 17:4, 17; 18:7

God fearers were Gentiles who were attracted to Judaism, practiced some of its rituals such as tithing, prayers, and worship, but never completed the requirements for conversion to Judaism (e.g., circumcision). God fearers were attracted to Judaism's system of ethics and its devotion to one God.

Issue: What does your church require for full membership? What prevents some people from becoming full church members? What can you say to encourage such people to give themselves fully to Jesus and become a part of His body?

Gog and Magog *Person* Ezek. 38–39; Rev. 20:8

Gog and Magog are satanic leaders who fight against God's forces. Ezekiel may have been referring to Gyges, the king of Lydia, with Magog meaning "place of Gog." Revelation points to two apocalyptic leaders representing Satan's power. Victory over Gog reveals God's glory.

Issue: What forces does Satan have to fight against God's people? Who ultimately wins?

Golan   *Place*   Deut. 4:43; Josh. 20:8; 21:27; 1 Chron. 6:71

Golan was a city of refuge and of Levites east of the Jordan in the land of Manasseh. Those who committed accidental murder could flee there for refuge from the injured family's designated "redeemer."

Issue: What is biblical attitude toward murder?

Golgotha   *Place*   Matt. 27:33; Mark 15:22; John 19:17

Golgotha is an Aramaic or Hebrew name transliterated into Greek and then into English. It means "place of the skull" and was the location of Jesus' crucifixion.

Issue: The Bible claims that on the place of the skull, the Roman government crucified Jesus as a common criminal, but Jesus' followers came to understand the crucifixion as the agency through which Jesus gave Himself for the sins of the world. What does it mean that Jesus was executed as a common criminal? What does Golgotha mean in your spiritual walk with Christ?

Goliath   *Person*   1 Sam. 17:4

Goliath was a Philistine giant who challenged Israel to one on one combat. Young David accepted the challenge and killed him.

Issue: What resources does God need to gain victory in earthly battles?

Gomer   *Person*   Hosea 1–3

Gomer was the prostitute whom Hosea, following God's command, took as his wife. She symbolized the sin of Israel and the lack of faithfulness to God. She gave horrific names to her children, but God later changed them as Hosea took Gomer back.

Issue: How deep is God's love for you? How deep is yours for God?

Goodman   *Person*   Prov. 7:19; Matt. 14:14; 20:11; 24:43; Luke 12:39; 22:11

The KJV term for the head of a household is goodman.

Issue: Is the head of the household always masculine? How are household decisions made? What responsibilities should a person assume as head of a household?

Gopher Wood *Thing* Gen. 6:14

Noah used gopher wood to build the ark. The modern equivalent is not known.

Issue: What kind of lumber do you think would be best for building the big, awkward boat called the ark?

Gozan *Place* 2 Kings 17:6; 18:11; 19:12; 1 Chron. 5:26; Isa. 37:12

Gozan was a city-state in Syria to which the Assyrians exiled many of the Israelites in 732 BC and again in 722 BC.

Issue: How would you react if an enemy nation defeated your armed forces and sent you away to a foreign land with no hopes of return?

Habakkuk *Person* Hab. 1–3

Habakkuk was a prophet in about 600 BC who questioned God about divine justice and found that the person who is justified lives by faithfulness.

Issue: The book of Romans draws from the words of Habakkuk. Martin Luther later used the idea of justification by faith to propel the Reformation. In what way is this meaningful for you? Are faith and faithfulness the center of your relationship with God?

Habor *Place*   2 Kings 17:6; 18:11; 1 Chron. 5:26

Habor is a town on the Akkadian River, a tributary of the Euphrates, where the Assyrians settled Israelite exiles after the victories of 732 BC and 722 BC. See Gozan.

Issue: What issues of social, economic, and religious life do you face when you must suddenly move to an entirely different culture? How is your faith in God involved?

Hacaliah *Person*   Neh. 1:1; 10:1

Hacaliah was the father of Nehemiah.

Issue: What pressures and achievements does one gain through one's children's accomplishments?

Hadad *Person*   1 Kings 11:14–25; 1 Chron. 1:30–51

Hadad was the throne name of the kings of Edom. Each king, at his enthronement, took on the traditional name of the kings of that country, even though he had a private, personal name.

Issue: What is the significance of a king assuming a traditional name upon ascending the national throne? What are contemporary examples of someone taking a traditional name as the person comes into a position of power?

Hadad *Thing*   Canaanite Religion

Hadad was the storm god of the Canaanites and the chief god at Ugarit.

Issue: What brings a people to serve more than one god and to have a hierarchy among the deities?

Hadad-rimmon *god*   Zech. 12:11

Hadad-rimmon was apparently a Canaanite god connected with mourning ceremonies, harvest rites, or dying and rising god rites. Hadad-rimmon is literally two divine names joined into one.

125

Issue: What parts do religion and worship play in individual or community mourning?

Hadassah *Person* Est. 2:7

Hadassah was the original Hebrew name of Esther.

Issue: How does a change of names affect a person?

Hadoram *Person* 2 Chron. 10:18

Hadoram was the official under King Rehoboam who was in charge of corvée labor, that is, work gangs summoned by the government and given no choice except to accept the assignment. Hadoram was killed by the Israelites when he attempted to collect tribute from them. See Josh. 9:21; 1 Kings 5:13–15; 9:15; 12:18.

Issue: How does one accomplish a political task among people strongly opposed to the task and to the sponsors of the task?

Haggith *Person* 2 Sam. 3:4; 1 Kings 1:5, 11; 2:13; 1 Chron. 3:2

Haggith was the wife of David who gave birth to his son Adonijah in Hebron, not in David's later capital in Jerusalem. Adonijah instigated a rebellion against David in Hebron.

Issue: How would you respond to a spouse whose child openly rebels against you?

Halah *Place* 2 Kings 17:6

Halah was the city-state in northern Mesopotamia that received Israelite exiles after the Assyrian victories in 732 BC and 722 BC.

Issue: How should a country treat the armies and citizens of nations it defeats in battle?

Halak   *Place*   Josh. 11:17; 12:7

Halak was the southern limit of Joshua's conquest marches, and was perhaps located at Jebel Halak, forty miles southwest of the Dead Sea, in Edom.

Issue: What issues face a town or state that lies on the borderline of an enemy town or state? How are religious issues involved?

Half-shekel Tax   *Thing*   Ex. 30:13, 15; 38:26; Matt. 17:24

The temple levied a half-shekel tax annually on Israelites twenty years and older in connection with atonement rituals. See Didrachma.

Issue: How can a religion justify financial taxes levied for spiritual atonement?

Hallel   *Thing*   Pss. 113–18

Hallel is a song of praise. One collection appears in Psalms 113–18 as the Egyptian Hallel, and another in 120–36 as Great Hallel. See Hallelujah.

Issue: List the elements of music and of experience that create true praise to God. How do you use music to worship God?

Hallelujah   *Thing*   Pss. 104:35; 105:45–106:1; 106:48; 111:1; 112:1; 113:1, 9; 115:18; 116:19; 117:2; 135: 1, 21; 146:1, 10–147:1; 147:20–148:1; 148: 14–149:1; 149:9–150:1; 150:6; Rev. 19:1, 3–4, 6

Hallelujah is a Hebrew term that has been transliterated syllable by syllable into English meaning "praise (pl) Jah" (Jah is the short form of Yahweh). It is used in both individual and congregational worship.

Issue: Do you experience differences between individual worship and congregational worship? What special terms do you use to praise God?

Ham   *Person*   Gen. 5:32; 9:20–29; 10:6

Ham was Noah's son, who found his father naked and drunk. God then cursed Ham's son, Canaan (the father of the Canaanites). Ham means "hot" in Hebrew.

Issue: In what ways do children show respect for parents today? How do they show disrespect? What is fair punishment?

Haman   *Person*   Est. 3–9

Haman was the Persian official who jealously tried to get Mordecai, Esther's uncle, killed but eventually was himself the subject to capital punishment.

Issue: What authority and what limitations does the state have in punishing criminals? What justifies capital punishment?

Hamor   *Person*   Gen. 33:19; Josh. 24:32

Hamor, "donkey" or "ass," was the father of Shechem, who raped Dinah, Jacob's daughter. Jacob's sons tricked Hamor and Shechem into having their men circumcised and, during their recovery, Simon and Levi attacked them. See Dinah.

Issue: Violence against women still happens today. How should we handle it? What can the church do to support victims and their families?

Haname[e]l   *Person*   Jer. 32:7–12

Jeremiah bought a plot of land in Anathoth from his uncle, Hanamel, in a symbolic act illustrating that the land would again be valuable.

Issue: Can you describe other symbolic acts through which God reveals His plans for His people?

Hananeel   *Thing*   Neh. 3:1; 7:2; 12:39; Jer. 31:38; Zech. 2:8; 14:10

Hananeel was a tower marking the northern wall of Jerusalem. Nehemiah repaired it.

Issue: Who in your church is responsible for the upkeep of the church, repairing and rebuilding as needed?

Hanani *Person* Neh. 1:2; 7:2

Nehemiah's brother Hanani was in Jerusalem and reported the sad conditions there to Nehemiah while Nehemiah served the Persian king in Persia.

Issue: Is nepotism ever helpful and advisable for a nation?

Hananiah *Person* Jer. 28:8–17

Hananiah was a prophet from Gibeon who opposed Jeremiah and tried to humiliate him before the people. His name means "Jah is gracious." Jeremiah needed a divine word against the Gibeonite prophet but did not receive one immediately.

Issue: How do you prove a word is from God and thus true?

Hananiah *Person* Dan. 1:7

Hananiah was the Hebrew name of Daniel's friend, Shadrach, who was cast into the fiery furnace.

Issue: Why do people change their names?

Hananiah *Person* Neh. 7:2

Another Hananiah was the trustworthy and reverent leader whom Nehemiah set up as the ruler and administrator of the temple fortress.

Issue: What gifts and qualities must an administrator have? Name good administrators God has set up in your church.

Hanes *Place* Isa. 30:4

Hanes was an Egyptian city to which Israel sent administrators and diplomats seeking help in the war against Assyria.

Issue: What role does political strategy and maneuvering play in God's plans to deliver His people?

Hannah *Person* 1 Sam. 1:2

Samuel's mother, Hannah, suffered ridicule as in her barren old age, she prayed fervently for a child. Her name means "grace." She sang Hannah's Song (1 Sam. 2) and dedicated her son to God's service in the temple at Shiloh.

Issue: Must a barren woman blame her condition on God? Can God fill the barren womb with new life? What part does prayer play in this situation?

Hanukkah *Thing* John 10:22

Hanukkah is the Festival of Lights or Festival of Dedication celebrating the victories of Judas Maccabeus in 167/165 BC over Antiochus Epiphanes, the Seleucid leader who had captured and polluted the Jerusalem temple. Judas repaired and repurified the temple. Then he had the priests set everything in holy order. The eight-day festival begins on the 25th day of Kislev (November-December) and represents the only festival in the Jewish calendar that does not appear in the Hebrew Bible.

Issue: How do you explain the concept of holiness in worship, relating even to the place of worship? Does your church have any traditions or practices related to keeping a sense of material and spiritual holiness in relation to the place of worship?

Haran *Person* Gen. 11–12

Haran was the brother of Abraham and the father of Lot who died before Abraham migrated westward.

Issue: How do you respond when you realize that you have missed an opportunity to be in a very special event such as the separation of Abraham to start a new people? Or an even less important but still important event for your family?

Haran *Place* Gen. 11–12; 24; 27:43; 28:10; 29:4; 2 Kings 19:12; Isa. 37:12; Ezek. 37:23; Acts 7:2, 4

Haran was a city on the Balik river in northern Mesopotamia where Abraham's family stopped when they answered God's call to go to Canaan. Haran was the chief center for worship of the moon god, Sin.

Issue: Can you trace a journey you have taken with God in which you discovered surprising stops and delays along the way? Do you still return to these special stopping places occasionally?

Harod *Place* Judg. 7:1

Harod was the place God chose for Gideon to test his troops, to see how they drank water, and to see if they were ready for battle.

Issue: Is it good or bad to test God?

Harosheth-hagoiim *Place* Judg. 4:2–16

Harosheth-hagoiim, or the "Forest of the Nations," was the mustering region for Sisera's armies.

Issue: How does a command to put to Herem (total destruction) or to kill all enemy personnel affect an army and its leaders?

Harpoon *Thing* Job 41:7

A harpoon is a pointed weapon used to hunt sea creatures. God remains sovereign and in control of all animals and all weapons.

Issue: Should nations today work to control weapons' increase? Or should we surrender and attempt to lead the world in killing power?

Hashabiah *Person* 1 Chron. 26:30

Hashabiah was the family of Levites, based in Hebron, who were authorized to carry out God's business in the king's service.

Issue: What is the relationship between religion and politics? What influence should one have on the other?

Hauran   *Place*   Ezek. 47:16–18

Hauran was the region marking the northeastern boundary of Israel after the exile.

Issue: Does God's fulfillment of His promises of restoration always mark the land expectations of Israel exactly?

Havvoth-jair   *Place*   Num. 32:41; Deut. 3:14; Judg. 10:4; 1 Chron. 2:23

Havvoth-jair was a group of thirty to sixty villages southeast of the Sea of Chinnereth that was captured and ruled by Jair and his sons.

Issue: What is the significance in naming leaders other than Joshua as conquerors of part of Israel's land?

Heavenly Father   *God*   Matt. 5:48; 6:14, 26–32; 15:13; 18:35; Luke 11:13

"Heavenly Father" is the intimate designation for God that Jesus used to demonstrate His relationship to God and to portray God as one who provides for our needs, forgives sins, sustains what He created, and sets an example for us to follow.

Issue: Where do you find a moral example to follow in day to day living?

Heber   *Person*   Judg. 4:11, 17

Heber was the Kenite who removed himself from Moses' clan and was in a treaty relationship with Jabin of Hazor. Heber's wife Jael became a surprising hero by killing Sisera, Jabin's general. See Jael.

Issue: Are we surprised when women take charge of heroic roles? Why?

Hegai   *Person*   Est. 2:8–15

Hegai was the eunuch who administered the harem for King Ahasuerus of Persia. He did a special favor for Esther.

Issue: Should believers in God expect to receive special favors from government officials?

Heli *Person* Luke 3:23–24; compare Matt. 1:16

Heli was the father of Joseph and the earthly grandfather of Jesus.

Issue: Explain the importance of Jesus having no earthly father.

Hellenism *Thing* Greek History

Hellenism is a term that refers to the philosophy and lifestyle of the early Greek thinkers that was eventually adopted to some extent by the western world and to some extent by the eastern world of Israel. Basic dualism, which saw the world as composed of competing powers of good and evil, was a central tenet.

Issue: To what extent do you see the world from a dualistic standpoint?

Hephzibah *Person* Isa. 62:4

Hephzibah, or "my delight is in her," was a symbolic name for Jerusalem.

Issue: How can God destroy the Holy City and then claim to delight in it?

Herbs, Bitter *Thing* Ex. 12:8; Num. 9:11

Bitter herbs are the part of the Passover menu to remind Israel of the bitter life they endured in Egypt. Bitter herbs probably included lettuce, chicory, eryngo, horseradish, and sow thistle.

Issue: Do your memories look at the bitter points of life or at the deliverance that God has brought you from such bitter experiences?

Herem	*Thing*	Deut. 2:34; 3:6; 7:2, 26; 13:15, 17; 20:17; Josh. 2:10; 6:17–18, 21; 7:1, 11–13, 15; 8:26; 10:1, 28, 35, 37, 39–40; 11:11–12, 20–21; 19:38; 22:20; Judg. 1:17; 21:11; 1 Sam. 15:3, 8–9, 15, 18, 20–21; 1 Kings 9:21; 20:42; 2 Kings 19:11

Herem is a Hebrew term appearing eighty-eight times in the Bible. It described a battle strategy in which all or a designated portion of spoils from a battle were dedicated to God and destroyed by fire. Most instances of the practice of herem appear in connection with the conquest of Canaan.

Issue: How can you apply such teaching to modern existence without finding license to destroy all your enemies? What kind of God would issue such battle orders?

Hermes	*Thing*	Acts 14:12

Hermes was the Greek god who was the messenger and public spokesperson for the rest of the Greek gods. The people of Lystra identified Paul with Hermes.

Issue: What skills do you have that people might compare with that of the gods? Do you take credit and praise, or do you easily credit God for all your skills?

Hermogenes	*Person*	2 Tim. 1:15

Hermogenes, or "born of Hermes," was the name for a man who followed Paul but apparently deserted him while Paul was in prison in Ephesus.

Issue: What will be the fate of someone who follows God for a while but then turns his or her back on God?

Herodians	*People*	Matt. 22:16; Mark 3:6; 12:13

The Jews in the Roman period who supported the policies of Herod and thus of Rome were known as Herodians.

Issue: How does a believer determine which political group to support?

Herodias *Person* Matt. 14:3, 6; Mark 6:17, 19, 22; Luke 3:19

Herodias was the daughter of Aristobulus and Bernice. She married Philip, her father's half brother, and had a daughter, Salome. Philip's brother Herod Antipas wooed Herodias away so she divorced Philip and married Antipas. John the Baptist denounced the divorce and eventually paid for it with his head, at the request of Salome.

Issue: What does the Bible teach about marriage and divorce?

Herodium *Place* Ancient History

Herodium was a combination fortress and palace that Herod the Great built four miles southeast of Bethlehem and ten miles south of Jerusalem. Herodium served Herod as an exotic villa, an architectural masterpiece, a personal monument visible from afar, and a tomb. Herod was buried there in 4 BC. Rome captured and destroyed it in AD 72. The massive structure is not mentioned in the Bible.

Issue: How do people prevent high government officials from spending money to build monuments to their egos rather than to meet the people's needs?

Heth *Person* Gen. 10:15; 23; 1 Chron. 1:13

Heth was the great-grandson of Noah and the original father in Hittite genealogy.

Issue: How does one explain the relationship between personal names and geographical or clan names in the Bible?

Hezir *Person* 1 Chron. 24:15

Hezir was the leader of one of twenty-four courses of Israelite priests. His name means "wild pig."

Issue: Why is an Israelite priest named "pig"? How did a major part of the Jewish priesthood form a connection of any type with pigs?

Hiddekel *Place* Gen. 2:14

Hiddekel refers to the third river flowing out of the Garden of Eden. It is often understood to be the Tigris.

Issue: God's original garden provided water for the entire universe. How?

Hiel *Person* 1 Kings 16:34

Hiel rebuilt Jericho, resulting in the fulfillment of Joshua's curse (Josh. 6:26) and the death of two of Hiel's sons.

Issue: God fulfills His Word, including the curses His messengers place on other people, actions, and places. What is another example of God fulfilling a curse?

Hierapolis *Place* Col. 4:13

Hierapolis was a city in southwest Phrygia one hundred miles east of Ephesus, twelve miles northwest of Colossae, and six miles north of Laodicea in modern Turkey. Hierapolis means "holy city." The town was a worship center for several gods, including the Anatolian mother goddess worshiped locally under the name Leto. The church in Hierapolis was apparently founded by Paul's compatriot Epaphras.

Issue: What advantage does a city receive from being the worship center for several gods? What disadvantage?

Higgaion *Thing* Ps. 9:16

Higgaion is the transliteration of the Hebrew term meaning a particular type of sound like whispering, meditating, strumming a stringed instrument (Pss. 19:14; 92:3; Lam. 3:62), or "meditation."

Issue: How do you and your church utilize music in public and private worship? Why do some churches refuse to allow the use of musical instruments in worship?

Hin *Thing* Ex. 29:40

A hin is a liquid measure equaling one-sixth of a bath or a liquid gallon.

Issue: What difference does it make that we do not know the exact equivalent to biblical measures?

Hippopotamus *Thing* Job 40

See Behemoth.

Hobab *Person* Num. 10:29; Judg. 1:16; 4:11

Hobab is an alternate name for Moses' father-in-law—Reuel and Jethro are other names for him. Hobab may instead refer to Moses' brother-in-law.

Issue: How do you think biblical characters got more than one name? What significance does it have?

Hoglah *Person* Num. 26:33; 27:1; 36:11; Josh. 17:3

Hoglah was one of the five daughters of Zelophehad who set their case before Moses and gained property rights for women.

Issue: Why should women not have the right to own property? Should some limitations or conditions be placed on their rights?

Hoopoe *Thing* Lev. 11:19; Deut. 14:18

A hoopoe is an unclean bird known for its unusual sound and for being filthy because it feeds on dunghills.

Issue: What do we learn from the Hebrew system of clean and unclean animals?

Hophni *Person* 1 Sam. 1:3; 2:34; 4:4, 11, 17

Hophni was the disobedient priest, son of Eli and brother of Phinehas, who took the ark of the covenant into battle, resulting in the ark's capture and Hophni and Phinehas being killed.

Issue: What are the ethical expectations God places on His ministers as seen in the contrast between Samuel and Eli's sons?

Hophra *Person* Jer. 44:30

Hophra was an Egyptian ruler also known as Apries. He was a treaty partner of Zedekiah of Judah; however, his army could not lift the Babylonian siege of Jerusalem. The Egyptian troops mutinied in 570 BC.

Issue: What value do international alliances have? What role does God play in such alliances?

Horam *Person* Josh. 10:33

Horam was the King of Gezer who unsuccessfully supported Lachish against Joshua.

Issue: What right does a ruler have to throw his army into battle when he knows thousands will be killed?

Hosanna *Thing* Ps. 118:25; Matt. 21:9, 15; Mark 11:9–10; John 12:13

"Hosanna" is the traditional cry asking God to come as the saving King to deliver His people. It is applied to Jesus in His Palm Sunday entrance into Jerusalem.

Issue: Have you asked Jesus to save you and promise you eternal deliverance?

House of the Forest of Lebanon *Thing* 1 Kings 10:17, 21; 2 Chron. 9:16, 20

The House of the Forest of Lebanon was a great hall within Solomon's palace in which valuable golden treasures were stored. Large beams of cedar imported from Lebanon dominated the architecture. Enemy kings often raided the hall to collect the treasures.

Issue: Where are your treasures collected? Are they safe from enemies? What do you consider a treasure?

Huldah   *Person*   2 Kings 22:14; 2 Chron. 34:22

Huldah was a prophet, the wife of Shallum. Temple personnel brought newly discovered law scrolls to her. She proclaimed judgment on the nation but peaceful death for Josiah.

Issue: How do you understand and apply the many words of judgment in the Bible? What calls forth such oracles of doom?

Hunchback   *Person*   Lev. 21:20

A hunchback is a person with a physical deformity who is not allowed to serve as priest.

Issue: How do you respond to people with physical or mental deformities? Does your church provide for ministries to recognize and incorporate such people into the fellowship?

Hur   *Person*   Ex. 17:10, 12; 24:14; 31:2; 35:30; 38:22; Num. 31:8; Josh. 13:21; 1 Chron. 2:19–20, 50; 4:1, 4; 2 Chron. 1:5; Neh. 3:9

Hur was an associate of Moses who helped Aaron hold up Moses' hands while Joshua led the battle against Amalek. Hur joined Aaron in deciding cases while Moses ascended the mountain of revelation.

Issue: How does the church solve disputes between or among members? Do you need to help set up a process for doing so?

Hyena   *Thing*   Isa. 13:22; 34:14; Jer. 50:39

A hyena is a striped, flesh-eating, stocky nocturnal animal that digs out graves. It is identified by its moaning sound. Hyenas could be tamed as pets. They are used metaphorically to speak of desolate nations enduring God's judgment. God could compare a hyena to someone's inheritance that was quickly destroyed.

Issue: Are you or some other church member as destructive as a hyena, eating up everything of value?

Hymenaeus *Person* 1 Tim. 1:20; 2 Tim. 2:17

Hymenaeus was a gospel worker with Paul and Timothy whose shipwrecked faith Paul had to note to Timothy. His changed lifestyle led Paul to give Hymenaeus over to Satan. Apparently this refers to excommunication from the church until the church could love him back to faith and fellowship. One part of his false teaching claimed the promised resurrection had already occurred.

Issue: Can a person leave the church and maintain some type of salvation experience with Jesus? What do you think it means to hand someone over to Satan?

I

Ibzan *Person* Judg. 12:8–10

Ibzan was one of Israel's "minor judges," originally from Bethlehem. He followed the royal practice of accumulating wives.

Issue: What type of lifestyle does a national leader have the right or responsibility to live? Why?

Ichabod *Person* 1 Sam. 4:21

Ichabod was the son of Phinehas and grandson of Eli. His name means "where is the glory?"—a symbolic note that his disobedient father was about to die as the ark of the covenant was captured.

Issue: What causes God to take His glory away from His people? What symbolizes the presence or absence of the glory today?

Iconium *Place*   Acts 13:51; 14:1, 19, 21; 16:2; 2 Tim. 3:11

Iconium was the administrative center in the Roman province of Galatia in modern southeastern Turkey. Paul and Barnabas stopped there on their mission travels where Paul was persecuted.

Issue: Christians continue to face persecution in many parts of the world. Would you be willing to suffer physically and emotionally for God? Would you still retain your faith and devotion to Christ?

Iddo *Person*   2 Chron. 9:29; 12:15; 13:22

Iddo was an otherwise unknown prophet whose writings and prophecies served as a source for the author(s) of Chronicles.

Issue: How does the use of sources by the Chronicler fit into your theory of biblical inspiration and authority?

Idumea *Place*   Mark 3:8

Idumea refers to the land from Hebron southward across to Philistine cities, incorporating ancient Edomites forced westward by invading Arabs. The Herod family came originally from Idumea.

Issue: How do you react when another person or persons take your property away from you? What causes one group to become enemies of another?

Igal *Person*   Num. 13:7

Igal was a spy representing the tribe of Naphtali in investigating the land before Israel entered it. He represented the majority voice in urging Moses not to enter the land.

Issue: What does a church or an individual do when they know the majority is wrong?

Igal   *Person*   2 Sam. 23:36

Another Igal was apparently a foreigner from Zobah and one of David's thirty elite warriors.

Issue: What role should we allow foreign immigrants to play in our nation?

Ijon   *Place*   1 Kings 15:20; 2 Kings 15:29; 2 Chron. 16:4

Ijon was a city whose name means "ruins." Located on the northern end of Huleh Valley in Naphtali's territory, it was a trading stop on the highway from Palestine to Syria. Encouraged by Asa of Judah, Ben-Hadad of Syria opted out of a treaty with Baasha of Israel, attacked Ijon, and stopped Baasha's intrusion into Judah. Later Tiglath-pileser of Assyria also captured the city.

Issue: When is it correct to break a promise with one person or group and establish a new promise with the enemy?

Illycrium   *Place*   Rom. 15:19

Illycrium is the Roman province that represented the northwest limit of Paul's ministry when he wrote Romans. It is located between the Danube and the Adriatic Sea.

Issue: Paul established plans for his mission travels and ministry, even though he remained open to God's intervention. Do you have some type of ministry plan for your work inside and beyond the church, or do you simply wait for an opportunity to arise?

Immanuel   *Person*   Isa. 7:14; Matt. 1:22–23

Immanuel was the name of the baby to be born in Isaiah's day, symbolizing God's presence with His beleaguered people. Baby Jesus gave final fulfillment to the symbolic prophecy when He was born.

Issue: In what way can you speak of an original fulfillment of a prophecy and a final fulfillment of the prophecy centuries later?

Immortality *Thing* Hab. 1:12; Rom. 1:23; 2:7; 1 Cor. 15:53–54; 1 Tim. 1:17; 6:16; 2 Tim. 1:10

The quality of being that assures a person will never die is called immortality. Only God is immortal by nature. Humans are all subject to death until they believe in God and receive eternal life.

Issue: God promises eternal life. Are you sure you have eternal life?

Ink *Thing* Jer. 36:18; 2 Cor. 3:3; 2 John 12; 3 John 13

Ink was a substance composed of soot, lampbrick, and gum arabic. Ink was used for writing on papyrus. Ink made with nutgalls mixed with iron sulfate stuck to parchment better.

Issue: God used many types of materials for creating and preserving His Word—carving into stone, etching into leather, inking into parchment. How did God's inspired writers maintain the accuracy and readability of texts and inscriptions because they can be damaged or fade over time?

Inn *Place* Gen. 42:27; 43:21; Jer. 9:2; Luke 2:7; 10:34

An inn in the Old Testament was a camping place without a roof but near a water supply where anyone from individuals up to armies could spend the night. The New Testament inn referred to a guest room or place in a courtyard where travelers could find water for themselves and their animals and could spend a night. In New Testament times, public inns could be dangerous places.

Issue: Does the contemporary church offer any ministry that resembles public inns for travelers? Does a church need to offer such a ministry in today's culture? What similar ministry might the church extend?

Innocents, Slaughter of *Things* Matt. 2:16–18

Jealous King Herod sought to murder Jesus to prevent Him from taking over the throne of Judea. Herod ordered all children two years and under to be killed. This action came to be known as the Slaughter of the

Innocents. The language of this story resembles that of the plagues in Egypt where the firstborn boys were slaughtered.

Issue: What is the value of children? How far should adults go in exercising their authority over children? What does your church do to demonstrate its love for and valuation of children?

Irijah *Person* Jer. 37:13–14

Irijah was a Judahite soldier who captured Jeremiah and turned him over to the king's officials because Irijah thought Jeremiah betrayed Judah to the Babylonians.

Issue: Both Irijah and Jeremiah intended to serve God with their actions. How is one sure he or she knows God's will when others oppose them strongly?

Iscah *Person* Gen. 11:29

Lot's sister Iscah was part of Abraham's extended family.

Issue: How does it feel to be a basically unknown member of a famous family?

Ishbaal *Person* 2 Sam. 2–4; 1 Chron. 8:33; 9:39

Ishbaal was the original name of Saul's son, meaning "man of Baal," though the Hebrew text reads Ishbosheth, "man of shame." Chronicles refers to Eshbaal, "man of Baal." Either the tradition or the scribes did not want to attribute a Baal name to an Israelite leader and so substituted "shame" for Baal.

Issue: What does your name signify? Do you know of people in your family or beyond who have what you would consider undesirable names? What would you do if you had such a name?

Ishbibenob *Person* 2 Sam. 21:16–17

Ishbibenob was a Philistine soldier who threatened to kill David but instead met death at the hand of Abishai. Some textual differences in the

EXPLORING THE UNEXPLAINED

passage may indicate he belonged to a group of Rephaim or giants or was a follower of the god Rapha.

Issue: What do you do when another person places death threats on your head? Do you have a support group as strong and loyal as Abishai?

| **Ishbosheth** | *Person* | 2 Sam. 2–4 |

See Ishbaal.

| **Italian Cohort** | *Persons* | Acts 10 |

An Italian cohort was a Roman military unit devoted to archery. Fully equipped, they would include one thousand men. Cornelius led this particular unit in Acts. See God Fearer.

Issue: How do you regard a military unit stationed far from home defending a foreign country? How differently do you feel concerning a local unit of the armed forces? Why?

| **Ithiel** | *Person* | Prov. 30:1 |

Ithiel was apparently a student for whom Agur first collected and taught his section of Proverbs. Many scholars emend the Hebrew text or try to translate the present text with verbs rather than proper nouns:

Thus says the man: I am weary, O God, I am weary, O God. How can I prevail? (NRSV)

The man's oration to Ithiel, to Ithiel and Ucal: (Holman Christian Study Bible)

The pronouncement of mortal man: "I am not God; I am not God, that I should prevail. (NAB)

The skeptic swore, "There is no God! No God!—I can do anything I want! (Message)

Someone cries out to God, "I am completely worn out! How can I last? (CEV)

This man's utterance to Ithiel: "I am weary, God, but I can prevail (TNIV)

God is not with me, God is not with me, and I am helpless. (TEV)

I am more boorish than anyone, I lack human discernment; (Complete Jewish Bible)

Issue: Why does God not give us a pure text free of copyist's mistakes? How do you explain the authority of Scripture when we have a translation for a verse of which no one is confident? See Agur.

Ittai *Person* 2 Sam. 15:19–22; 18:2–12

Ittai was a Philistine soldier who proved his loyalty to David and became one of the top three leaders of David's armies. He refused to harm the rebelling Absalom.

Issue: Name biblical heroes who were not native Israelites. How can their example speak to modern discussions of the role of foreigners in your country? What about in your church?

Jaazaniah *Person* 2 Kings 25:23–25

Jaazaniah was an army captain who joined Ishmael in opposing Gedaliah, the governor the Babylonians appointed over Judah after Jerusalem fell in 586 BC.

Issue: How does a country, especially one subject to a victorious enemy, decide on their political and military leaders?

Jabez *Person* 1 Chron. 4:9–10

Jabez was a man who prayed to God for blessing, land, presence, and protection and was immediately answered.

Issue: How quickly do you expect God to respond to your prayers? What do you ask for in most of your prayers?

Jabin *Person* Josh. 11:1–5; Judg. 4

Jabin was the king of the Canaanites residing near Hazor. Jabin is apparently a dynastic name carried by at least two Canaanite kings, both of whom the Israelites defeated.

Issue: What are the advantages of dynastic succession, a form of government in which a son or daughter inherits the title from his or her parents? What are the disadvantages?

Jachin *Thing* 1 Kings 7:21

Jachin and its counterpart, Boaz, were pillars set up in front of the temple, possibly symbolizing the entryway for the deity.

Issue: Does your church have a ritual or architectural feature that reminds worshipers that God has entered the sanctuary and is ready for your worship?

Jackal *Thing* Job 30:29; Pss. 44:19; 63:10; Isa. 13:22; 34:13; 35:7; 43:20; Jer. 9:11; 10:22; 14:6; 49:33; 51:37; Lam. 4:3; 5:18; Ezek. 13:4; Mic. 1:8; Mal. 1:3

A jackal is a ravaging animal that, biblically, lives among ruins and signifies destruction. It is known for its distinctive moaning sound.

Issue: What symbolizes destruction and ruin for you? Does God have the right and the power to destroy us if He so chooses?

Jael *Person* Judg. 4:17; 5:24–27

Jael was the wife of Heber, a Kenite who had an alliance treaty with Jabin of Canaan. Jael ignored the treaty by enticing Jabin's general Sisera into her tent. She lured Sisera to sleep and drove a tent peg through his head. By doing so, she gains the glory the Israelite general Barak should have won.

Issue: What drove Jael to break Heber's treaty with the Canaanites? In how many instances does a woman win glory and praise by accomplishing a task originally assigned to a man? Is it good or bad for a woman to act like Jael and gain such praise?

Jah or Yah   *God*   Isa. 12:2; 26:4

Jah or Yah is the abbreviated form of the divine name, J(Y)ahweh.

Issue: By what name do you address God? What does the use of different names for God signify?

Jair   *Person*   Judg. 10:3–5

Jair was one of the "minor judges" who ruled Israel twenty-two years. He accumulated thirty sons and thirty cities.

Issue: Do rulers have the right to great power and large families? What should be the relationship between a powerful political family and personal wealth?

Jairus   *Person*   Mark 5:22

Jairus was a synagogue official whose daughter Jesus raised from the dead.

Issue: In what way is death final? In what way is death only another stage in life?

Jakeh   *Person*   Prov. 30:1

Jakeh's son, Agur, was a writer of proverbs. See Ithiel.

Issue: Agur seems to join Solomon and a few others as authors of Proverbs. What significance does this fact have for the theological understanding of Scripture?

Jannes and Jambres *Persons*   Ex. 7:11–12, 22; 2 Tim. 3:8–9

Jannes and Jambres are the names that later tradition assigned to the two Egyptians who opposed Moses. They became legendary examples of sinful behavior.

Issue: What will future generations remember and retell about you? What are you doing now to build a reputation for the future?

Japheth *Person*   Gen. 5:32; 6:10; 7:13; 9:18, 23, 27; 10:1–2, 5, 21; 1 Chron. 1:4–5

Japheth, a son of Noah, treated his drunken father with respect and, along with Shem, gained a blessing while Ham was cursed.

Issue: Is respect for parents still expected by God? How do you instill respect for parents in children's behavioral patterns?

Jarmuth *Place*   Josh. 10

Jarmuth was a town in southern Judea that joined Jerusalem, Hebron, Eglon, and Lachish in fighting Gibeon and Joshua. During battle, God answered Joshua's prayer and made the sun stand still.

Issue: Does God intervene in any way in modern warfare and international conflicts? What evidence do you have for your position?

Jashar, Book of *Thing*   Josh. 10:12–13; 2 Sam. 1:17–27; 1 Kings 8:12–13

The book of Jashar is a collection of early Israelite poetry used by the writers of Joshua, Samuel, and Kings. Its poems celebrate God's saving actions in Israel's history.

Issue: What collections do your family cherish and how do they help you remember family history? At what times do you as a family go through this collection together? Does the collection cause any problems in the family?

Jashen   *Person*   1 Kings 8:12–13

Jashen, whose name means "sleepy," was an outstanding military leader in David's elite corps of thirty.

Issue: How does a military hero gain the name of "sleepy"? Do you have any interesting names or nicknames in your family? What do these names say about their name bearer?

Jashobeam   *Person*   1 Chron. 11:11; 12:6; 27:2

Part of David's Three, Jashobeam used his spear to kill three hundred enemy troops.

Issue: What makes a military hero great—successful strategy, surprise attack, or massive killing of the enemy? Why did you make this choice?

Jason   *Person*   Acts 17:1–9

Jason was the owner of the house where Paul stayed in Thessalonica. When Paul disappeared, the authorities persecuted Jason.

Issue: Would you willingly bear persecution in place of another believer, or would you cop a plea of ignorance, helping authorities find the leader of your movement?

Jazer   *Place*   Num. 21:32; 32:35; Josh. 13:25; 21:39; 1 Chron. 26:31–32; Isa. 16:8–9; Jer. 48:32

Jazer was an Amorite city-state that Joshua captured on his way through the wilderness. The tribe of Gad settled there, and Joshua set it up as a city for Levites.

Issue: Discuss the concept of divine and human freedom. Why did tribes settle east of the Jordan when God had apparently promised the Israelites only the area west of the Jordan, as seen in Josh. 22?

Jaziz   *Person*   1 Chron. 27:31

Jaziz was David's chief shepherd of the flocks.

Issue: How do you evaluate or treat government employees before you meet them personally? Is it too easy to stereotype certain classes of people? What group do you most easily stereotype or categorize?

Jebus *People* Josh. 15:63; 18:28; Judg. 1:21; 19:10; 1 Chron. 11:4

Jebus is the name of the tribe of people who lived in what we call Jerusalem before David captured it. The city of Jebus lay on the boundary of Benjamin and Judah.

Issue: Do you know the history of your town? Has it had other names earlier in its history? What caused the change? What makes you most proud of your town?

Jecoliah *Person* 2 Kings 15:2; 2 Chron. 26:3

Jecoliah was one of three queen mothers who exercised influence in Jerusalem. The others were Jehoaddan and Nehushta.

Issue: Jerusalem apparently had a special position and role expectation for the mother of the reigning king. How do you see her exercising influence? How do women exercise political influence today? Which system do you prefer? Why?

Jeconiah *Person* 1 Chron. 3:16

Jeconiah is the alternate name of King Jehoichin of Judah, who was exiled by Nebuchadnezzar.

Issue: Do you have special nicknames for your leaders, bosses, or supervisors? In what situations would you use such a name? When would you refrain from using the nickname? Why?

Jediael *Person* 1 Chron. 12:20

Jediael was the military deserter who left the Mannasseh troops to fight on David's side in Philistia.

Issue: When is it proper for a person to desert a post and join the competition? Have you ever done this in any realm of life: business, church, sports, or friendships? Why?

Jedidiah   *Person*   2 Sam. 12:25

Jedidiah, which means "Beloved of Yah," was the name that God, through Nathan the prophet, told David to name the son born to Bathsheba after the death of the child of adultery. The more common name for the child is Solomon.

Issue: David and Bathsheba suffered great loss and grief over the death of their illegitimate son. Having punished them, God then proclaimed His love for the child Solomon or Jedidiah. Have you ever felt God's punishment? Has God restored His relationship with you in a surprising, concrete manner? How did you respond in each instance?

Jeduthan   *Person*   1 Chron. 25:1; 2 Chron. 35:15; Pss. 39; 62; 77

David appointed Jeduthan and his descendants as temple musicians and as prophets. Here, music accompanies prophesy.

Issue: Describe the connection of music with preaching, prayer, and worship. Does one of these dominate the others in your worship services? Why? Can you help change things?

Jehdeiah   *Person*   1 Chron. 27:30

Jehdeiah, whose name means "Yahweh rejoices," was in charge of David's donkeys.

Issue: What is the best job you can ever have? Is it the one bringing the most prestige and money or the one to which God has called you? What jobs would you refuse to take?

Jehiah   *Person*   1 Chron. 15:24

Jehiah was the man who guarded the ark when David had it brought to Jerusalem.

Issue: Why was it important to guard the ark? Today does anyone hold any similar or corresponding position? In what way is modern discussion over the nature of Scripture similar to this responsibility?

Jehiel   *Person*   1 Chron. 26:21

Jehiel was a Levite who managed the priestly treasury under David.

Issue: Do modern churches ever find trouble in managing their assets and accounts? What kind of action do such churches need to take?

Jehiel   *Person*   1 Chron. 27:32

Jehiel was a tutor or advisor to David's sons.

Issue: Who has the most influence on your children? What are they teaching your children?

Jehoiada   *Person*   1 Chron. 27:34

Jehoiada is the person who replaced Ahithophel as David's advisor.

Issue: To whom do you go for advice? Have you ever had a trusted advisor turn against you? What do you do then?

Jehoiada   *Person*   2 Kings 11:4–20

Another Jehoiada was the high priest who protected Joash and installed him as king in place of Athaliah.

Issue: How does your community and/or church deal with abusive parents who are so selfish that they harm their children to gain personal "advantage"?

Jehonathan   *Person*   2 Sam. 15:27, 36; 17:17, 20

Son of Abiathar the priest, Jehonathan informed King David of his son Absalom's plans when Absalom drove David out of Jerusalem.

Issue: How does it feel to have a son rebel against you and seek to take away all the power and influence you have? How would you respond?

Jehonathan   *Person*   2 Sam. 21:21–22

Another Jehonathan was the nephew of King David, who slew a giant from Gath.

Issue: A person's accomplishments are often hidden in the shadow of more famous people. What have you accomplished that most people do not recognize? How do you respond to being unjustly ignored?

Jehonathan   *Person*   Judg. 18:30

A third Jehonathan was the founder of the priesthood in the sanctuary at Dan. He is seen by later tradition as a descendant of Moses.

Issue: How can a hereditary priesthood be condemned as corrupt? Has anyone ever publically criticized you as believing or practicing in some way that should be condemned? How do (or would) you respond?

Jehonathan   *Person*   2 Chron. 17:8

Jehonathan was the name of a Levite that king Jehoshaphat sent to teach the law in the cities of Judah.

Issue: With modern emphasis on separation of church and state, what can the church do to teach the Word of God to the people of our generation?

Jehoshaphat, Valley of   *Place*   Joel 3:2

The "Valley of Jehoshaphat" was the symbolic name that Joel used to describe the location of God's final judgment on His disobedient people. Final judgment is often pictured in a valley known for military encounters.

Issue: Do you believe in a final divine judgment as God faces all people in a valley of decision? What will be the verdict on you when the judgment comes? Why?

Jehosheba *Person*   2 Kings 11:2; 2 Chron. 22:11

Jehosheba was the aunt of king Joash and the sister of King Ahaziah. She hid Joash from Athaliah for six years so that Athaliah would not kill him.

Issue: Can you name someone specifically who is a champion of children's rights? Do you know someone who has protected a child's life from an ambitious, power hungry relative?

Jehovah *God*   Ex. 6:3

Jehovah is a relatively modern rendering of the name of God, Yahweh. Confusion concerning the pronunciation of the holy name comes from the fact that it was considered blasphemous to pronounce God's name. The Hebrew text has four consonants (Y H W H) without the vowels for the name of God. Instead early scribes added the vowels for adonai (*adonay*), the Hebrew word for lord. This practice created a reminder that every time the text has the word YHWH, the reader is to pronounce the word *adonay*. If one pronounces the word with the written consonants and vowels the word is *yahowah*. Using the German system of spelling and pronunciation with the y pronounced as a j and the w pronounced as a v, we get the word *Jehovah*.

Issue: Do you have habits you follow to maintain a sense of awe and reverence as you talk about God and His holy name?

Jehovah (Yahweh)-Jireh *Place*   Gen. 22:14

Jehovah-Jireh, "Yahweh will provide," is the name Abraham gave the place where God provided a sacrifice in place of Isaac.

Issue: Have you experienced a moment of true need and seen God provide exactly what you needed? What does this say about the nature of God?

Jehovah (Yahweh)-Nissi *Place*   Ex. 17:15

Jehovah-Nissi, or "Yahweh is my banner," is the name Moses gave to the altar he built after God led him to defeat the Amalekites.

Issue: Do you have a special place where you can go and remember a special victory God has brought in your life? How do you celebrate at that place?

Jehovah (Yahweh)-Shalom   *Place*   Judg. 6:24

Jehovah-Shalom, or "Yahweh is peace," is the name of the altar Gideon constructed after destroying the altar to Baal that his father had made.

Issue: Have you had a special moment of need where God brought peace into your troubled life? How do you remember and celebrate this life-changing moment?

Jehovah (Yahweh)-Shamma   *Place*   Isa. 60:19–20; Ezek. 48:35; Rev. 21:3

Jehovah-Shamma, or "Yahweh is there," is Ezekiel's name for the rebuilt Jerusalem.

Issue: Do you have a holy place in your life where you repeatedly find God's presence? What times do you go there? Why?

Jehovah (Yahweh)-Tsidekenu   *Person*   Jer. 23:6; 33:16

Jehovah-Tsidekenu, or "Yahweh is our righteousness," is the name for Jeremiah's promised future king of Judah.

Issue: Do you have a favorite name for our God? In what ways do you use that name?

Jehozabad   *Place*   2 Kings 12:21

Jehozabad was a conspirator who joined in the assassination of King Joash of Judah.

Issue: What government official has been assassinated in your time? Is such deadly conspiracy ever justified?

Jehozadak *Person* 1 Chron. 6:14–15

Jehozadak was the high priest when Babylon exiled Judah in about 587 BC. He was the father of the high priest, Joshua, who returned from exile with Zerubbabel.

Issue: Have you ever been in charge of something that collapsed as a total failure? How did you feel? How did you respond?

Jehucal *Person* Jer. 37:3

Jehucal was the messenger of king Zedekiah as he ascended the throne. King Zedekiah sent Jehucal to ask Jeremiah to pray for him. He apparently wanted Jeremiah to ask blessings on his political policy, which depended on Egypt against Bablyon.

Issue: Is God's messenger expected to favor one political group over against another? Why?

Jephthah *Person* Judg. 11–12

Jephthah was an early judge of Israel who made a quick vow to God that cost his daughter's life. He told God he would sacrifice the first thing that came out of his house to meet him if God would give him victory in battle. His daughter was the first to appear.

Issue: Have you made a rash promise or a vow that you deeply regretted later? Did you feel obligated to keep the vow? Why?

Jeshua *Person* 2 Chron. 31:15

Jeshua was the priest under Hezekiah who helped distribute food to Levitical cities from the collection of tithes and offerings in Jerusalem.

Issue: Do you think clergy are underpaid or overpaid? What can you do to bring justice to the situation? Are you giving tithes and offerings to God?

Jether Person Judg. 8:20

Jether, son of the judge Gideon, refused his father's request to slay enemy leaders.

Issue: When is it acceptable to go against parents' wishes? Would Jether have been justified in following his father's command?

Joanna Person Luke 8:3; 24:10

Healed by Jesus, Joanna, or "Yahweh's Gift," supported His ministry through her financial gifts. Her husband Chuza was a steward for King Herod. She was also part of the group of women who first told the disciples about the empty tomb.

Issue: What roles do women play in the New Testament? What roles do they not play? Why? What ministries do women perform for your church?

Job Person Job 1–42

Job is the central figure in the book named for him. His story is difficult for people to interpret and understand because it is the account of a very righteous and blessed man who loses everything because God allows the accuser (the satan) to test Job's devotion to God seemingly on a whim. Through the course of the book, Job's friends visit him and assert that the righteous are blessed but the wicked suffer. They encourage Job to repent, but he denies that he has done anything wrong. In the end, God restores everything to Job and more. The book grapples with the traditional wisdom that only the wicked suffer and deals with the age old question "why does God allow innocent people to suffer?"

Issue: We are constantly faced with suffering in our world, yet God is all-powerful. Why do you think good people suffer? What answer do you find in the book of Job? Is there any easy solution to why sometimes the wicked prosper, while the righteous suffer? How is God connected to these events?

Johanan   *Person*   2 Kings 25:23; Jer. 40–43

Johanan was a Judean leader who supported Gedaliah at Mizpah immediately after the exile in 586 BC. He warned Gedaliah of Ishmael's assassination plans. When the assassination occurred, Johanan rescued captives from Ishmael, asked Jeremiah for advice (but did not follow it), and, fleeing to Egypt, took Jeremiah with them.

Issue: Why would you find the Word of God for your situation and then do exactly the opposite?

Joiarib   *Person*   Ezra 8:16–17

Joiarib was a wise Levite whom Ezra sent to gain needed priests for the Jerusalem temple.

Issue: How can your church help increase the supply of ministers for the church in days when fewer volunteers are available?

Jokshan   *Person*   Gen. 25:2–3

Jokshan, or "trap" or "snare," was a son of Abraham and the ancestor of the Arabian tribes east of the Jordan. He linked Jew and Arab together in his own descendants.

Issue: Do you see any possible solutions to the Arab/Israelite conflict today? What would it be?

Jonadab   *Person*   2 Sam. 13

David's nephew, Jonadab, outlined for Ammon the way to take advantage of Tamar and told the grieving David that only his son Ammon was dead.

Issue: What causes conflict, jealousy, and attack among family members? How do you avoid such actions and feelings?

Jonath-elem-rechokim   *Thing*   Ps. 56

Jonath-elem-rechokim is a musical notation in the title of Psalm 56, apparently dealing with a dove. English translations provide several renderings such as "For the choir director: according to 'A Silent Dove Far Away' or 'Dove on Far-off Terebinths.'"

Issue: What evidence or directions does the Bible give the church concerning the music it uses to worship God?

Jubal   *Person*   Gen. 4:19–21

Jubal was a primordial man, the son of Lamech, and was connected to the invention of musical instruments.

Issue: What instruments should be used in the service of worship to praise God? Which should not be used? Why?

Julia   *Person*   Rom. 16:15

Paul greeted Julia at the end of his letter to the Romans. Her Roman name may indicate some connection with the emperor's staff.

Issue: How could the gospel be proclaimed and accepted in a pagan government staff? Do we know famous or important people with whom we need to share the gospel?

Julius   *Person*   Acts 27

Julius was a Roman centurion assigned to carry Paul from Antioch to Rome. He protected Paul and treated him kindly.

Issue: In what ways does God use unbelievers to protect His people and to bring the gospel message into new, difficult places? Are you praying for people in a difficult place who have not accepted the gospel?

Junia   *Person*   Rom. 16:7

Junia was a relative of Paul. Her connection with Christ was older than Paul's, and Paul referred to her as outstanding among the apostles. Andronicus was apparently her husband. This woman in this verse is among the strongest evidence some scholars use to support female ministers and apostles.

Issue: What roles did woman serve in during New Testament times? What does that say about their role in the church today?

Jushab-hesed *Person* 1 Chron. 3:20

Jushab-hesed, "mercy is brought back," was a descendant of David and the son of Zerubbabel. He helped keep the messianic hope alive during and just after the exile.

Issue: Describe various ways in which God keeps alive the hope He has given His people of a messianic return, a true kingdom of God, and eternal life. What would make someone lose this hope in our day?

Justus *Person* Acts 18:7

Justus was a God-fearing Gentile in Corinth who opened his home to Paul after the synagogue leaders asked Paul to leave.

Issue: Name countries or individuals that persecute God's people today. What can you and your church do to support these persecuted believers?

Justus Barsabbas *Person* Acts 1:23

Justus Barsabbas was the man nominated to replace Judas Iscariot as the twelfth disciple, but he was not elected.

Issue: How does the church choose its leaders? How does the church ensure that people not chosen for one office are incorporated into the church's ongoing ministry?

Kab *Thing* 2 Kings 6:25

The kab is a measurement mentioned once in the Old Testament and equals about a quart or a liter.

Issue: Knowledge of biblical measurements is not essential for productive Bible study. What is essential?

Kadesh-on-the-Orontes   *Place*   Ancient History

Kadesh-on-the-Orontes was the site just north of Damascus of an important international battle between Ramesses II of Egypt and the Hittite armies that took place about 1274 BC, bringing an international truce and eliminating efforts to conquer Palestine. The battle established Egyptian control over Palestine, while the Hittites continued to control the northern city-states.

Issue: What two nations exercise as much international control today as did the Egyptians and Hittites? What do you think will be the ultimate result of the competition between these two super-power nations?

Karkor   *Place*   Judg. 8:10–11

Named for "soft, level ground," the mountain village of Karkor in eastern Gilead formed the arena for Gideon's attack on the Midianites. Three hundred Israelites, with the help of God, defeated fifteen thousand Midianites.

Issue: Military victories are not based on arithmetic. What victories have you won simply because God was on your side?

Kenite   *Person*   Gen. 15:19; Num. 24:21; Judg. 1:16; 4:11, 17; 5:24; 1 Sam. 15:6; 27:10; 30:29; 1 Chron. 2:55

Kenites were from a tribe whose name means "smith" and so probably worked as itinerant blacksmiths. They worked in southeastern Judah, land that God promised Abraham. Moses' father-in-law Jethro was a Kenite. Some scholars think Jethro had a strong hand in introducing Moses to the worship of Yahweh and that he had strong ties to the Midianites.

Issue: What type of relationship do you have with your in-laws? Are you able to gain wisdom from them? Do you show any signs of resenting them?

Kethubim   *Thing*   Ancient Texts

The Kethubim is the third section of Jewish scripture and includes Psalms, Proverbs, Job, Song of Songs, Ruth, Lamentations, Ecclesiastes, Esther, Daniel, Ezra, Nehemiah, and 1–2 Chronicles.

Issue: How much of the Hebrew Bible do you actually read and study? Does God want to speak to you through material you are not reading?

Keturah   *Person*   Gen. 25:1–6; 1 Chron. 1:32–34

Keturah was Abraham's wife (Gen. 25) or concubine (1 Chron. 1) after the death of Sarah. Their six children represented the primary ancestors of the tribes east and southeast of Palestine.

Issue: God works all peoples north and south, east and west into His world plan. The ongoing struggle of Palestine and Israel has its origin with Abraham's children. What plan do you think God has for the Jews and Arabs? What does Scripture teach us about dealing with people whom we disagree with?

Keziah   *Person*   Job 42:14

Keziah, "Cassia" or "Cinnamon," was the second daughter born to Job after God restored his resources. She and her two sisters were the most beautiful women in the land.

Issue: Does God act justly with His people? Did Job and his new daughters receive their just reward from God? Have you questioned God's justice? Why?

Kibroth-hattaavah   *Place*   Num. 11; 33:16; Deut. 9:22; Ps. 78:30–31

Kibroth-hattaavah was Israel's first stop on leaving Sinai. There they received God's quails but begged for the meat of Egypt. Eating too much led to an epidemic in which many died. Thus the place is called "graves of lust" or "graves of craving."

Issue: The church often ignores the sin of gluttony. Does your church attack the sin of gluttony and the danger of obesity in any manner?

Kohath *Person* Gen. 46:11; Ex. 6:18–20

Kohath was the second son of Levi and the father of Amram, Izhar, Hebron, and Uzziel, who were the original heads of the priestly branches.

Issue: How do God's worship leaders gain their positions—through educational requirements, heredity, or election? What biblical evidence do you have for your answer?

Korah *Person* Num. 16

Korah was a leader of the rebellion against the leadership of Aaron and Moses in the wilderness. God caused the earth to open up and swallow Korah, Dathan, and Abiram.

Issue: How does your church handle crises of leadership?

L

Laish *Place* Judg. 18:7

Laish was a town in northeast Palestine known as a quiet and peaceful place until the tribe of Dan chose it for a new home, occupied it, and renamed it Dan.

Issue: Was Dan justified in taking over the city of Laish? When, if ever, is one group justified in God's sight in occupying another nation's land? How do military occupation narratives of the Old Testament inform military actions today?

Lamb of God *Thing* Ex. 12; Lev. 14; Isa. 53:7; John 1:29; Heb. 10:5–7

"Lamb of God" is a messianic title by which John the Baptist identified the one to follow him, namely Jesus. The title carries Passover connotations, the lamb being the chief sacrifice of the Passover, and John used the term right before the Passover to emphasize its connections.

Issue: Have you accepted Jesus as the Lamb who has died for your sins? What have you received from the Lamb of God?

Lamech *Person* Gen. 4:18; 5:25, 29

Lamech, or "powerful," was the son of Methuselah and the father of Noah. He was the first to practice polygamy, or at least bigamy, and the first to show personal pride.

Issue: Pride goeth before a fall. Can you testify to a time when pride led to disaster in your life? Why is pride so destructive?

Land of Forgetfulness *Thing* Ps. 88:12

"Land of Forgetfulness" is a poetic expression describing Sheol, or the life after death.

Issue: Who goes where after death? What assurance do you have of a blessed life after death? Is your faith and trust in God?

Last Supper *Thing* Matt. 26:20–35; Mark 14:12–31; Luke 22:14–38; John 13:1–17:26; 1 Cor. 11:17–34

The Last Supper was the final meal that Jesus celebrated with His disciples, wherein He again warned them of His coming death and dismissed the traitor Judas to do his wicked deed. He showed the symbolic meaning of drinking wine and eating bread, the Eucharist, as He established His new covenant with His followers.

Issue: The central act of Christian worship summons worshipers to experience and remember what Jesus did on the cross and to recommit to a life unto death of serving Jesus. What occurs in your heart as you celebrate the Lord's Supper?

Lazarus *Person* Luke 16:19–31

Lazarus was the principal character in Jesus' parable about the rich man and the beggar. Poor Lazarus died and went to heaven, while the rich man died and entered torment. The rich man asked Lazarus to bring him a drop of water, but the separation of the two arenas made that impossible. The rich man prayed for help for his brothers before it was too late for them, but God said they already had heard the testimony that should lead them to belief and heaven.

Issue: Heaven and hell are biblical descriptions of life after death. Do you stand with Lazarus or with the rich man and his brothers? Do you trust in Jesus or in tradition that ignores the afterlife and its requirements?

Lazarus *Person* John 11

Another New Testament Lazarus was the brother of Mary and Martha. Jesus hesitated when he died before going to him and raising him from the dead. His resuscitation prefigured Jesus' own death and resurrection. Lazarus experienced only resuscitation, or being raised from the dead by someone else's agency only to die again, not resurrection as being raised from the dead by one's own agency to live forever.

Issue: Do you believe in life after death? Are you willing to believe in Jesus for eternal life? How would you describe life after resurrection?

Lebonah *Place* Judg. 21:19

Lebonah was a place used to locate the apparently less-well-known Shiloh, where an annual feast took place. It was a grape-producing area.

Issue: Why do people hold a recurring festival at a place to which directions must be given?

Leb-qamai   *Thing*   Jer. 51:1

Leb-qamai means "Chaldeans," or "Babyonians," through literary chicanery. Literally "the heart of those who rise against me," it results from the Masoretic scholars adding vowel points to an unpointed Hebrew text. The text originally represented a Hebrew code called "Athbash," in which a letter represents a corresponding letter starting at the other end of the alphabet. In English A would equal Z, B would equal Y, C would equal X, and W would equal D.

Issue: Does the church speak in codes today that only members can understand? How can we straighten up our language of proclamation and teaching so the outside world can understand and intelligently respond to us?

Leech   *Thing*   Prov. 30:15

A leech is a blood-sucking animal that is used here to represent greed and insatiable appetite.

Issue: Human greed spans the human race. What appetites do you need to rein in and say, "Enough"?

Leek   *Thing*   Num. 11:5

A leek is an onion-like vegetable prized in Egyptian menus. Eaten raw, it prompted memories the Israelites held on to as a reason to return to Egypt rather than endure manna in the wilderness.

Issue: The ability of the human mind to concoct memories that extend far past reality is well-known. What "good-old-days" thoughts detour you from reality and misshape present goals and dreams?

Legion   *Thing*   Matt. 26:53; Mark 5:9, 15; Luke 8:30

A legion is a large collection of a set of objects. Built on the imagery of the Roman military "legion," it could include from 4,500 to 6,000 skilled military personnel. Here *legion* is used to express the greatness of the number of demons in an evil army.

Issue: Can a person be controlled by thousands of demons? What supporting evidence do you have? Have demonic forces ever challenged you?

Lemuel *Person* Prov. 31

Lemuel was a foreign king of an obscure land apparently named Massa. His name apparently means "Belonging to God." Lemuel recites proverbial wisdom learned from his mother, apparently a queen of the foreign country.

Issue: Did God lead His people to collect and incorporate into Scripture wise words stemming from foreign royalty against wine, women, and the mistreatment of the poor?

Lentil *Thing* Gen. 25:34; 2 Sam. 17:28; Ezek. 4:9

Lentils, one of oldest vegetables cultivated, are legumes used in stews and bread and as a part of a soldier's rations.

Issue: Biblical foods kept soldiers and families healthy. What changes should occur in your diet?

Leviathan *Thing* Job 3:8; 41:1; Pss. 74:14; 104:26; Isa. 27:1

The Leviathan is a fearful primeval inhabitant of the deep waters with several heads. This twisting, dragon-like animal appears in the literature of other nations dating back to the third millennium BC. As with other language and images of neighboring nations, Israel adopted different ways to picture chaotic conditions that humans fear. The Bible witnesses to human fear and lack of power in the face of the Leviathan, while showing that God made it as a creature to play in the seas and to show His creative power over the most frightening of beings.

Issue: God holds more power than does any creature on earth or any machinery or robotic tool, or any military force that might oppose Him. Think of the things great and small that stop you in your tracks with fear and dismay. Can God easily overpower anything you can dream up?

Levite's Secondary Wife (Concubine) *Person* Judg. 19–21

A concubine or secondary wife of an unnamed levite from Ephraim suffers rejection from her man and returns to her father in Bethlehem. The levite goes to get her and bring her back. On the return journey he decides to stay in Gibeah of the Benjaminites, where the pair is not shown hospitality until finally an alien takes them in for the night. The citizens of Gibeah demand that the levite be sent out to be sexually abused, but the Levite and his host instead send the woman out in the levite's place. The levite goes out in the morning and finds that she was abused all night. He throws her on his donkey, takes her to Ephraim, cuts her body into twelve pieces, and sends one to each tribe, starting intertribal warfare.

Issue: Sexual abuse runs throughout history. At times, ordained ministers are the worst culprits. How can the church protect its members from abusers? How should the church teach its people how to behave biblically towards each other and respect each other?

Life, Book of

See Book of Life

Lilith *Thing* Isa. 34:14

According to Isaiah, Lilith was a female demon who would find a resting place along with nighttime scavenger animals in the wilderness. In later Jewish tradition, Lilith appears as Adam's first wife who leaves him because she refuses to be subservient. Eve becomes Adam's second wife. Authors have used the character of Lilith in books and television shows. See Night Monster.

Issue: How much do you know about the demonic world? How many of the traditions about demons that we know from popular culture come from ancient superstition and folklore?

Lily of the Testimony (Covenant) *Thing* Ps. 60

The Book of Life is used here as tune information for the proper recital of Psalm 60.

Issue: Information about musical life in Israel remains quite scarce. Every bit helps our understanding. Have you ever spent time singing the Psalms to whatever tune you can make up? What kind of worship experience did that prove to be?

Linus   *Person*   2 Tim. 4:21

Linus was a companion of Paul who sent greetings to Timothy. Some doubtful tradition identifies him as the first bishop of Rome.

Issue: How do you deal with early church tradition that was not admitted to the biblical canon? How do you think such tradition arose? On what basis do we accept or reject it?

Lois   *Person*   Acts 16:1; 2 Tim. 1:5

Lois was the grandmother of Timothy and mother of Eunice. The two women were commended for their faith in God. The Jewish women believed in Christ and raised Timothy to become a believer even though his father was an unbelieving Gentile.

Issue: The Christian family can be a strong instrument in bringing children to Christ when only one spouse is a believer or when only one spouse raises the child. How are you doing at helping children know more about and trust more in Jesus?

Lord of Hosts   *God*   Ancient Texts

The most common title for God in the Old Testament, appearing about 285 times, is the "Lord of Hosts." This title pictures God as the head of the heavenly council and a general leading the heavenly and earthly armies.

Issue: This title shows the nature of God as the most powerful force in the created order and as a leader of an army who wins bloody victories on earth. How do you incorporate this strong description of God into your picture of the God who is defined as "love"?

Lord's Day   *Thing*   Acts 20:7–12; 1 Cor. 16:1–2; Rev. 1:10

Sunday, the Lord's Day, is the first day of the week, the day on which the early church worshiped and participated in the Lord's Supper. The Jewish calendar would put the evening of the first day on Saturday while the Roman calendar places it on a Sunday.

Issue: We can see a movement from the Sabbath worship of the Old Testament on the sixth day to a New Testament worship on Christ's day. Can you explain why the early church began to worship on the first day of the week?

Lord's Supper   *Thing*   Matt. 26:26–29; Acts 2:42; 1 Cor. 11:20

Jesus instituted the Lord's Supper with His disciples on the evening before the crucifixion. The Lord's Supper includes participating in the eating of bread and the drinking of the fruit of the vine to remind the church of all that Christ has done for us, delivering us from sin by His death.

Issue: What meaning, if any, does the Lord's Supper have in your life? Have you committed your life to serve the crucified and risen Lord?

Lo-ruhamah   *Person*   Hos. 1:6

Lo-ruhamah was the name that God told Hosea to give his daughter. It means "no mother's mercy." God used the prophet's family as a symbol of God's message of judgment on Israel.

Issue: How do your children's names and actions reflect God's love and mercy on you and your family? In what ways does your family express God's mercy to other people?

Lubim (Libyans)   *People*   2 Chron. 12:3; 16:8; Jer. 46:9; Ezek. 30:5; Dan. 11:43; Nah. 3:9

Lubim is a somewhat indistinct term for modern day Libya, the lands adjoining the southern Mediterranean coastland, west of Egypt. The people of these lands were often hostile to the Egyptians. Sheshonq I (biblical Shishak) became an Egyptian general and then established the Libyan

Dynasty over Egypt from about 945 to 550 BC. Phoenicia, Greece, and Rome took turns occupying Libya.

Issue: During the time of ancient Israel, many nations were vieing for power along the Mediterranean. Does a person need to know the players in the various battlefields to understand biblical history?

Lucifer *Thing* Isa. 14:12

"Lucifer" is translated from a Hebrew term for the Day Star or Shining One. This term was often used for deities but here it is used in reference to the prideful king of Babylon who overstepped his limits, assumed the powers of the gods, and sought to become like the most high God. As punishment, he has fallen into the worm-infested Sheol where he is too weak to talk. The term "Lucifer" came into play in the Vulgate, or Latin translation, which translated "Day Star" as "Lucifer." Interpreters then began to use the verse as a description of the fall of Satan, where Satan is an earthly king, not a demonic, fallen angel.

Issue: What are some of the assumptions we make about benefits and entitlements that we should receive without effort or earning? If world emperors have no entitlements, why should we? Do you need to check your attitude toward what you deserve to have and receive?

Lucius *Person* Acts 13:1

Lucius was a prophet from Cyrene who became one of the leaders of the church in Antioch of Syria. This means that an African was among the first leaders of a pivotal church in the New Testament.

Issue: What is the ethnic and racial composition of New Testament church leadership? Is it possible in your church or in many others to create a body that ignores race or ethnicity and elects members and leaders according to the leadership of the Holy Spirit? Or have different races and ethnicities become so culturally different in worship styles and leadership expectations that we are doomed never to unite again?

Lucius *Person* Rom. 16:21

Another New Testament Lucius was a relative of Paul who sent greetings to Rome.

Issue: How does the New Testament handle nepotism? Should church leadership include blood relatives on their staff? What are the advantages and disadvantages of having relatives on one's staff?

LXX *Thing* Ancient Texts

The Septuagint, or LXX (the Roman numerals for seventy), is the earliest translation of the Hebrew Old Testament into Greek, with different readings, more books, and a different structure to certain sections than is found in the original. See Apocrypha.

Issue: Modern language Bibles generally follow the Septuagint's order of books: the law, history, writings, and the prophets over the Hebrew order: the law, the former prophets, the latter prophets, and the writings. If we follow the LXX model in this issue, why do most Protestants not include the extra sections that appear only in Greek? What difference would it make in our walk and worship?

Lydia *Person* Acts 16:14

Lydia was the first European to become a Christian under Paul's ministry. A dealer in purple cloths and clothing, she was financially secure and probably helped support Paul's ministry.

Issue: What is the relationship between the church and the wealthy? Too many churches want to minister to the poor and the middle-class and miss opportunities to bring some of the world's most needful people— the rich—to Christ. Does your church have a plan to reach those with the deepest pains? What access do you have to talk to the rich?

Lysias *Person* Acts 23:26

Lysias was the Roman army officer who protected Paul so that he could speak before the governor, Felix.

Issue: Representatives of the Roman government considered themselves the mightiest forces ever gathered by any nation in history. God used one of their officers to protect Paul from the Roman army, Roman courts, and radical Jewish protestors seeking Paul's life. What signs do you see that God is still at work protecting His people around the globe?

Lystra *Place* Acts 14; 16:1

Lystra was apparently Timothy's hometown and a transportation center. There, recognizing a crippled man's faith, Paul called on him to stand and walk. The amazed crowd identified Paul with the messenger god Hermes and Barnabas with Zeus. People from Antioch and Iconium, seeking to add Jewish practices to Paul's gospel, incited a crowd to stone Paul until he almost died.

Issue: Opponents constantly demanded that Paul add circumcision and other Jewish practices to the gospel of freedom in Christ. Today, what types of practices and beliefs do people seek to add to salvation by grace through faith? What is the temptation that such practices bring?

Maacah *Person* 2 Sam. 3:2; 1 Chron. 3:2

Maacah, which possibly means "dull" or "stupid," was the name of David's wife and Absalom's mother.

Issue: Church ministry should be conscious of inner feelings of people with unusual names. What atrocious names have parents given people you know? How do people who have to bear such names respond to them?

Maccabees *People* 1 and 2 Maccabees

The Maccabees were the family of Mattathias, a faithful Jewish priest who rejected the Hellenistic lifestyle imposed on Jews by Antiochus

Ephiphanes, the Seleucid king who trashed the Jewish temple in 168 BC. The Maccabeans were the last Jews to gain Jewish self-government in Israel until 1948.

Issue: The Maccabean wars represent a very important period in Jewish history, yet it is known only through books from the Apocrypha, whose history many Protestants accept while refusing to grant their canonical authority. What do you see as the relationship of the Maccabean books to the Bible? Why?

Macedonia *Place* Acts 16

Macedonia was a Roman province in the northern part of Greece, west of the Adriatic Sea. There, faithful to a vision from God, Paul first carried the gospel to Europe and to the city of Philippi in about the year AD 50.

Issue: Paul is the prime example of fulfilling Christ's call to carry the gospel to the nations. People strongly anchored in other faiths and systems now seek to prevent Christian mission work around the world, while Christian apathy threatens to turn formerly Christian nations into agnostics and atheists. What can you and your church do to regain the mission zeal Paul exhibited?

Machpelah *Place* Gen. 23:9, 17, 19; 25:9; 49:30; 50:13

Machpelah, or "the double cave," is a place near Hebron where Abraham bought a burial plot for his family. Sarah, Abraham, Isaac, Rebekah, Leah, and Jacob were all buried there, possibly along with other members of the family.

Issue: Different individuals respond differently to burial ceremonies and burial plots. What features of funerals have you seen that you want incorporated into your own burial? What features do you not want included? Why? Are the members of your family, especially the older ones, content with plans made for their future home-going celebration?

Magi   *People*   Dan. 2:2, 10; Matt. 2; compare Acts 8:9; 13:6, 8

The Magi were astrologers well-versed in interpreting the positions of the stars in relationship to earthly events. They hailed from some unknown eastern country, possibly Babylon, Persia, Arabia, or even Assyria. Linguistic evidence suggests they were Persian fire priests of Zoroaster. Other evidence points to Babylonian magicians and sorcerers as their origin.

Issue: Taking over beliefs from other religions, as is so popular around the world today, is disastrous. Spiritualists and others fascinated by Far Eastern religions find emotional solace and individual experiences but do not deal with the basic human needs of forgiveness and eternal life. What modern adaptation of Eastern religions have you been tempted at some time to follow?

Magistrate   *Person*   Acts 16; 18:12–17

Magistrates were local city officials elected by adult male citizens from the financially and socially elite. It was a prestigious, unpaid position, and usually lasted for a one-year term. Magistrates made judicial, financial, and administrative decisions, sometimes a bit arbitrarily, paying special favor to Roman citizens. They were responsible to the Roman governors.

Issue: What kind of local system best ensures the needs and will of the people are met without favoritism and injustice? How would you evaluate your city or county government? How would you improve things should you be elected?

Magnificat   *Thing*   Luke 1:46–55

The song Mary sang in the presence of Elizabeth is called the Magnificat. It is a song praising her savior God for using her to fulfill His promises to His people.

Issue: Are you aware of the actions God is taking to bring blessing to you, your family, and beyond? How do you explain them to others? How do you express your gratitude to God? How do you fit your life with Him into God's larger plan of salvation for His people?

Magor-missabib   *Thing*   Jer. 20:3

Magor-missabib, or "terror on every side," is the name Jeremiah gave to Pashur after the priest had the prophet arrested, beaten, and put in stocks.

Issue: Both Pashur and Jeremiah claimed to be divine messengers bringing God's message to the nation, but no one had a criterion for determining which person had a true message. How does your church make decisions when qualified and chosen leaders strongly disagree?

Mahalath   *Person*   2 Chron. 11:18

Mahalath was the granddaughter of David and the wife of King Rehoboam.

Issue: The person holding a strong political and social position may receive hardly a word in later history. How much fame and fortune do you need to feel life is worthwhile? Will anyone try to keep your story alive after you have departed this life?

Maher-shalal-hash-baz   *Person*   Isa. 8:1

Maher-shalal-hash-baz was the ambivalent name that Isaiah gave his son, meaning "belonging to speedy is the spoil, quick the plunder." Who will speedily plunder whom? Does this proclaim salvation or destruction for Judah? The choice of name warns King Ahaz of Judah not to depend on Samaria or Assyria for help. Isaiah is warning that God will shortly destroy Israel and Damascus.

Issue: On whom do you depend for help in decision making? How does God's Word help? Or do you try to interpret world powers and situations?

Mahlah   *Person*   Num. 26:33; 27:5–12; 36:11; Josh. 17:3

Mahlah was one of the five daughters of Zelophehad. When he died, they pleaded with Moses for inheritance rights to family property, and Moses gave them the rights.

Issue: Has your family found itself involved in inheritance disputes in court? What was the central issue? How did you get the case solved? Why did Zelophehad's daughters go to Moses to decide?

Mahlon   *Person*   Ruth 1:2, 5; 4:9, 10; 1 Sam. 17:12

Ruth's Moabite husband, Mahlon, named "sickly," died in Moab and left Ruth a widow.

Issue: Do you have memories of one or more family members who died at a young age? What suffering did this cause for you and/or the family? Did religious tradition help you solve your situation or make it worse?

Makkedah   *Place*   Josh. 10:11, 29; 12:16; 15:41

Makkedah was a Canaanite city named "place of shepherds" that joined an alliance against Joshua after Israel made a treaty with Gibeon. Joshua trapped the coalition forces in the caves of Makkedah.

Issue: Human alliances may appear to be the way to victory, but they may also be a way that God uses to more easily defeat His enemies. Have you had experiences of agreements you later wished you had never made?

Malchishua   *Person*   1 Sam. 14:49; 31:2; 1 Chron. 8:33; 9:39; 10:2

Malchishua, a son of Saul, named "my king is salvation," was killed in battle with the Philistines at Mount Gilboa.

Issue: Saul's son looked to political and economic success, not to military defeat and death. How hard is it when you do not realize your high expectations?

Malchus   *Person*   Matt. 26:51; Mark 14:47; Luke 22:50–51; John 18:10

Malchus was the servant of the high priest whose ear Peter sliced off. Jesus restored it, after chastising Peter.

Issue: Do you tend to act before you decide? Jesus taught Peter to think through the results before acting in haste. In what ways do you need to learn that lesson?

Malefactor *Person* Luke 23:32–33, 39

Malefactor is the KJV translation used to describe criminals. Taken from Latin, the word describes a person who gradually develops a habitual evil character through wrong decisions, actions, and companions.

Issue: Describe people you have seen gradually become malefactors. How are they different than when you first knew them? How can they reverse the process?

Mammon *Thing* Matt. 6:24; Luke 16:9, 11, 13

Mammon is a term that means personified evil or an all-encompassing term for worldly possessions controlled in ungodly manner.

Issue: What deciding factors win out when you and your family have important decisions to make? What chance does God have of leading you to a decision when expectations of wealth and fame enter the picture?

Manna *Thing* Ex. 16; Num. 11; John 6

Manna, literally "what is this," was the food God provided Israel to sustain them during their years of wilderness wandering. Each person had exactly as much as they needed when he or she finished gathering the manna. The story shows God's care for Israel. In the book of John, Jesus explains that He is the bread of Life.

Issue: Do we tend to want more than God gives? Does God tend to give what we need to meet physical and spiritual needs rather than what we might ask for?

Manoah *Person* Judg. 13; 14:1–5, 10, 19; 16:31

Manoah was the father of Samson. He prayed with his barren wife for a son. The answering messenger insisted that the pregnant mother and future son must maintain rituals that are similar to those of the Nazirites. Manoah and his wife could not make Samson keep his vows. Samson killed himself when he destroyed the building where the Philistines had gathered to make a sacrific to the god Dagon. By this act, Samson killed more Philistines than he ever had in his lifetime. Manoah's final biblical act is his participation in the burial of Samson.

Issue: How does someone parent a child who is wild from the start? In what way is the Bible a guidebook to parenting? In what way has the Bible helped you in parenting the children God has given you? How does the church and the church family respond to those who can't have children or do not choose to have children?

Mara *Person* Ruth 1:20–21

Mara, or "bitter," is the name Naomi chose in response to her life situation after the loss of her husband and sons.

Issue: How does a person respond in public to bad fortunes such as the loss of family? Does your community have a tradition about dress, visitation, place of the funeral, etc.? Do you feel uncomfortable with any of the traditions? Can you avoid having such traditions included in your own last rites?

Marah *Place* Ex. 15:22–23

Marah, or "bitterness," is the third location of Israel in the wilderness, where people complained about the bitter water. Moses obediently put a stick of wood into the stream to purify the water.

Issue: Are you always looking for something to complain about? Do people have reason to call you "bitter"? What can you do to gain a sweeter outlook on life?

Maranatha *Thing* 1 Cor. 16:22

Maranatha, "come, oh Lord," is an Aramaic expression transliterated into Greek and then into English. Two Aramaic words appear here: *mar*,

Lord and *atha,* come. It is open to several translations and meanings, depending on how one divides the letters:

maran atha   either "Our Lord/Master has come," or
"Our Lord/Master is coming" or
"Our Lord/Master will come."

marana tha   "Our Lord/Master, come!"

Such language represents the hope of the early church, its ties to the cross, and its ties to Paul's letters claiming to be victors and expressing their strong hope for Christ to return.

Issue: Untranslated Aramaic in the Bible points beyond literary Greek of most writings to Aramaic oral tradition, showing the authenticity of the language of hope in the New Testament. On what do you base your hope for eternity? Is it more than hope but real assurance?

Mariamne   *Person*   Matt. 2:16–18

Mariamne was the granddaughter of high priest Hyrcanus II. Wife of King Herod, she was executed in 27 BC at the behest of her husband. Two of their children were later executed in AD 7.

Issue: To what lengths will the church and/or religious leaders go to gain apparent legitimacy in their office? When is it legitimate not to follow the will of the "electorate" in seating leadership?

Martha   *Person*   Luke 10:38–42; John 11–12

Martha was a part of a family of disciples of Jesus. Her brother Lazarus was allowed to die before Jesus resuscitated him. The two sisters, Martha and Mary, model devotion to different tasks a disciple can perform.

Issue: Each sister and Lazarus stood dedicated to serve Jesus. Was one type of service superior to another? Does your church have trouble with people wanting to see their service as superior to that of others? How can you help these people?

Matthias *Person* Acts 1:23, 26

Matthias was the person the early Jerusalem church chose through casting lots to replace Judas Iscariot as one of the twelve disciples, or eyewitnesses of Jesus' ministry.

Issue: Is casting lots the one and only scriptural method for making decisions among God's people? What would be the alternative?

Mattithiah *Person* 1 Chron. 15:18, 21; 16:5; 25:3, 21

Mattithiah was a Levite musician whom David appointed to lead the lyre players.

Issue: Who should lead various parts of a church's music ministry? How should the church select them?

Mazzaroth *Thing* Job 38:21

Mazzaroth is a transliteration of the Hebrew term referring to the stars and constellations, with no clarity as to the exact stars or constellations intended.

Issue: Do you expect to find truth by consulting astrological maps or horoscopes? Why?

Medad *Person* Num. 11:26–27

Medad remained in the wilderness camp during the congregational meeting but still received the spirit and prophesied. Moses overruled Joshua and encouraged Medad (and his partner Eldad) in their prophecy.

Issue: What causes jealousy among leaders in God's people? How do church leaders deal with disputes among leadership? Can a person support a wrong cause and still emerge as a strong leader in the church?

Megilloth *Thing* Ancient Texts

Megilloth is a plural term (singular: Megilla) that refers to five brief writings of Scripture that are read during Jewish festivals. They include the

Song of Songs, which is read at Passover; Ruth, which is read at Shavuot, or Pentecost; Lamentations, which is read on the ninth of the month Ab, commemorating when the temple was destroyed; Ecclesiastes, which is read during Succoth, booths, or tabernacles; and Esther, which is read at Purim, the festival commemorating Esther's deliverance of the Jews.

Issue: What value do you find in following a prescribed order of Bible study and reading? Would you prefer a looser schedule that lets you choose what seems most applicable at the moment?

Mehuman *Person* Est. 1:10

Mehuman was the trusted servant of King Ahasuerus of Persia.

Issue: When has God surprised you by working out His plans through people you would never suspect?

Melchizedek *Person* Gen. 14:18; Ps. 110:4; Heb. 5:6, 10; 6:20–7:1; 7:10–21

Melchizedek was a priest from Salem (later Jerusalem) of the God Most High to whom Abraham paid tithes and to whose priestly order Hebrews assigns Jesus.

Issue: In what ways is Jesus a priest, and why does Hebrews say He follows after the order of Melchizedek? How does Jesus relate to the Jewish priesthood?

Memucan *Person* Est. 1:14–21

Memucan was an advisor of King Ahasuerus of Persia during the time that the Persian leader dealt with his wife Vashti.

Issue: In what way do men have the right to control the life of their spouse, even to the point of humiliating her? How should a humiliated spouse respond?

Mene, mene, tekel, upharsin   *Thing*   Dan. 5

"*Mene, mene, tekel, upharsin*" were the fearsome words that a disembodied man's hand wrote on the wall of King Belshazzar's palace when he and his drunken guests celebrated their victory by drinking from golden vessels taken out of the Jerusalem temple. The meaning of the words is somewhat unclear, though Daniel interpreted them using wordplay, turning the nouns into passive verbs to mean "numbered, weighed, and divided," and used that to predict the kingdom's downfall.

Issue: God's means of revelation come in unexpected ways to unsuspecting recipients. Does God continue to interrupt normal daily life with new directions for His people?

Meni   *Thing*   Isa. 65:11

Meni is the name of a false god of fortune that Isaiah described as being worshiped by Jews, often translated as "destiny" or "the number."

Issue: Where do you look for luck or fortune? Is it gambling, the stock market, a stroke of luck, or some mysterious deity? Where does the Bible point you for the best of all fortunes?

Men Pleasers   *People*   Eph. 6:6; Col. 3:22

"Men pleasers" is a term the Bible uses for people whose basic goal in life is to win popularity and do what they desire rather than listening to and obeying God.

Issue: The center of life is either pleasing people or pleasing God. What is your center?

Merab   *Person*   1 Sam. 14:49; 18:17, 19; 2 Sam. 21:8

Merab, the daughter of Saul who is sometimes listed as Michal, was promised twice to David as a wife. She later married Adriel.

Issue: How easily can marriage become a bargaining game to see which family can get the most out of the arrangement? Do you know of weddings today made more for social rewards than for covenant commitment and love before God?

Meroz   *Place*   Judg. 5:23

Meroz was an otherwise unknown town or region condemned in the Song of Deborah for not supporting Israel's army.

Issue: Unknown participants and regions may play a greater role in history than historians discuss. What factors have played a role in the growth or loss of significance for your own home community?

Mesha   *Person*   2 Kings 3

Mesha was a king of Moab who paid high tribute or taxes to Israel until he revolted. This king was made famous to the modern world by the discovery of the Mesha Stele, or Moabite Stone.

Issue: Can international foreign policy be conducted without one nation gaining great advantages over other nations through tribute, taxation, and economic policy?

Meshach   *Person*   Dan. 1–3

Meshach was a friend of Daniel who endured the fiery furnace because he and his friends stood up against the demands of pagan worshipers and leaders.

Issue: Can a person facing persecution and even death for participating in God's work expect God to bring immediate, automatic deliverance? What evidence supports your position?

Methuselah   *Person*   Gen. 5:21–27; 1 Chron. 1:3; Luke 3:37

Methuselah, whose name means "man of the javelin" or "worshiper of Selah" (a god), was the son of Enoch, who walked with God, and the grandfather of Noah. He is the oldest human, as the Bible says he died at the age 969, the year of Noah's flood.

Issue: Does the length of a person's life mirror a person's significance or importance? Who is the oldest person you know? What has that person accomplished on earth?

Micaiah   *Person*   1 Kings 22; 2 Chron. 18

Micaiah was a prophet of God who opposed four hundred court prophets of King Ahab of Israel when he predicted Ahab's defeat and death. He had a vision of a member of the heavenly council becoming a lying spirit to delude the four hundred court prophets.

Issue: Discerning God's will is not a simple process. We fight against evil powers and lying spirits. How do you determine the divine will when you have to make a decision?

Michael   *Angel*   Dan. 10:13, 21; 12:1; Jude 1:9; Rev. 12:7

With Gabriel, Michael is one of the only angels in Scripture with a name. Michael guarded Israel against their enemies, especially Persia. He is to lead the angelic host against Satan, casting Satan's forces out of heaven.

Issue: God's power and resources always have the upper hand in battling satanic forces. What faith do you have that God will lead you through times of trial and hardship? Have you experienced God's deliverance? What do you believe about angels?

Michal   *Person*   1 Sam. 14:49; 18:20, 28; 19:11–17; 25:44; 2 Sam. 3:13–14; 6:16, 20–23; 1 Chron. 15:29

Michal, Saul's daughter, married David at a price of one hundred Philistine foreskins. She later came to despise David. See Merab.

Issue: Human relationships are fickle. Have you been in a relationship that suddenly turned bad? What did you do? What would you do if a relationship turned bad today?

Michtam (Miktam)   *Thing*   Pss. 16; 56–60

Michtam is a mysterious term in Psalm titles. It denotes which musical tune to use or the title of the hymn.

Issue: The Psalms gradually developed musical notations for many of the individual pieces. Gradually, the levitical choirs and probably even lay worshipers learned the pieces by the musical tune or the title. Singing well-known hymns becomes a central means of teaching church beliefs. What does this indicate for modern church music ministries?

Midwife *Person* Gen. 35:17; 38:28; Ex. 1:19

A midwife helps deliver babies. Midwives plotted against Pharaoh by not killing babies as Pharaoh commanded and by helping protect the baby Moses.

Issue: People whom the world considers unimportant find special places in the stories of God's plan to preserve and deliver His people. Without faithful midwives, we would have no Moses. Whom do you know who is seemly unimportant but has a special place in God's plans?

Milcah *Person* Gen. 11:29; 22:20, 23; 24:15, 24, 47

Milcah, or "queen," was Abraham's niece, the wife of his brother Nahor and grandmother of Rebekah.

Issue: A family tree contains many entries about whom only one or two sentences can be written, but that does not rob such people of importance and meaning for the family. What rank do you hold on your family tree?

Millennium *Thing* Rev. 20

The millennium refers to a period of one thousand years during which Satan is bound.

Issue: What persecution must God's people face, and what hope do we have of deliverance? Must you have a specific theory of the millennium to maintain realistic hope in God's final deliverance?

Miriam *Person* Ex. 15:20–21; Chron. 6:3; Mic. 6:4

Miriam was the sister of Moses who fetched her and Moses' mother to raise the baby for Pharaoh's daughter. A prophet, she led in singing the victory song after Israel crossed the sea, but later joined Aaron in opposing Moses' marriage to an Ethiopian.

Issue: When did racial prejudice enter among God's people? Can we be prejudiced against one group and find another group prejudiced in the same way against us? What can we do to avoid personal prejudice?

Mishael *Person* Dan. 1–2

Mishael, literally "who is what God is?" is the Hebrew name for Daniel's friend who was known among his captors as Meshach. He provides a faithful example of trust in God, knowing no one is like God. See Abednego.

Issue: Daniel and his three friends strengthened one another against temptation. Who or what group supports you in times of persecution, suffering, and temptation?

Mnason *Person* Acts 21:16

Mnason was a disciple from Cyprus who befriended Paul on his final voyage to Jerusalem.

Issue: Friendship includes taking care of a person's needs even when the person is in trouble or facing persecution. What truly friendly acts have you done recently?

Mordecai *Person* Esther

Mordecai, or "little man," stood tall as he followed God's instructions and rescued Esther and the Israelite people from Haman's deadly plot.

Issue: Which is the greater gift or possession: physical strength and ability or ties to God enabling one to obey the Heavenly Father? How do you gain the latter gift?

Moreh *Place* Gen. 12:6; Deut. 11:30; Josh. 24:26; Judg. 7:1

Moreh was an important cult site for the patriarchs and early Israel. Abraham, Jacob, Moses, and Joshua were connected with the worship there, emphasizing covenant and commandment.

Issue: Do you have a traditional worship site to which you return repeatedly? What brings you back? How does visiting there change your life and relationship with God?

Moriah *Place* Gen. 22:2

Moriah was where God sent Abraham to sacrifice Isaac and was the mount on which God told David to have Solomon build the temple.

Issue: Does God continue to lead people to important places and show where altars to Him should be built?

Mouse *Thing* Lev. 11:29; 1 Sam. 6

A mouse is a small rodent that, in biblical times, brought plague. God showed His power and relieved sufferers of the plague.

Issue: What animal or disease corresponds today to the Old Testament mouse and plague? What relationship does God have with sufferers of cancer, HIV, or other complex maladies?

Mule *Thing* 2 Sam. 13:29; 18:9; 1 Kings 1:33, 38, 44; Ps. 32:9

The mule was a valued work animal that Israel and Judah imported to use especially in the mountains. Mules were seen as unclean because they cannot reproduce, being a cross between a horse and a donkey. The mule also symbolized the power of royalty.

Issue: Animals have reputations for certain contributions to human society, even those with stigmas against them. What animals can you think of that receive both blame and praise in different segments of modern culture?

Muth-leben   *Thing*   Ps. 9

Muth-leben, literally "death of the son," apparently refers to the tune by which one sang this psalm.

Issue: How do we use music and other rituals to deal with death, especially unexpected death like that of a child? How would you change most funeral services today?

Myra   *Place*   Acts 27:5–6

Myra was a large city in Lysia in Asia Minor where Paul stopped on his way to Rome.

Issue: Paul continued talking about the gospel even as he rode to Rome to face Caesar and possible death. What stops us from talking about the gospel?

Mysia   *Place*   Acts 16:7–8

Mysia is the northwest region of Asia Minor, including Adramyttium, Assos, Pergamum, and Troas. Paul met opposition there, and eventually headed away to Macedonia.

Issue: Missionaries and churches face difficult decisions as they seek to find the exact places where God wants a team to work. Do we seek places where response is good and the church grows, or do we seek to make sure all places hear the gospel, no matter the immediate response?

Naamah   *Person*   1 Kings 14:21, 31; 2 Chron. 12:13

Naamah was the Ammonite wife of Solomon and the mother of Rehoboam.

Issue: What happens when you or your children become involved in activities with a group of people who will obviously lead you or them away from God? How do you respond in such a situation? Name some of the groups you have in mind.

Naaman *Person*   2 Kings 5; Luke 4:27

Naaman was a Syrian soldier, stricken with a skin disease, who at first refused to follow the advice of Israelite prophet Elisha. He eventually went to Elisha, then lowered himself in the dirty Jordan River and was healed.

Issue: What racial, ethnic, linguistic, educational, economic, or other characteristic defining a group of people do you distrust and feel superior to? What changes of attitude do you need to make?

Nabal *Person*   1 Sam. 25:3–39; 30:5; 2 Sam. 2:2; 3:3

Nabal, whose name means "fool," refused to help David, drew his wife Abigail's ire, and died in a drunken furor. His widow then married David.

Issue: What makes a person so self-centered that he appears to others to be a fool? Does alcohol or anything else rob you of your senses to the point that you act foolishly?

Naboth *Person*   1 Kings 21:1–19; 2 Kings 9:21, 25–26

Naboth, whose name means "sprout," upheld Israelite property law and frustrated the plans of King Ahab to take over property for the monarchy. This eventually lead to the death of Ahab via Jehu.

Issue: Naboth pitted tribal inheritance law against a royal understanding of control over all needed property. Even today arguments persist over what right the state has to take over private lands for public needs. How does the Bible deal with issues of ownership?

Nadab   *Person*   Ex. 6:23; 24:1, 9; 28:1; Lev. 10:1–7; Num. 3:2, 4; 26:61; 1 Chron. 24:2

The sons of Aaron the priest, Nadab and his brother Abihu shared priestly responsibilities until they made improper offerings and were sentenced to death by fire.

Issue: Does your church have any complaints about how the minister uses his or her time? Does the minister do things some members think are improper? How do you handle this issue?

Nahash   *Person*   1 Sam. 11:2; 12:12; 2 Sam. 10:1–5; 1 Chron. 19:1–2

Nahash was the king of the Ammonites who attacked Jabesh-gilead and opened the way for Saul to consolidate his power and holdings. David had various relationships with members of the Ammonite royal family.

Issue: Political partners and treaties cannot be guaranteed to remain firm in changing political scenes. Does your political stage show people who make and break alliances when it is to their advantage? How do you deal with such people?

Nahor   *Person*   Gen. 11:22–26, 29; 22:20–24

Nahor was the name of two different men in Abraham's family tree, connecting the patriarch's ties between Judah and Syria.

Issue: Do you tend to emphasize the unity and local nature of your family or its widespread multi-national elements?

Nain   *Place*   Luke 7:11–15

In Nain, a town named "pleasant" in southwest Galilee, Jesus healed a widow's son.

Issue: What is the connection between human petition, or desire and divine action, that helps certain people while others suffer?

Naioth *Place* 1 Sam. 19:18–24

Naioth was the site of Samuel's school of the prophets, where Saul and his messengers exercised ecstatic prophecy.

Issue: How much charismatic action does your church allow or encourage in its services? What is the biblical evidence for their position?

Naomi *Person* Ruth

The widow Naomi is the central figure of the book of Ruth. Her name moves from "my pleasantness" to "bitter" as she loses her family, moves to a foreign country to avoid famine, then returns back home for a second chance and becomes an integral part of the messianic line of Israel.

Issue: Do God's people have a plan to give meaning and hope to broken families? What is your role in such a plan?

Nathanael *Person* John 1:45–49; 21:2

One of twelve apostles in John's gospel, Nathanael was replaced in the list by Bartholomew in the other Gospels. Jesus pointed to Nathanael's sincerity and honesty. Amazed by Jesus' remembering seeing him under the fig tree, Nathanael confessed Jesus as Son of God and King of Israel.

Issue: No actions of Nathanael are reported. He does not even make three of the lists, yet he belonged to Jesus' inner circle. How would you feel if you were Nathanael? Can you accept yourself for who you are and go about your ministry without trying to make someone's brag list?

Nathane(e)l *Person* Num. 1:8

Nathanel was the leader of 54,400 men of the tribe of Issachar. He was a major tribal leader with strong numerical numbers who was otherwise unknown.

Issue: How important is it to be known by strong numbers? What else would you like to see in the record?

Nathane(e)l *Person* 2 Chron. 17:7–9

Nathanel was a Judean leader delegated by King Jehoshaphat to teach God's law in the Judean cities.

Issue: Would you like for your child to become a teacher of God's law to God's people? How can you encourage that?

Navel of the earth *Thing* Judg. 9:37; Ezek. 38:12

The phrase, navel of the earth, is traditional language that adds a bit of mystery to the narrative by reminding us of the place where the earth is tied to the heavens.

Issue: Traditional language carries baggage with it. With any one particular use, the reader must determine how much of the original tradition carries on into the current context. What does the phrase evoke for you?

Nebo *Place* Num. 33:47; Deut. 32:49; 34:1; 1 Chron. 5:8

Mount Nebo, a mountain over four thousand feet above sea level near the Jordan, is a place from where a person can see much of the Promised Land. It was a point of contention as to who controlled it. From its peak, Moses got a final view of the land he would never enter.

Issue: Moses got only a glance at the goal of his life. Why? What huge goals have you set up? How close are you to accomplishing your goal? How would you respond to someone who robbed you of any chance of achieving your goal?

Necho, Pharaoh *Person* 2 Kings 23:29–35; 2 Chron. 35:20, 22; 36:4; Jer. 46:2

Pharaoh Necho was an Egyptian ruler (609–594 BC) whose army captured and killed King Josiah of Judah. Nebuchadnezzar of Babylon then defeated Necho at Carchemish in 605 BC.

Issue: Ambitions can be quickly cut off. How can you make sure that your endeavor comes from God before you act?

Necromancy *Thing* Lev. 19:31; 20:27; Deut. 18:11; 1 Sam. 28:3–25; Isa. 8:19–20; 29:4

Necromancy is the practice of seeking knowledge of the future through consulting the dead. A forbidden activity for Israel, crucial moments still brought out people who claimed to communicate with the dead. The most famous was Saul seeking Samuel through the witch of Endor. See Endor.

Issue: People continue to employ numerous means of seeking knowledge of and control over the future. Are you interested in divination, tarot cards, witches, ghosts, etc.?

Needle *Thing* Matt. 19:24; Mark 10:25; Luke 18:25

Needles are household sewing instruments that Jesus used in one of His enigmatic parables, saying no one can force a camel through the eye of a needle. Jesus used magnificent hyperbole to warn the rich of their plight when relying on riches and not faith.

Issue: Do you control your wealth, or does it control you? The world has identified you as rich. Will you show the world the ways Jesus wants you to use wealth?

Nehelam *Person* Jer. 29:24–32

Nehelam was a false prophet who wrote letters from the Babylonian exile accusing Jeremiah of being false.

Issue: Why do God's ministers have to quarrel with one another and call one another names? How does your church handle situations when ministers publically disagree with each other? What causes such disagreements?

Nehushta *Person* 2 Kings 24:8

Nehushta, which translates as "serpent" or "bronze," was the queen mother of Judah during the reign of her son King Jehoiachin and was one of the first to enter exile. Her name may indicate the worship of a bronze serpent god.

Issue: What offices or traditions do we have to take advantage of the knowledge and wisdom of our older ladies? What temptations lead them to follow the opposite direction? Does your church have programs or plans to prepare women for leadership?

| Nehushtan | *Thing* | 2 Kings 18:4 |

Nehushtan was a bronze serpent that Hezekiah finally removed from the temple. It was connected with Moses' serpent in the wilderness (Num. 21:8–9). See Bronze Serpent.

Issue: Do you or your church have traditional items you have always used in worship? How close is such a tradition coming to being an object of worship?

| Nepheg | *Person* | 2 Sam. 5:15; 1 Chron. 3:7; 14:6 |

We know nothing about David's son, Nepheg.

Issue: How does a person feel who has no connections or accomplishments among a famous family? Have you ever felt like the only one around who has accomplished nothing?

| Nephilim | *People* | Gen. 6:1–4 |

Stories from long ago tell us about the Nephilim, a race of gigantic people. When you get near one, you feel like a tiny grasshopper (Num. 13:33). Their name means "fallen ones" which in its pre-Israelite form may refer to fallen in death.

Children of humans and angels, they appeared on earth when the sons of God, which refers here to fallen angels, gave in to their desire for the daughters of men. These giants reached fifteen feet tall. Fear of the Nephilim drove the Israelite spies to recommend that Israel not try to enter the Promised Land. Because of their fear, Israel endured forty years in the wilderness with only Joshua and Caleb allowed to enter the land. In the New Testament, Nephilim become fallen, sinful angels put in prison by God (2 Peter 2:4; Jude 6).

Judith describes their punishment along with the Sodomites (20:5) for uncleanness. Resemblance to the Greek Titans does not reflect growth or borrowing of the Nephilim or giants tradition, but represents access to the same source(s).

Literature written during the Second Temple period referred to the giants and Nephilim frequently. Born in the vast house of God, they perished for lack of knowledge and wisdom (Baruch 3:26–28). See Enoch.

Issue: Tradition is filled with frightening horror stories of gigantic warriors. Be careful to note the reaction of your children to stories you tell or read, letting the children see the good side of the story rather than the fearful one. Why would the Bible want to scare us?

Nereus   *Person*   Rom. 16:15

Nereus was a Roman believer named for the Greek god of the sea.

Issue: Should believers change their names if they in any way conflict with strong Christian theology?

Nergal   *Thing*   2 Kings 17:30

Nergal was the Mesopotamian god of the underworld whose worship resettling Mesopotamians brought with them as they resettled the exiled northern kingdom.

Issue: Defeat in battle does not indicate the defeat of God and the need to forsake God for another. God can use our defeats to humble us and to start over with others. Can you think of an instance where it seems like God has lost? How was it resolved?

Nergal-Sharezer   *Person*   Jer. 39:3, 13

Nergal-Sharezer was a Babylonian military leader who helped destroy Jerusalem in 586 BC. A son-in-law of King Nebuchadnezzar, he helped take over the Babylonian throne at the death of Evil-merodach. He lost his life during the battle with Medes in Taurus Mountains.

Issue: Rebels and usurpers may rule for a space of time, but in the end, God puts them in their place. Is someone attempting to squeeze you into personal disagreements and fights? How will you respond?

Neriah   *Person*   Jer. 32:12, 16; 36:4–32; 43:3, 6; 45:1; 51:59

Neriah was the father of two important members of Jeremiah's ministry team: Baruch the scribe and Seraiah the quartermaster.

Issue: What is successful parenting? Is otherwise unknown Neriah a model parent for us because of the success of his children, or do we need a different measure for success?

Nero   *Person*   Ancient History

Dominating and cruel, Nero was a Roman emperor (AD 54–68). He began his rule at age thirteen. He is not mentioned in the Bible, but was a strong influence on it nonetheless. Nero had his own mother murdered. He blamed Christians for the great fire in Rome for which he himself may have been responsible. He strenuously persecuted believers who opposed his debauchery and who, at times, labeled him as the antichrist. He eventually lost virtually all loyalty and respect and ended up committing suicide.

Issue: Major historical issues strongly affected the church but were not mentioned in Scripture. To understand Scripture, you must understand the history behind the canon. What resources do you use to understand biblical history?

Nethaniah   *Person*   1 Chron. 25:1–2

Nethaniah was one of a company of musical prophets whom David appointed to relay God's Word through the playing of percussion instruments.

Issue: In what way do musicians enhance worship? Can songs relay God's word to a congregation more effectively than a sermon can at times? Why?

Nethinim   *People*   1 Chron. 9:2; Ezra 2:43, 58, 70; 7:7, 24; 8:17, 20; Neh. 3:26, 31; 7:46, 60, 73; 10:28; 11:3, 21

Nethinim is the collective name for temple servants and slaves who were assigned the most menial of cult responsibilities. They were often foreign prisoners of war.

Issue: What is proper treatment for present or former prisoners of war? What type of ethical agreements should we enter into in regard to treating enemy soldiers?

Nibhaz   *Thing*   2 Kings 17:31

Nibhaz was an otherwise unknown god brought to Samaria and the Assyrians by foreigners forcibly settled there.

Issue: What objects of worship do we almost unconsciously adopt as our culture changes and new groups are added to it?

Nicanor   *Person*   Acts 6:5

Nicanor was one of seven Greek-speaking believers that the early church set aside to minister to Greek-speaking widows in the Jerusalem church.

Issue: What groups in your church or town need special ministries from your church by special people who understand the needs and know how to communicate? See Stephen.

Nicodemus   *Person*   John 3:1–9; 7:50; 19:39

Nicodemus was a member of the Jewish Sanhedrin who came searching for Jesus by night and learned that he must be born again.

Issue: Who is the expert? You may have belonged to the church all your life, served in several church offices, never failed to attend church meetings, and still not understand the basic elements of faith in Jesus. Explain the new birth to someone today. Are you certain that you have been born again?

Nicolaitans | *People* | Rev. 2

Nicolaitans were a heretical sect whose false teaching the book of Revelation condemned. What the Nicolaitans believed is unclear.

Issue: False teaching often comes in strong, attractive packages argued persuasively by attractive, charismatic leaders. Teachers made famous by media and other channels so enchant you with their oratorical skills that you fail to recognize the heretical error of their ways. How can you be sure you are not falling for heretical teaching?

Nicolaus | *Person* | Acts 6:5

Nicolaus was a proselyte into Judaism who became a Christian believer and was chosen as one of seven Greek-speaking leaders to minister to the needs of the Greek-speaking widows.

Issue: What qualifications does the Bible give for the church to use in choosing leaders of ministry to different groups? What skills do you have that best qualify you to help a ministry with a specific type of people?

Night Monster (Lilith) | *Thing* | Isa. 34:14

Isaiah refers to a night monster, or succubus, a mysterious visitor in the night—bird or beast—that was feared for its ability to drain life away but easily disposed of by people. Often equated to Lilith, the supposed first wife of Adam in later Jewish traditions. See Lilith.

Issue: Does the inability to interpret exactly what a word or two in this text means cause problems? How do you explain that God's Word has words whose meaning forces us to guess a bit, since we cannot be sure?

Nimrod | *Person* | Gen. 10:8–9; 1 Chron. 1:10; Mic. 5:6

Nimrod, whose name means "we shall rebel," is the son of Cush, or Ethiopia, who built the kingdom of Babel so that Micah refers to Assyria as the land of Nimrod.

Issue: Primeval history explains circumstances on the international scale and describes international relationships on the basis of ancient heroes. What heroes would you raise up as the dominant forces in your international scene? What nation exercises the greatest influence on you?

Nimshi *Person* 1 Kings 19:16; 2 Kings 9:2, 14, 20; 2 Chron. 22:7

Nimshi was an ancestor of the terror-raising Jehu. The Hebrew "son of" can be translated to mean father, grandfather, or male ancestor.

Issue: A new generation may ruin the family reputation. There is no telling the renown and respect Nimshi held until it was undone by the murderous acts of Jehu. How have you treated your ancestors' reputation? How can you guide your children to maintain the family name?

Nippur *Place* Ancient History

Nippur was a major center of ancient Sumer dating back to 4000 BC. The nation of Sumer, more specifically the city of Ur, was Abraham's birthplace. It lay fifty miles southeast of the ancient city of Babylon and approximately one hundred miles south of modern Baghdad, Iraq.

Issue: Our heritage reaches far back across many countries and many centuries. Learning of ancient civilizations helps us to understand the greatness of the human race through the centuries. In what ways can you better understand yourself in the light of Sumerian and other ancient civilizations? How can these nations help our generation maintain humility and responsibility?

Nisan *Thing* Neh. 2:1; Est. 3:7

Nisan is the first month (March-April) of the post-exilic Jewish calendar.

Issue: As world powers gain and lose control of other nations, the subjugated countries adopt and then reject certain parts of the dominant culture, such as calendars beginning in the spring or fall or holidays connected with traditional worship rites. What dates on the Christian calendar have been borrowed from other cultures?

Nisroch   *Thing*   2 Kings 19:37; Isa. 37:38

Sennacherib, the king of Assyria, either worshiped Nisroch, or it is an intentional misspelling of another god's name, such as Marduk.

Issue: Why would biblical writers intentionally misspell the name of foreign gods?

No (No-Amon)   *Place*   Jer. 46:25; Ezek. 30:14–16; Nah. 3:8

No was a major Egyptian city (also called Thebes or the modern Luxor) paired with nearby Karnak on the east side of Nile in southern Egypt. Ashurbanipal of Assyria destroyed the city in 661 BC.

Issue: A city may celebrate itself for centuries, but God, in His time, can bring come-uppance to a proud people. The empty cathedrals of Europe remind us of the brevity of cultural and religious dominance. Do we truly live in post-Christian America?

Noadiah   *Person*   Neh. 6:14

Noadiah was a prophet who tried to dissuade Nehemiah from rebuilding Jerusalem's walls.

Issue: Does someone in your church work out of self-interest and try to keep the church from moving forward in new ways? How do you deal with them?

Nob   *Place*   1 Sam. 21:1; 22:9–19; Neh. 11:32; Isa. 10:32

Nob was a city near Jerusalem whose sanctuary and priesthood replaced those of Shiloh in about the year 1000 BC. Saul killed eighty-five priests of Nob for helping David.

Issue: Clergy do not stand apart from revenge. Does your church hold stories of past fights among clergy groups? Can you do something to bring peace and mutual care to your ministers?

Nod   *Place*   Gen. 4

Nod was an unreachable land where Cain was relegated to wander after killing Abel.

Issue: Sin brings punishment including isolation from other people in unfamiliar territory. What specific punishment have you received for your sin? Have you asked God to forgive and restore you?

Nunc dimittis   *Thing*   Luke 2:29–32

Nunc dimittis, the Song of Simeon, was Simeon's prayer for the baby Jesus. It gains its title from the first words of the Latin translation. God through His Holy Spirit had promised Simeon he would not die until he saw the Messiah. Having seen Jesus in the temple, Simeon pronounced that he was ready to be dismissed from the living.

Issue: Are you ready for God to dismiss you since you have seen Jesus, asked for forgiveness, and received His salvation?

Nympha (Mymphas)   *Person*   Col. 4:15

Nympha was a woman (although possibly a man, because the Greek could refer to either) who hosted a house church in Laodicea and received Paul's greetings.

Issue: Hospitality to God's people is a marvelous spiritual gift that can bless many who know or do not know Jesus. Have you invited an unbeliever to dinner recently?

Obed   *Person*   Ruth 4:13–17; Matt. 1:5; Luke 3:32

Obed, the son of Boaz and Ruth, was an ancestor of Jesus. His name remains known and in print because he was the ancestor of both David and Jesus.

Issue: Have your parents accomplished something significant so that you need to maintain their memory? Do you exercise a great enough faith that you will have a permanent place in the roll call of Jesus' faithful witnesses?

Obed-edom *Person* 2 Sam. 6

Obed-edom was a Philistine who showed loyalty to David, kept the ark of the covenant at his house, and experienced prosperity.

Issue: God blesses foreigners who obey Him. Have you seen God's blessings come down on people who do not outwardly exhibit faith in Jesus?

Obil *Person* 1 Chron. 27:30

Obil cared for David's camels.

Issue: How do you view an overseer of camels for the king? What people today do you admire because of the position they hold? What people do you look down on because of the position they hold? How do you respond to people who hold no position at all?

Oholah *Person* Ezek. 23

Oholah was the name of the woman in Ezekiel's parable representing the religiously adulterous and unfaithful Samaria. She is paired with Oholibah, representing Jerusalem.

Issue: What is religious adultery? How is it manifest in modern life?

Oholiab *Person* Ex. 31:6; 35:34; 36:1–2; 38:23

Oholiab was the craftsman who assisted Bezalel in creating the wilderness tabernacle.

Issue: How does God use artistic skills to enhance the worship of His people? Do you appreciate the people in your church who quietly enhance weekly worship for you by using artistic and aesthetic skills?

Oholibah *Person* Ezek. 23

See Oholah.

Olympas *Person* Rom. 16:15

Olympas was a person in Rome whom Paul greeted.

Issue: Paul had access to a multitude of names as he wrote his letters and greeted recipients, even in churches he had never visited. Do you need to cultivate the ability to remember names and encourage people by using their name?

Omega *Thing* Rev. 1:8, 11; 21:6; 22:13

Omega is the last letter in the Greek alphabet. It is frequently paired with Alpha, the first letter, to indicate the totality of reality, especially when applied to God the Father and God the Son as encompassing all reality. The Bible teaches a monotheistic religion in Trinitarian form, meaning one God has appeared in three forms or persons—Father, Son, and Spirit.

Issue: In what way is the modern church tempted to overemphasize one person of the Trinity or ignore another? Do we fear the charismatic Spirit, overplay the sovereignty of the Father, or miss the present work of the Son?

Onan *Person* Gen. 38

Onan, whose name means "power," refused to follow the practice of Levirate marriage, which instructed him to marry his widowed sister-in-law and to raise up sons for his deceased older brother. God punished his disobedience with death.

Issue: No one stands above God's law. When God issues a command, do you follow even if you do not completely understand why?

Onesimus *Person* Col. 4:7–9; Philem. 16

Onesimus was an escaped slave for whose protection Paul pleaded in his letter to Philemon, Onesimus's master.

Issue: Christian love for believers often overruns the letter of the law, seeking mercy and reinstatement rather than precise punishment. Do you know of someone against whom you continue to hold a grudge rather than accepting as a Christian convert? What action should you take?

Onesiphorus   *Person*   2 Tim. 1:16–18; 4:19

Onesiphorus, Paul's companion from Ephesus, showed loyalty to Paul no matter the personal cost.

Issue: Loyal disciples and ministers help people no matter the personal cost or shame involved. Do you demonstrate consistent loyalty to your church and its ministers even when you may have to pay a price for such faithfulness?

Ophel   *Place*   2 Chron. 27:3; 33:14; Neh. 3:26–27; 11:21

Ophel was the place in Jerusalem where the "city of David" was built. It lay south of the temple mountain and represented the oldest settlement area in Jerusalem.

Issue: Certain areas of a city or region gather an aura of mystery and holiness through past history. Does a part of your sanctuary gather visitors in your city because of its age and history? Does this prove to be an asset or a liability for your mission?

Oreb   *Person*   Judg. 7:25; 8:3; Ps. 83:11; Isa. 10:26

Oreb was the Midianite officer whom Gideon defeated and killed.

Issue: The size of an army does not determine the outcome of the battle. What spiritual battles have you seen in which God carried you to victory despite overwhelming odds?

Orion   *Thing*   Job 9:9; 38:31; Amos 5:8

Orion is a heavenly constellation whose brightness and power, according to Job and Amos, cannot match that of Yahweh, the God of Israel.

Issue: What can humans see or find that matches the power and glory of God? What modern inventions and technological wonders can be lifted up in comparison to God's power?

Orpah   *Person*   Ruth 1:4, 14

Naomi's Moabite daughter-in-law, Orpah, returned home in response to Naomi's pleading, while Ruth, the other daughter-in-law, went with Naomi into Israel.

Issue: Making a choice that differs from that of another person may be perceived as wrong. Orpah made a sensible decision, but it differed from Ruth's. Have you faced a situation where you made an unpopular though reasonable decision?

Othniel   *Person*   Josh. 15:17; Judg. 1:13; 3:9, 11; 1 Chron. 4:13; 27:15

Othniel, Caleb's son-in-law, served as Israel's first "judge."

Issue: Sometimes the woman or man you marry matters more than the person you are. Did Othniel earn his opportunities or did he get them because he married into Caleb's family? Does acclaim go to the deserving in your family or to the person who married right? How does that affect you?

P

Pad(d)an-aram   *Place*   Josh. 15:17; Judg. 1:13; 3:9, 11; 1 Chron. 4:13; 27:15

Padan-aram is the portion of Syria from which Abraham moved to Canaan and the place to which Abraham sent his servant to find a wife for Isaac. Jacob fled there for refuge from Esau, and there he married Leah and Rachel.

Issue: Do you or do you and your family have a sanctuary place where you go to review family traditions and to ensure that all is well in the family? Is this a place where family feuds can be resolved?

Palms, City of *Place* Deut. 34:3; Judg. 1:16; 3:13; 2 Chron. 28:15

A popular name for Jericho was the City of Palms.

Issue: Does your town have a slogan name that you use for advertising and popularizing? What is the value of such a name?

Palti *Person* 1 Sam. 25:44; 2 Sam. 3:15–16

Palti was the second husband of Michal after David. When David demanded Michal back, Palti followed all the way, weeping, until Abner ordered him to return home.

Issue: David wanted Michal to legitimate his succession to Saul. Do you know of marriages broken up by political maneuvering? What does such maneuvering do to people caught in the middle?

Pamphylia *Place* Acts 2:10; 13:13

Pamphylia was the province in Asia Minor, now southern Turkey, where John Mark left Paul and Barnabas.

Issue: Can you stay the course? John Mark could not endure the physical or psychological stress involved in missionary work. Have you had to abandon a project because you did not have the physical or psychological stamina to complete it? Does that mean God is through with you, or is God waiting to give you a second chance as He did John Mark?

Paphos *Place* Acts 13:6, 13

Paul, Barnabas, and John Mark visited Paphos, the capital of Cyprus, on their first missionary journey.

Issue: Does missionary strategy begin with visits to small areas where people may be more receptive to the gospel or with efforts in major cities where a large number of people may be targeted? What area do you mark out as your missionary target focus?

Parmenas   *Person*   Acts 6:5

Parmenas was one of the seven Greek-speaking believers that the Jerusalem church chose to minister to Greek-speaking widows.

Issue: Do you have special needs groups based on economic need, ethnicity, age, work opportunities, or marital status in your church or community? What can you do to begin a new ministry for people with special needs in your church?

Pasdammin   *Place*   1 Chron. 11:13

Pasdammin was the site of David's victory over the Philistines. It lies between Socoh and Azekah.

Issue: Causes that appear hopeless come out victorious when God goes to work. What hopeless cause or impossible circumstance have you seen God deliver you from?

Pathros   *Place*   Isa. 11:11; Jer. 44:1, 15; Ezek. 29:14; 30:14

Pathros is the transliteration of the Egyptian term for Upper (that is, southern) Egypt between Memphis and Elephantine. The prophets show that God's judgment and God's restoration reach all the way down into Upper Egypt.

Issue: God's activities with His people have no geographical limits. We too often see God as the God of America or the God of the Western world, or as the God of Dixie. In what ways do you almost unconsciously place limits on God? Why?

Patmos   *Place*   Rev. 1:9

Patmos is the small island southwest of Miletus where John was exiled and where he wrote the book of Revelation.

Issue: Exiled for Christ seems language and reality of long ago, but closer investigation finds thousands of prisoners and martyrs in our era who simply kept their faith in Christ. What group do you know that continues to imprison and kill Christians? What can you do about this situation?

Patrobas *Person* Rom. 16:14

Patrobas was a faithful believer to whom Paul sent greetings in his letter to the Romans.

Issue: One mention is all most people get in Scripture. What would you feel like if you found yourself worthy of being mentioned in Scripture? Such recognition is not awarded for achievement but quietly mentioned for faithfulness. Would you prove faithful enough that an important Christian leader would honor you by mentioning you as a person of faith?

Pax Romana *Thing* Ancient History

The Pax Romana, or the Roman Peace, was a period of time from 27 BC to AD 180 when the Roman government was able to establish peace across its vast empire. This allowed people like Paul to more easily travel roads and seaways with their message. Roman Peace does not appear in the Bible, but it establishes the cultural background for every event mentioned in the New Testament.

Issue: In what ways did Rome's Pax Romana enable Christian missions? Do you know of any ways it hindered the Christian movement? What role did emperors like Nero play in this era?

Pekod *Place* Jer. 50:21; Ezek. 23:23

Pekod was the home of the Aramean tribe on the eastern bank of Tigris River. Jeremiah and Ezekiel called for their destruction as part of the punishment of Babylon. The consonant formation of PKD means punishment in Hebrew, so a word play is at work here.

Issue: Do you like to play with words? What kind of word games have you devised to help people understand God's Word?

Pelethites *People* 2 Sam. 8:18; 15:18; 20:7, 23; 1 Kings 1:38, 44; 1 Chron. 18:17

The Pelethites were mostly foreign soldiers whom David employed to protect him and to carry out special missions. They may have had ancestral ties with sea peoples kin to the Philistines. They maintained loyalty to Solomon.

Issue: Why do rulers so often employ elite foreign soldiers in their personal bodyguard and elite units? Can you name other such groups, such as the Swiss Guard? Does this indicate some problems at the deepest levels of trust?

Peninnah *Person* 1 Sam. 1:2, 4

Peninnah was the second wife of Elkanah and thus a rival of Hannah, his first wife, who prayed for a child and finally received Samuel from the Lord.

Issue: How does polygamy produce jealousy and rivalry? In the modern world, why do people cheat on their spouses and think nothing will come of it?

Peor *Place* Num. 23:28; 25:3, 5, 18; 31:16; Deut. 4:3; Josh. 22:17; Ps. 106:28

Peor is the Moabite mountain where Balak brought Balaam to curse Israel, and where God blocked the plan. Israel later fell to temptation and worshipped the god Baal-Peor.

Issue: Places where God shows His power in the most obvious ways often become sources of greatest temptation. What places do you find deliciously tempting even though in the past, God has used those places to bless your life? What is the greatest temptation you are facing right now?

Pergamum *Place* Rev. 1:11; 2:12

Pergamum was the major city of religion, culture, and commerce in Asia Minor, fifteen miles from the Aegean Sea and where one of the seven churches of Revelation worshiped. It was an established leader in making parchment for writing and as a medical center. The church there was praised for its faith.

Issue: What church do you know that Christ can praise for its faith even in the midst of persecution and controversy? Do we too often praise our churches for accomplishing much too little?

Persis   *Person*   Rom. 6:12

Paul greeted Persis in his letter to Romans and recognized her for her hard work for the Lord.

Issue: What constitutes hard work for the Lord? Whom do you know in the church that you would say works very hard for God? What criteria do you use to measure this? Who has the right to commend or condemn someone else?

Pethahiah   *Person*   Neh. 11:24

Pethahiah was a Jewish leader who advised the Persian king about matters in Jerusalem.

Issue: What is the distinction between representing your people by advising a foreign king and betraying your people by serving on the foreign king's staff as they rule over your people? Do you know of situations today where a person's service approaches treason? What can be done to help the situation?

Pethor   *Place*   Num. 22:5; Deut. 23:4

Pethor was the distant home of Balaam, the prophet whom Balak tried to hire to curse Israel in the wilderness. It lies across the Euphrates sixty miles northeast of Aleppo, meaning that Balaam traveled about four hundred miles to see the Israelites he was to curse.

Issue: God's enemies may travel far and work hard to oppose God's people, but in the end, God's will for His people prevails. What opposition to God have you seen develop and then lose all power in the face of God's actions? Have you ever faced an enemy of God? What happened in the encounter?

Pharpar *Thing* 2 Kings 5:12

Pharpar was the Syrian river in which Naaman, the Syrian general afflicted with a skin disease, wanted to wash, rather than in the muddy Jordan where Elisha sent him.

Issue: Have you ever had a better plan than the one God showed you? How did you respond? What did you discover in the end? What do you do now when God shows you a plan?

Phicol *Person* Gen. 21:22, 32; 26:26

Phicol was the commander of the Philistine army under Abimelech when both Abraham and Isaac tried to protect themselves by passing their wives off as their sisters.

Issue: Both Abraham and Isaac tried to manipulate Abimelech by swearing in God's name. You cannot use God's name and God's person to try to manipulate God when you know what you are doing is wrong. Remember a time when you schemed against God with a plan to manipulate Him and protect yourself? What was the outcome?

Philadelphia *Place* Rev. 1:11; 3:7

Philadelphia was a city in the province of Lydia in western Asia Minor. John commended the church there for persevering in the faith.

Issue: On what occasion has your faith been strongly tested? How did you remain faithful despite the desperate situation? How would you react if you faced another desperate situation?

Philetus *Person* 2 Tim. 2:17–18

Philetus was a teacher who tried to convince the early church of the heretical belief that the final resurrection had already occurred. See Hymenaeus.

Issue: How do you test the doctrine you hear at church, at Bible study groups, in the mass media, and in popular books? Are you skilled enough at reading Scripture that you can test what you hear and what you read?

Philip's Family *People* Acts 21

On Paul's final return to Palestine, he stopped in Caesarea at the home of Philip the evangelist and his four daughters, who were Christian prophets.

Issue: What is a Christian prophet? Distinguish prophet from pastor or teacher or evangelist or elder. Which officers does your church have? Why not the others?

Philologus *Person* Rom. 16:15

In his letter to the Romans, Paul greeted and praised Philologus, whose name means "lover of words" or "lover of learning."

Issue: Paul consistently greeted and praised people through his letter-writing ministry. What kind of ministry of encouragement do you conduct with fellow believers—letter writing, calling, emailing, personal visits, sharing a meal, etc.? In what ways do you need to improve in this area? Do you have to have the gift of hospitality before you can do this?

Phlegon *Person* Rom. 16:14

Phlegon, whose name means "burning," was another believer that Paul greeted in Romans.

Issue: Some people live out their name. Here is a believer apparently burning with zeal. Whom do you know whose life matches their name? Do you know someone given a nickname because of their lifestyle? Our name is "Christian" or "little Christ." Do you live up to that name?

Phoebe *Person* Rom. 16:1–2

Phoebe was a woman from Cenchrea whom Paul recommended to the church at Rome as a true servant or deacon of the church.

Issue: Does Paul accept women in ministry as deacons? What evidence do you have to answer this question? What women in your church would you recommend as highly as Paul recommended Phoebe?

Phoenix *Place* Acts 27:12

Phoenix was the harbor town in Crete's southeastern coast that the crew taking Paul to Rome hoped to reach for the winter.

Issue: Have you ever set a goal and failed to reach it with disastrous results? How did you react to your failure? Has God helped you overcome the failure?

Phygelus *Person* 2 Tim. 1:15

Phygelus, whose name means "fugitive," left Paul while Paul was imprisoned.

Issue: Has someone you depended on for help forsaken you in the midst of trouble? How did you react? Have you given up on a task and deserted your companion or leader at an important time? Why? Have you worked to mend the relationship?

Pi-Beseth *Place* Ezek. 30:17

Pi-Beseth was the Egyptian administrative center forty-five miles northeast of Cairo upon which Ezekiel proclaimed judgment.

Issue: What do we learn about God when He constantly announced judgment on nations far and wide? What is the extent of God's control over the nations and cities of the world? In what ways does God exercise that control today?

Pihahiroth *Place* Ex. 14:2, 9; Num. 33:7–8

Pihahiroth was Israel's early camping place after leaving Egypt.

Issue: How could Israel survive in the early days of leaving Egypt? Have you ever been lost or wandered in unknown territory? How did you find your way? Do you credit God in any way for helping you?

Pilate's Wife *Person*   Matt. 27:19

Pilate's wife, who is unnamed, sought to get her powerful husband to withdraw from any dealings with Jesus because of a vision she had.

Issue: How do you respond to dreams that you or members of your family have? Do you continue with an activity, or do you follow the dream? Why?

Piram *Person*   Josh. 10:3, 23

Piram, named "wild ass," was the king of Jarmuth who joined four other kings in opposing Joshua after Israel's treaty with Gibeon.

Issue: Have you ever formed a coalition to fight for a cause? Did the coalition work well? What results did you have?

Pishon *Place*   Gen. 2:11

Pishon was a river that flowed out of the Garden of Eden but is not identified with any current river.

Issue: God created the entire universe and provided for the needs of all its inhabitants. What elements of creation most amaze you? Can we believe in God as Creator without being able to accurately describe everything He created?

Pithom *Place*   Ex. 1:11

Pithom is one of the two supply cities that Israelite slaves built for the Egyptian pharaoh.

Issue: How do you respond to the hard work that someone else forces you to accomplish? Has there been another time in your life when you've wished to get back to such labor, like the Israelites in the wilderness longed to return to Egypt?

Pleiades   *Thing*   Job 9:9; 38:31; Amos 5:8

The Pleiades, the Seven Sisters, is a star cluster in the constellation Taurus. The seven of the brightest stars of the Pleiades are named for the Seven Sisters of Greek mythology: Sterope, Merope, Electra, Maia, Taygeta, Celaeno, and Alcyone. The remaining two brightest stars are named for the parents of the Seven Sisters: Atlas and Pleione. In ancient Israel the Pleiades were used for predicting weather and guiding ships.

Issue: God shows His unique power by using the stars. How do you respond when you gaze at the evening sky?

Pontus   *Place*   Acts 2:9; 18:2; 1 Peter 1:1

First Peter was written to the church in Pontus, a Roman province in Asia Minor south of the Black Sea.

Issue: The Christian mission reached Pontus quickly after Pentecost. What places today are responding quickly to the gospel? How is your own country responding to the gospel? What can you do to help the gospel spread more quickly at home and across the sea?

Potiphar   *Person*   Gen. 37:36; 39:1

Potiphar was an Egyptian official who bought Joseph as a slave from the Midianites, but put him in prison when his unnamed wife lied about Joseph seducing her.

Issue: Why do people lie? What brings you the greatest temptation to lie? How do lies hurt you and other people?

Potiphera(h)   *Person*   Gen. 41:45, 50; 46:20

Potiphera was the priest of the Egyptian sun god Ra in Heliopolis whose daughter Joseph married.

Issue: How can we justify Joseph's marriage into the family of an Egyptian priest of a pagan god?

Prochorus   *Person*   Acts 6:5

Prochorus was a leader among the Greek-speaking believers in the Jerusalem church. They elected him as one of seven to minister to Greek-speaking widows.

Issue: To whom does your church provide food and other benevolence items? Can you think of ways to improve on your ministry to the poor, hungry, homeless, etc.?

Puah   *Person*   Ex. 1

Puah was the midwife in Egypt who helped the Israelites bypass the pharaoh's command to kill the babies.

Issue: Do you obey the commands of the earthly commander or of God? Can you give an example of following God's rather than human orders?

Publius   *Person*   Acts 28:7–8

Publius was the highest public official on the island of Malta, where Paul was shipwrecked on his way to Rome and was bitten by a snake.

Issue: Some mission strategists witness to top government officials as the beginning point of their mission strategy. In what situations would you think that strategy would work? What is the danger of such strategy?

Pudens   *Person*   2 Tim. 4:21

Pudens was a Roman believer who sent greetings to Timothy.

Issue: Paul continually sent his young compatriots across the Roman Empire, communicating with other churches to find out how widespread problems may be and how other churches were solving their problems. How does a modern church learn new ways of facing and solving problems that arise?

Purah   *Person*   Judg. 7:10–11

Purah, a servant of the judge Gideon, went with Gideon to spy on and listen to the Midianite camp in order to alleviate Gideon's fears.

Issue: What mission or situation has caused you to fear more than any other? Who helped you in this situation? How was God involved?

Purim   *Thing*   Esther

Purim is the annual Jewish festival that commemorates Esther's deliverance of the Jews from the persecution of Haman.

Issue: List the holidays you celebrate as a family, a church, a town, a state, or a nation. How do you use these to teach your family the meaning and origin of the traditions that have established the values and beliefs by which you live?

Puteoli   *Place*   Acts 28:13

Puteoli was a major seaport on the Bay of Naples, serving Rome. Paul landed in Puteoli on his way to Rome to testify before Caesar.

Issue: Join in Paul's journey as he finally came to land. What evidence did he have on his side? What evidence stood against him? How do you feel on the brink of a major event in your life when you know it is only a stepping-stone to an even more important event?

Quartus   *Person*   Rom. 16:23

Quartus, whose name means "fourth," sent greetings to the church at Rome. Tertius in the preceding verse is "third" and may have been a brother.

Issue: Why do families give a child the exact same name the father bears? What are the advantages? What are the problems involved?

Queen of Heaven   *Thing*   Jer. 7:18; 44:17–25

The Queen of Heaven was a goddess who tempted Israel, especially the Israelite women, with promises of fertility and prosperity. As archaeology shows, Israelite women apparently formed images of nude goddesses to worship.

Issue: Prosperity and fertility are basic desires of the human heart. Modern-day preachers and teachers too often offer a prosperity gospel with too many promises and not enough expectations. In what ways do you expect material prosperity from God?

Quirinius   *Person*   Luke 2:1–2

See Cyrenius.

R

Ra(a)mses   *Place*   Ex. 1:11

Ramses was the city that Israelite slaves were building for the Egyptians just prior to the Exodus.

Issue: There is a great scholarly debate concerning the date of the exodus because there is no archaeological evidence that easily connects to the written traditions in Exodus. Many might question your faith in the Bible when no evidence outside the Bible exists for an event. How do you respond to people who question your faith in the Bible?

Rab-mag   *Person*   Jer. 39:3, 13

Rab-mag was the title of Nergal-sharezer, an advisor close to the Babylonian king.

Issue: If you compared the power and influence of the Rab-mag to that of Jeremiah, who had the most power? What evidence do you have for your answer?

Rabsaris *Person* 2 Kings 18:17; Jer. 39:3, 13

Rabsaris was the title for a major advisor to the king of Assyria, especially in military matters. The man in this position often headed a delegation seeking unpaid tribute.

Issue: Refusal to pay tribute to the imperial power signified rebellion. When is political/military rebellion justified?

Rabshakeh *Person* 2 Kings 18–19; Isa. 36–37

Rabshakeh was the title of important advisors to the king of Assyria. The man in this position acted as an ambassador, presenting messages of the king to foreign vassals.

Issue: Different officials held different titles, but they all represented the power and authority of the king of Assyria. Christians are called as ambassadors for Christ, to represent Him in every relationship and transaction in which we are involved. What is your ambassadorial assignment today?

Raca *Thing* Matt. 5:22

Raca is a word of contempt, labeling someone as empty or ignorant. Jesus placed it next to "fool" as language not to use in talking of someone else.

Issue: Your mouth is a burning fire ready to scorch another person. What sets you off to call someone else names? Will you ask Jesus to cleanse your mouth today?

Rainbow *Thing* Gen. 9:12–17

The rainbow is a symbol of God's promise that He will never again destroy all humans via a flood, no matter their wickedness.

Issue: God's promises, in a way, place limits on God—self-imposed limits that benefit people. Some of His promises, such as this one, appear to conflict with simple scientific explanations of phenomena such as the rainbow. In your own reading and meditation, what relationship do you see between science and biblically based Christian faith?

Ramathaim   *Place*   1 Sam. 1:1

Samuel's birthplace was Ramathaim.

Issue: Home can be a place of refuge or a place of jealousy and spite. Samuel's home was a place of dissatisfaction, blame, and competition before his birth. How would you describe your home life when you were a child? Did you ever experience a major transformation? What type of home life have you developed for your family and friends?

Ramath-lehi   *Place*   Judg. 15:14–17

Ramath-lehi was a place whose name means "raised jawbone." It is where Samson used a donkey's jawbone to kill one thousand Philistines.

Issue: Samson played lone ranger with his enemies and with God. He never joined forces with anyone else or with a conscripted army of any kind. Do you sometimes decide working with other people is too slow and cumbersome? In the end, do you accomplish more by yourself than with other people?

Reba   *Person*   Num. 31:8; Josh. 13:21

Reba was the king of the Midianites whom Moses defeated, allowing parts of Israel to expand east of the Jordan.

Issue: God is free to adjust His plans. He promised land west of the Jordan to Israel, then agreed with some Israelites that they could live east of the Jordan. Have you seen God respond to you, your family, or your church in a way that appears to alter previous plans? What does such divine flexibility teach you about God?

Rechab *Person* 2 Sam. 4:1–12

Rechab was a Benjaminite who plotted with his brother to kill Ish-bosheth, Saul's son and the claimant to the throne of Saul. Hearing of their deed, David ordered them killed.

Issue: Human logic and human expectations do not win out in human encounters with God. We too often try to get ahead of God and do things our way rather than His way. Can you recall an experience where you became impatient with God and wanted to get something done before He opened the door to do it?

Resheph *Thing* Deut. 32:24; 1 Chron. 7:25; Job 5:7; Pss. 76:3; 78:48; Song 8:6; Hab. 3:5

A Near Eastern deity about whom much is speculated and little known, Resheph appears to be associated with metalworking and with the underworld.

Issue: Hebrew biblical passages take up the language of foreign gods and their attributes to describe Yahweh's superiority. What kind of language does the church borrow today to clarify the nature of our God? Do we ever face the temptation to let the borrowed language lead us to worship the idolatrous god?

Reuel *Person* Ex. 2:18; Num. 10:29

One tradition names Moses' father-in-law Reuel, in comparison to Jethro in another tradition.

Issue: Some people go by two names, often due to different "social circles" in which they run. Can you name people who go by different names within different social circles—childhood community, college, athletics, or adult life? How and why do such double names function?

Rezin *Person* 2 Kings 15:37–16:9

Rezin was a king of Aram (Syria) who formed a coalition of kings against Assyria, stopping first to force Jerusalem to join the coalition.

Issue: When does the status quo become so bad that you want to organize a revolt and change everything? If you had the authority and power, what is the first thing you would change?

Rezon   *Person*   1 Kings 11:23–25

Rezon was an official of Hadadezer of Zobah in Syria. Rezon fled with a rag-tag army and established his own Syrian kingdom in Damascus. He became known as an enemy who troubled Solomon for most of Solomon's rule.

Issue: Rezon is known more for whom he opposed than for what he accomplished. Do you know someone who is more a troublemaker than a person of accomplishments? How do you respond to such people? Do you really find hope in changing their attitude and actions?

Rhoda   *Person*   Acts 12:13

Rhoda left the prayer meeting, convened to pray for Peter's release from prison, to answer a knock at the door, then slammed the door in Peter's face in her excitement to tell everyone he was there.

Issue: Emotions, not intelligence and logic, control so many of our actions. Share an experience in which you let emotions grab control so that you did something totally illogical. What positive roles do emotions play in the life of the church?

Riblah   *Place*   2 Kings 23:33; 25:6–21; Jer. 39:5–6; 52:9–27

Riblah was the town or military camp in Syria near the Orontes River where Pharaoh Necho of Egypt imprisoned King Jehoahaz of Judah. It is also where Nebuchadnezzar of Babylon took the rebellious King Zedekiah of Judah, executed his three sons, and blinded the king.

Issue: What do we learn from history about rebellion? Judah's kings constantly found reasons to rebel. Are you of a rebellious spirit? What do you rebel against? Why?

Rimmon   *Place*   2 Kings 5:18

Rimmon is one name for the chief god of Syria, who is also known as Hadad.

Issue: How do gods change their names? Do the characteristics of one god get absorbed or incorporated into another god (for instance, the Greek god Zeus and the Roman god Jupiter)? Does a quick look at your checkbook and calendar confirm your Christian devotion or testify that another "god" has absorbed your religious practice?

Rizpah   *Person*   2 Sam. 3:7; 21:8–11

Rizpah was Saul's secondary wife, whom his general Abner confiscated to make his own wife. She set up a vigil watching over the bodies of her slain sons until David had them buried.

Issue: How do you show faithfulness to the memory of the dead? Should all people follow the same standard and tradition, or should each have the freedom to choose how to maintain and express memory?

Ruhamah   *Person*   Hos. 1:6; 2:1; 1 Peter 2:10

Ruhamah was the symbolic name meaning "pitied" or "given a mother's love" which God gave Hosea for his daughter after the family returned to God. Originally, Hosea called her Loruhamah, or "not pitied."

Issue: Do people in your family give nicknames that reflect something about the person like Freckles, Stormy, Sweetness, Tough One, Little Professor, Strawberry, etc.?

S

Sabaoth   *God*   Rom. 9:29; James 5:4

Sabaoth, or "lord of hosts," is a divine title transliterated into Greek and then into English.

Issue: Why does the God of Jesus have a military title that shows Him as commander of a victorious army? Is it a paradox that the God of Love is God of Might? See Lord of Hosts.

Sabbath Day's Journey *Thing* Acts 1:12

The length of the limits a Jew may walk on the Sabbath, no more than about one-half mile, is called the Sabbath Day's Journey. The Rabbis computed the distance by joining the interpretation of Ex. 16:29 and Josh. 3:4.

Issue: What is obedience? Whom would you obey? Why?

Salamis *Place* Acts 13:5

Cyprus' most important center, Salamis, lies on the east coast. There was a strong Jewish settlement with more than one synagogue located there.

Issue: For Paul, the easiest place to begin witnessing was in the Jewish synagogue, where the people understood the claims he was making for Jesus. What is the easiest spot for you to start in your witnessing for Jesus?

Salmone *Place* Mark 15:40; 16:1

Salmone was the point that marked the eastern end of Crete. There, Paul boarded a large grain ship sailing from Alexandria to go to Rome.

Issue: Paul never demanded entitlements. He accepted whatever class and berth people were willing to give him. What benefits do you feel you have earned and are entitled to? Will you go only if you receive your entitlements?

Salome *Person* Mark 15:40; 16:1; compare John 19:25

Salome was the wife of Zebedee the mother of James and John, and possibly an aunt of Jesus. She helped prepare Jesus for burial.

Issue: The Gospels do not specify precise relationships among the characters introduced but does show the importance of women like Salome in Jesus' ministry. How faithful would you have been as you saw Jesus hanging on the cross? Would you have run with the men or stayed and ministered with the women?

Salt, Valley of *Place* 2 Sam. 8:13; 2 Kings 14:7; 1 Chron. 18:12; 2 Chron. 25:11; Ps. 60:0

The Valley of Salt was a pass southeast of the Dead Sea where David established his reputation by killing eighteen thousand Syrians (sometimes the text is changed to Edomites). Later, King Amaziah killed ten thousand Edomites there.

Issue: How do you make a name for yourself? Many people continue the way the kings of old used to do; they kill and destroy as much as possible. What kind of name do you want to leave to posterity? What is the best way to do that?

Samaritan(s) *People* Luke 9:52; John 4:9–40; Acts 8:15, 25

Samaritans were people who lived in the northern kingdom after its destruction by the Assyrians in 721 BC. They were largely made up of people of mixed belief, mixed ethnic background, and mixed culture. They built their own temple at Shechem and only believed the first five books of Scripture were inspired.

Issue: Samaritans and Jews did not get along because of their different beliefs about Scripture and because some Jews did not consider Samaritans to be true descendants of Israel. Do we mistrust people we consider to be different? How should we behave if we follow the example of Jesus?

Samgar-nebo(u) *Person* Jer. 39:3

Samgar-nebo was a Babylonian official who entered Jerusalem as it fell to the Babylonian armies.

Issue: A line of Babylonian officers suddenly appeared to join in the last part of capturing Jerusalem after the siege and battles. How often do people try to participate in a celebration and want to gather glory when an entirely different group has taken all the risk in battling the enemy and winning the battle? How often do church people want to be headline celebrators without risking anything in the battle? What can the church do to prevent this?

Sanballat *Person* Neh. 2:10, 19; 4:1, 7; 6:1–14; 13:28

Sanballat was the governor of Samaria, whose Akkadian name means "The god Sin has healed," but whose children were named after Yahweh, the God of Israel. This suggests he was a partaker in Jewish worship. He tried to stop Nehemiah's rebuilding of Jerusalem.

Issue: How and why does a person use religion as a political tool rather than as a personal relationship? Do you or members of your church become much more active in church affairs when political elections approach? Do people use church contacts to benefit their business? Do they appear to measure success in business and personal terms rather than in gospel-spreading and living terms? What can you do about this?

Sanhedrin *Thing* Matt. 5:22; 10:17; 26:59; Mark 13:9; 14:55; 15:1; Luke 22:66; John 11:47; Acts 4:15; 5:21–41; 6:12, 15; 22:30–23:1; 23:6–28; 24:20

The Sanhedrin was a Jewish council made up of seventy-one members and headed by the High Priest. It included both Pharisees and Sadducees. The Sanhedrin exercised strong authority in Jewish affairs under the Romans but could not execute a prisoner. Stephen's stoning is an exception.

Issue: Sometimes political, judicial, or church groups exercise authority for so long and so stringently that they neglect to remember the limits on their authority. Does your church have people causing trouble because they continue to exercise unauthorized authority?

Saph *Person* 2 Sam. 21:18

Saph was a giant who was killed by David's men in the Philistine wars.

Issue: Why were giants opposed to David and his people? Is it just happenstance that Israel does not seem to include great physical specimens in their army? Does it always seem that battles involve some great element of injustice?

Sardis *Place* Rev. 1:11; 3:1, 4

Called dead in Revelation, Sardis was a city with a famous temple to Artemis. There was a strong Jewish contingent there with their own synagogue and gymnasium, which shows a strong degree of assimilation of Greek culture within the community.

Issue: What happens when people of one religion are assimilated into another religion? Where have you seen Judaism or Christianity virtually absorbed by another religion or lifestyle? What causes this?

Satan *Person or Thing* Num. 22:22, 32; 1 Sam. 29:4; 2 Sam 19: 22; 1 Kings 5:4; 11:14, 23, 25; 1 Chron. 21:1; Job 1:6–9, 12; 2:1–4, 6–7; Ps. 109: 6, 20, 29; Zech. 3:1–2

In Hebrew the word *satan* means accuser, adversary, or enemy. The word can be used with or without the definite article *the*. In Numbers and Chronicles the word appears without the definite article refers to the "messenger of Yahweh" as an accuser. In the books of Job and Zechariah the definite article *the* appears with the word *satan*, so it refers to a specific enemy or accuser—the Satan. The noun with an article is the theologically important usage. Adding the article shifts the meaning to a specific individual who apparently has access to the heavenly divine council as seen in Job, where the heavenly accuser or adversary questions Job's credentials and motives. In Job and Zechariah the term refers to a specific member of God's council that is given the mission to act as a prosecuting attorney.

The New Testament refers to Satan thirty-five times and to the devil thirty-two times. During the period of the second temple, the idea of Satan as the embodiment of evil developed and we see that in the New Testament. Many parallel titles show the evil power of Satan or the devil: He is an enemy (Matt. 13:39), the evil one (Matt. 13:38), a tempter (Matt. 4:3; 1 Thess. 3:5), an adversary (1 Peter 5:8), the father of lies (John 8:44), a murderer (John 8:44), a liar (John 8:44), a deceiver (Rev. 10:9), an accuser (Rev. 10:10), and one disguised as an angel of light (2 Cor. 11:14).

Satan's power to tempt and harm individuals faces God's overwhelming opposition. God cast him out of heaven. His power is not absolute but can be resisted and will be taken totally away during the last days.

Issue: Why does evil exist? When you do something wrong, do you take responsibilty for your choices or do you say Satan made you do it?

Satrap	*Thing*	Ancient History

Satrap is the title of a Persian administrator that is equal to a governor of a territory. At its height, Persia had twenty satrapies; one, called Beyond the River, encompassed Israel and Syria.

Issue: Israel was governed by people from a foreign culture who promoted the rights and demands of a nation far away. Can you understand why many in the world today call Americans and the western world colonialists? In what way do we really help far-off lands, or do we rather manipulate them for our own good? What are some examples?

Scarlet	*Thing*	Isa. 1:18; Matt. 27:28; Heb. 9:19; Rev. 17:3–4; 18:12, 16

Scarlet is a specific color that is produced from the females of a type of louse, requiring about seventy thousand insects for one pound of dye. A colorfast dye, it provided a strong metaphor for sin and the cleansing of sin. The dye was also used only in expensive, luxury products. The dragon of Revelation exhibits an exorbitant lifestyle with all of the scarlet and purple connected with it.

Issue: Can you imagine yourself working with seventy thousand lice to get a pound of dye? Are you imagining unjust labor conditions that exhaust and frustrate you, especially since you get no part of the profit? Can you imagine how God must feel as He works with each one of us to get rid of our scarlet sin and cleanse us back to the perfect purity He desires in each of us? Do you have some scarlet spots in your life that you need to get rid of?

Sceva   *Person*   Acts 19:14

Sceva was a man who claimed to be a Jewish high priest but who lived in Ephesus. He and seven sons (or followers) tried unsuccessfully to mock Paul's prayers of healing. Instead, evil spirits overcame them, and they left the premises unclothed. Ironically, this brought honor to Paul and to the name of Jesus in Ephesus.

Issue: Christian healing does not come from secret formulas or actions. A person wanting to follow Paul must have the relationship with Jesus that Paul had. What relationship with Jesus do you have?

S(h)ebat   *Thing*   Zech. 1:7

Sebat (February-March) was the eleventh month on Babylonian calendar.

Issue: International relations can be confused as different countries use different calendars. Can you imagine extending our problems with daylight savings time to different languages and times?

Sela   *Place*   Judg. 1:36; 2 Kings 14:7; 2 Chron. 25:12; Isa. 16:1; 42:11

Sela was a place whose name means "rock," resulting in some translations calling it simply "rock" and others naming the place Sela. Amaziah of Judah captured the town and renamed it Joktheel. Sela is often equated with Petra, Edom's capital, though more recent study has placed it at es-Sela, two-and-a-half miles northwest of Bozrah and five miles southwest of Tafileh.

Issue: Sela represented the perfect defense system, high in the hills and surrounded by hard rock. It was believed that enemies could never take it, but one enemy had no trouble. At our most secure, we find ourselves weakest. At our weakest moment, we find the greatest courage. What experiences of strength in the midst of weakness or weakness at your strongest moment can you think of?

Selah-Hammahlekoth   *Place*   1 Sam. 23:28

David hid from Saul in Selah-Hammahlekoth in the wilderness of Maon. Modern translations usually translate the term: "Rock of Separation" (HCSB), "Dividing Rock" (REB), "Rock of Escape" (NRSV, NASB).

Issue: God's people cannot live in peace with one another and so go on hunting trips after each other. Why? Does your church have family feuds or troubles that you can help solve?

Selvedge   *Thing*   Ex. 26:4; 36:11

Selvedge is a term for a corner or edge of a garment or tent. It was used here as part of the wilderness tabernacle.

Issue: God wanted His dwelling place built just so. He also has very specific ways He wants His people to be. Have we become tattered at the edges and worn at the corners? Is it time to go back to the Creator and get Him to put us back together just like He wants us?

Sepharad   *Place*   Obad. 20

Exiles from Jerusalem lived in Sepharad, among other places such as Chebar in Babylon. The location of Sepharad is widely discussed by scholars without any agreement.

Issue: God promised through Obadiah that the exiles would return home and have places to live. Did the exiles believe the prophet? Does God speak a word of promise to you? How do you respond?

Seppohoris   *Place*   Ancient History

Seppohoris was the Roman administrative center of Galilee during Jesus' time. Modern archaeologists have uncovered an extraordinary Roman city with lavish buildings there.

Issue: Jesus would have known Roman buildings, Roman ways, and Roman extravagance. He was not simply a backwoods boy without knowledge of up-to-date Roman ways. How do you picture Jesus? As an urbanite or as a peasant?

Septuagint *Thing* Ancient Texts

The Septuagint is the earliest Greek translation of the Old Testament and includes several books of the Apocrypha. It was the source for many New Testament quotations of the Old Testament.

Issue: Most issues of establishing the exact spelling and wording of the original Old Testament are caused by translations in the Septuagint. Scholars have to make textual decisions on nearly each verse. How does this knowledge influence your reading of the Bible?

Seraphim *Thing* Isa. 6:2, 6

Seraphim are heavenly messengers whose image is taken from Egyptian throne decorations and who are described as agents bringing God's messages to His people. They have six wings.

Issue: Seraphim are angelic creatures who recognize and praise God and His holiness. How would you depict a seraph? In what ways do you recognize God's holiness? In what ways do you respond to it?

Sergius Paulus *Person* Acts 13:6–12

Bar-Jesus, a sorcerer, bothered Sergius Paulus, the proconsul of Cyprus. Paul blinded Bar-Jesus so he could not interfere with the presentation of the gospel.

Issue: What forces work in your life or in your church to prevent the pure presentation of the gospel message? Do you have faith to present God's message to nonbelievers? Do you fear what other people might think?

Seth *Person* Gen. 4:25–26; 5:3–8; 1 Chron. 1:1; Luke 3:38

Seth was the third son of Adam and Eve being born after Cain killed Abel.

Issue: What causes such animosity and anger between brothers? What can parents do to relieve the anger and jealousy?

Shaashgaz *Person* Est. 2:14

Shaashgaz was the eunuch who administered Xerxes's (Ahasuerus's) harem when Esther entered it.

Issue: What right does a king have to collect a harem of women and to physically deform people to make them acceptable as administrators of the harem? Are our ethical standards superior to those of a past age?

Shabbethai *Person* Ezra 10:15; Neh. 8:7; 11:16

Shabbethai was the official in charge of external business for the house of God. As a Levite, he explained the law that Ezra read, although he seems to have opposed Ezra's plan of divorce for many people.

Issue: How does one deal with the alarming number of divorces in this age? Do we as a culture have a built-in expectation of divorce rather than a commitment to marriage?

Shadrach *Person* Dan. 1:7; 2:49; 3:12–30

Shadrach, also known as Hananiah, was one of Daniel's three friends whose trust in God protected him from injury in the fiery furnace. See Abednego, Meshach.

Issue: A strong leader brings out faith from trusted followers. Whom do you have the opportunity to lead away from temptation and into a life of trusting confidence in God? Do you have the faith to be a leader, or must you depend on someone else?

Shamgar *Person* Judg. 3:31; 5:6

Shamgar was a mysterious judge of Israel who was credited with killing six hundred Philistines. His name apparently represents that of a foreign god, and no details are given about his battle(s) with the Philistines. He appears in between a notice ending Ehud's ministry and one describing Ehud's death. The normal framework around a narrative about a judge does not appear with Shamgar. The many ways he does not fit the pattern of the judges narrative bring mystery to the story.

Issue: Knowledge about God's chosen deliverers is not always available. The call is to meet God's criteria, not human qualifications. Can you be God's hero without anyone knowing where you came from or to where you're going?

| Sharon | *Place* | 1 Chron. 27:29; Song 2:1; Isa. 33:9; 35:2; 65:10; Acts 9:35 |

Sharon was a coastal plain running from Joppa to Mount Carmel. It was better suited for migrants than for established farmers.

Issue: Israel had long shoreline but no natural ports, and had to depend on Phoenicia and others for maritime shipping expertise. Do you have what, at first glance, appears to be a valuable resource but is gradually seen to be almost worthless? What do you do?

| Shasu | *People* | Ancient History |

The Shasu were a group of nomadic pastoralists who moved through Canaan and harassed Egyptian soldiers between 1500 BC and 1100 BC. They represented more of a social class than an ethnic group. The land of the Shasu was located originally in Transjordan. Some scholars see them as part of or forerunners to the Israelites leaving Egypt and entering Canaan.

Issue: Can the Shasu actually be a group involved in the Israelite occupation of Canaan? Is their activity in the south in Edom evidence for this? Is Yahweh somehow connected with this group of southern nomads? Are these part of the mixed multitude that Exodus mentions?

| Shear-jashub | *Person* | Isa. 7:3; 10:20–21 |

Shear-jashub is a mysterious and symbolic name that Isaiah gave his son at the behest of God. It means "a remnant will return." Whose remnant? Israel's or the enemy's? Return where? When? Is the return spiritual, meaning to repent?

Issue: Prophetic speech often has such symbolic terms with various meanings. The response of the audience often determines the meaning.

Do you find yourself, at times, mulling over God's Word or an experience with God and trying to figure out what it all means?

Sheba, Queen of *Person* 1 Kings 10

The Queen of Sheba was a famous, wealthy, Arabian queen who came to Jerusalem to substantiate stories of Solomon's wealth and wisdom.

Issue: Each culture has its own criterion for good food, spouses, and wisdom. Who is the wisest person you have known on earth? What evidence leads to that conclusion?

Shebat *Thing* Zech. 1:7

Shebat is the eleventh month in the Hebrew calendar.

Issue: Israel was somewhat late in developing its culture and civilization. Thus Israel borrowed many everyday items from neighbors like Egypt, Syria, Assyria, and Babylonia. Military defeat, at times, imposed cultural items such as calendar systems on Israel. This brings difficulty in dating events and dynasties in Israel. To bring God's authoritative message, must the Bible give a date we can reconstruct for every king and every event?

Shechem *Person* Gen. 34

Shechem the Canaanite prince fell victim to his own plot. He raped Jacob's daughter Dinah and then offered to marry her, leading Jacob and his sons to demand that the Shechemite men be circumcised as a dowry. While the men healed, Simeon and Levi entered the camp and killed them all.

Issue: Sexual desire and activity can lead people into deeper trouble than almost anything else. How do you train yourself to avoid sexual temptation? How do you discuss this issue with your children?

Sheerah *Person* 1 Chron. 7:24

Sheerah was the only woman in the Bible to build cities. She built three of them, lower Bethoron, upper Bethoron, and Uzzensherah.

Issue: What is important about a woman building cities? Is this a step toward encouraging women to use whatever talents they have in whatever sphere of life they find themselves?

Shekel   *Thing*   2 Kings 18:37; 19:2; Isa. 22:15; 36:3, 11, 22; 37:2

Shekels were the basic unit of weight and money, though coins as such were not made until late into the postexilic period.

Issue: Every culture has its own ways of exchange—straight trade, barter, scales, coins, currency, stocks, plastic, etc. With each step along the way comes new innovations in thievery. What can you do to protect yourself?

Sickle scythe   *Thing*   Deut. 16:9; 23:25; Jer. 50:16; Joel 3:13; Mark 4:29; Rev. 14:14–19

Farmers relied upon their short-handled sickle scythe made of flint or metal to harvest the grain crops and to fight close quartered battles. They are among earth's oldest tools; archaeologists date finds back to 8500 BC. Symbolically, the sickle represents judgment, especially the final judgment with Christ holding a sickle.

Issue: Few people see a sickle or scythe today. What has replaced them as central, necessary tools or instruments in your line of work?

Sikkuth (Sakkuth)   *Thing*   Amos 5:26

Amos warned Israel about worshipping the false god Sikkuth. The original reference may be to the Assyrian god Ninurta or the Greek god Saturn.

Issue: False worship comes from many sources. Finding people succeeding in worship or economics or politics and copying their worship style does not guarantee worldly success. Rather, all worship that excludes the God of Israel or includes someone besides the God of Israel is false, condemned, and on the path to eternal failure. How do you avoid false worship?

Silas *Person*   Acts 15:22–40; 16:19–38; 17:4–15; 18:5

Silas was a missionary companion of Paul and of Peter. The Jerusalem church sent him as part of the delegation to inform the Antioch church of the history made at the Jerusalem conference. With Paul in jail as they witnessed to the Philippian jailer, Silas probably served as Peter's scribe and may have resolved some of the disputes between Paul and Peter.

Issue: Silas was apparently well-educated but utilized his talents in the background, letting Paul or Peter get more public attention. Can backstage talents be as important or more so than center stage performances?

Simeon *Person*   Luke 2:25–34

Simeon was an elderly man who was staying by the temple to see Jesus as God had promised.

Issue: God can be trusted to do what He says and promises. Back to Abraham and beyond, people have tried to devise ways to show God as a liar. Each time, God fulfills His promises. Can you think of people who have tried to show God as a liar? How do you combat such falsehood?

Sim(e)on *Person*   John 6:71; 13:2, 26

This Simeon is notable only as Judas Iscariot's father.

Issue: A father is too often known by his son. How do you think Judas's father felt after Judas betrayed Jesus and hung himself? How did the church feel? How would you respond to Judas's father if you could speak to him?

Simon of Cyrene *Person*   Matt. 27:32; Mark 15:21; Luke 23:26

Simon of Cyrene was the man from the island of Cyrene who was conscripted into carrying Jesus' cross. He appears to be known in the church as he is identified by his sons Alexander and Rufus.

Issue: Simon was forced by Roman soldiers to carry the cross. How would you have reacted if Jesus had handed His cross to you and asked you to carry it? What if carrying the cross identified you as a follower of Jesus?

Simon the Brother of Jesus   *Person*   Matt. 13:55; Mark 6:3

People of Nazareth knew Jesus' brothers, including Simon, and did not think that the family could produce anyone close to being the Messiah. Jesus said those who believed in Him, not those He grew up in the same house with, were His family.

Issue: What is family? How does family leave an impression in a community? How does family show unity? Why did Jesus treat His earthly family in such ways? How close and unified is your family? What impression do your neighbors and townspeople have of your family?

Simon the Leper   *Person*   Matt. 26:6; Mark 14:3–7

Guests at Simon's house questioned the price of healing ointment that a woman used to anoint Jesus' head. Jesus said she was preparing Him for His burial. Surprisingly, Simon had a home where guests would come.

Issue: What priorities do you set for yourself and your family? Because you are scorned by some does not give you the right to scorn and scold others. Would you rather see the ointment spent for something else besides helping Jesus?

Simon the Magician of Samaria   *Person*   Acts 8:5–25

Simon was a highly regarded citizen of Samaria with a strong ego. The people looked on him as great. Then Philip came preaching Christ, healing, and bringing the Holy Spirit to people. Simon believed Philip's preaching, was baptized, and followed Philip. When he saw the power of the Holy Spirit, he offered money to have that power. Philip condemned him and commanded him to pray for forgiveness. Simon asked Philip to pray for him.

Issue: Religious power is God's gift of grace and the Spirit freely working in you. Do you experience the power of the Spirit in your life? How did you receive the Spirit?

Sim(e)on the Pharisee   *Person*   Luke 7:36–49

Simon the Pharisee was a man whose guests proved unforgettable. A sinful woman anointed Jesus and washed His feet. Simon shamed Jesus for letting an unclean woman touch Him. Jesus asked Simon if a person with few sins or a person with large sins would most appreciate forgiveness. Simon answered the one with great sins. Jesus then forgave the woman, stirring the crowd to ask who Jesus thought He was.

Issue: How much forgiveness do you need? Needing any at all is too much. Have you asked Jesus to forgive every bit of your sin? Or do you hide some as justified? Why not ask Jesus for forgiveness right now?

Simon the Tanner   *Person*   Acts 10:6

Simon, a well-known leather tanner in the coastal city of Joppa, seems to have been a believer since he provided lodging for Peter. On Simon's rooftop, Peter received the vision of the net of clean and unclean animals, by which God led him to preach to Cornelius, the God-fearing Roman soldier. Peter's missionary vision shocked everyone. This was a major beginning of the church's mission work beyond the Jewish race.

Issue: Peter had his mission beliefs expanded partly due to the hospitality of Simon. In what ways can you expand your mission participation to let God work among people who have not yet heard the gospel or responded to it? Talk with the mission leaders in your church about your desire to be more deeply engaged in the mission work of the church.

Simon the Zealot   *Person*   Matt. 10:4; Mark 3:18; Luke 6:15; Acts 1:13

Simon was a lesser-known disciple who is also called the Canaanite. Simon is not credited with any action in the Bible. He always stands at the next to last or last spot in the listing of the disciples.

Issue: Who keeps score in Christianity? Are you in front of most of your Christian friends, or must you admit some are more faithful to Jesus than you are?

Sinai, Mount   *Place*   Ex. 18—Lev. 27; Deut. 5

Moses received the Ten Commandments, other laws, and building directions on Mount Sinai, also called Mount Horeb. Its location remains a matter of scholarly debate. It remained in Jewish teaching as the most holy place in their history with the possible exception of the temple.

Issue: Take a Bible atlas or the maps in the back of your Bible. Find Sinai, probably at the bottom of a map of the Exodus to the southeast of Egypt. Does your map have an alternative location below the Jordan River? What feeling or thoughts do you have in realizing the most famous of mountains cannot be located for sure?

Sisera   *Person*   Josh. 11; Judg. 4–5

Deborah, Barak, and Jael defeated Sisera, head of the army of Jabin, king of Canaan. Jael went against her husband's Kenite treaty with Jabin. She lured Sisera into her tent, refreshed his thirst, let him rest, and nailed a tent peg through his head.

Issue: Jael used her feminine wiles to subdue a man. Is that ethical?

Sivan   *Thing*   Ancient History

Sivan (May-June) is the third month of Hebrew Calendar.

Issue: Living by others' calendars causes problems for parents trying to instill their own traditional culture into their children. Does Passover take place during the first, the seventh, or the tenth month? Other children might celebrate their festivals at different times from yours. How do you keep your children from becoming confused?

Slave Girl at Philippi   *Person*   Acts 16:16–26

The slave girl was used by her masters to make a profit through her demon-possession that enabled her to predict the future. When Paul cast out the demons, the masters retaliated by seizing Paul and Silas. Her masters then took them to the magistrates and had them jailed. This gave

God opportunity to shake the jail gates open so Paul could witness to the Philippian jailer.

Demonic possession does not provide a new spiritual gift but a new hindrance to what a human is trying to do. God has given Christ spiritual power over all demonic powers in the universe, a power God has provided as a continuing power in His church. Spiritual warfare continues in our world. Just to list the signs of demons seeking to conquer our world is proof enough. Sadly, a glance inside our churches shows the demonic activities of our world. Pray for God to reveal the powers fighting against us and to show us the weapons to fight such powers.

Issue: Why does Paul repeatedly relate stories of his triumph over demonic powers? He seemingly wants to focus his readers on divine powers over against human power and liberty. Have you had any experience with demonic forces?

So   *Person*   2 Kings 17:4

King Hosea of Israel appealed to Pharaoh So of Egypt for help against Shalmaneser of Assyria about 724 BC. There is no Pharaoh So outside of biblical history; rather this is probably referring to Pharaoh Osorkon IV or Pharaoh Tefnakhte.

Issue: The Bible shows Israel's mistakes as well as her accomplishments, but all events stand under God's expectations. The Bible uses names for foreign characters that may differ from the names known from sources outside of the Bible. What do you learn about the Bible from these statements?

Socoh   *Place*   Josh. 15:35; 1 Sam. 17:1; 2 Chron. 11:6–10; 28:18

Socoh, or "thorns," the camping site of the Philistines during the fight between David and Goliath, was a central area of protection on the road up to Jerusalem.

Issue: A place's name does not always indicate the place's importance. Do you come from a place of seeming insignificance? Is your life making that place significant for someone?

Sopater   *Person*   Acts 20:4

Sopater, whose name means "savior of his father," represented Berea in Paul's traveling party back to Jerusalem.

Issue: Sopater's name indicates he witnessed to and saved his own father. Do you have a relative to whom you need to witness about Jesus?

Sorek Valley   *Place*   Judg. 16:4

The Sorek "red grapes" valley was the home of Samson's Delilah.

Issue: What happens when a person wanders away from their home and into enemy territory? Do you have places you know you should not go and still feel a great desire to go there?

Sosthenes   *Person*   Acts 18:17; 2 Cor. 1:1

Sosthenes was the synagogue leader in Corinth who was beaten by the Corinthians because they were legally forbidden to persecute Paul. He was apparently Paul's compatriot in the writing of 2 Corinthians.

Issue: It appears that suffering eventually led Sosthenes to accept Christ and become a trusted associate of Paul. What incident in life encouraged you to accept Christ?

Spain   *Place*   Rom. 15:24–28

Paul's final missionary plans had the goal of reaching Spain, which tradition claims he achieved.

Issue: Each church and each believer should have a missions goal, whether that is reaching people at home or reaching people in far places. Are you praying and seeking ways to meet that goal or find that goal?

Spelt   *Thing*   Ex. 9:32; Isa. 28:25; Ezek. 4:9

Spelt is an inferior, hard-grained wheat that is planted on the edges of a field to prevent the intrusion of weeds. It is sown in the fall and harvested after barley.

Issue: What do you use to prevent weeds from entering your life? Are you willing to use inferior objects in your dedication to God's work?

Spider *Thing* Job 8:14; Isa. 59:5

A spider's web is used in the Bible to illustrate frailty and short life. Spiders' eggs are used to illustrate danger.

Issue: Is your life founded on materials as insecure as a spider's web?

Stachys *Person* Rom. 16:9

Paul greeted Stachys, whose name means "wheat" or "grain."

Issue: Naming of children is a serious business. Too often children endure ridicule and hardship because of the name their parents foisted on them. Do you know anyone who doesn't like his or her name? Why?

Stephanas *Person* 1 Cor. 1:16; 16:15–17

To downplay his role of baptizing over against preaching about Christ, Paul reminisced about baptizing Stephanas's family in Corinth. At the same time, Stephanas and his family were the "first fruits of Achaia," in other words, they were among the first converts. Stephanas served faithfully in Corinth and visited Paul with fellowship and material needs.

Issue: What is the role of baptism in your church practice? Who is permitted to perform baptism? What is the relationship between baptizing and salvation? What is your evidence?

Stephen *Person* Acts 6:1–8:1

Stephen was a Hellenistic, Greek-speaking Jew in Antioch. He was chosen as one of the seven to serve the Greek-speaking widows. He preached a major sermon that showed Jesus as the fulfillment of the Old Testament, causing the church to spread out beyond Jerusalem. Stephen became the first martyr when he was killed for his sermon.

Issue: Can a church happily join different cultures together in its membership without neglecting some or making some feel second-class or unappreciated? What different cultural backgrounds are represented in your church or your Bible study group? Do you faithfully minister to all groups according to their needs and include them in church leadership?

Sychar   *Place*   John 4

Sychar was a place named "falsehood," whose water supply was traced back to Jacob and called "Jacob's Well." There, Jesus showed the Samaritan woman that He is the "living water."

Issue: What group of people have traditionally been ignored and unwanted in your church? Are you making sure your church reaches out to all people? Explain how Jesus is living water.

Syntyche   *Person*   Phil. 4:2

Syntyche was a woman in a leadership position in the Philippi church whom Paul had to reprimand for being involved in an argument with Euodia.

Issue: Do leaders in your church continually argue and attack other members? What does the leadership do to prevent such behavior? Can you be a peacemaker in your church?

Syrophoenician   *Person*   Mark 7:26

Jesus first refused to heal the daughter of the Syrophoenician woman, betraying an old and negative attitude toward Gentiles. In response to her unrelenting faith, Jesus healed her, changing the focus in Mark's gospel to acceptance of all non-Jews, and showing that none are essentially unclean.

Issue: Read the passage carefully. Who is this Jesus who talks so radically and dismissingly to a woman before He finally fulfills her request? What does this passage teach you about Jesus and the gospel?

Syrtis *Place* Acts 27:17

Paul's Rome-bound ship appeared to be headed into quicksand and shallows in Syrtis, which was probably the Gulf of Sidra off the African coast and west of Cyrene.

Issue: Refusing to follow God's directions through God's inspired leader brings casualty. Is your church facing a major decision? You can get caught in the quicksands and shallows of life if you do not join together to find and follow God's directions.

Taanach *Place* Josh. 12:21; 17:11; 21:25; Judg. 1:27; 5:19;
1 Kings 4:12; 1 Chron. 7:29

Taanach was the site of the battle between Israel under Deborah and Barak and the Canaanites under Sisera and Jabin. It was a major transportation hub that protected the entrance into Samaria. Egyptian records show their god giving Taanach to the pharaoh, something the Bible does not mention. See 1 Kings 14:25–26.

Issue: A major military and commercial city finds few mentions in Scripture, showing that the Bible does not record history per se, instead passing by important events and important places to show how and where God works. What historical questions do you have that you might expect the Bible to answer? Are you willing to live in faith even when answers do not come?

Tabeel *Person* Isa. 7:6

Tabeel was the father of an otherwise unknown prince whom the kings of Israel and Damascus tried to put on the throne of Judea to force Judea into joining a coalition against Assyria. Isaiah warned against the coalition. The father's name in the text means "good for nothing," which is probably a scribal wordplay against the young man whose original name was probably "God is good."

Issue: International politics involves many strategies and actions in an effort to gain control. Making word plays on enemy leaders' names is one such action. Warfare is another. God's Word calls upon us to avoid "dirty politics" of all kinds and find His direction for personal, national, and international life. What are some examples of "dirty politics" that are taking place today?

| **Tabor** | *Place* | Josh. 19:22; Judg. 4:6–14; 8:18; 1 Sam. 10:3; 1 Chron. 6:77; Ps. 89:12; Jer. 46:18; Hos. 5:1 |

Tabor was a mountain six miles east of Nazareth that served as a cultic and military gathering place. Barak and Deborah gathered troops there. Tradition views it as the place for Jesus' transfiguration.

Issue: Much of Israel's early worship took place on mountains or in valleys without buildings. Does your church ever diversify its program to include worship in places displaying the wondrous beauty of God's creation? Would you suggest that to worship leaders?

| **Tabrimmon** | *Person* | 1 Kings 15:18 |

Tabrimmon was the father of Ben-hadad. King of Damascus, Ben-hadad formed strong relationships with the king of Judah shortly after 900 BC. He collected a large sum for tribute from Asa of Judah. Tabrimmon's name means "(The god) Rimmon is good."

Issue: God works His plans through foreign kings as well as through His own people. Can you discover God's hand in any sphere of international politics today?

| **Tadmor** | *Place* | 1 Kings 9:18; 2 Chron. 8:4 |

Tadmor was a camping place 150 miles northeast of Damascus, control of which allowed Solomon to control the major trading highways in the Middle East. Tributes and tariffs from the highways helped Solomon gain much of his wealth.

Issue: Solomon is known for his wisdom, wealth, worship place, and wives. Loving wealth and women brought him down so that his kingdom soon divided and his wealth dissipated under his successors. Do you have faith to seek God's wisdom and worship rather than following the popular crowd?

Tahpanhes *Place* Jer. 2:16; 43:7–9; 44:1; 46:14; Ezek. 30

Tahpanhes was an Egyptian city near the country's eastern border. Jeremiah used it as a symbol of Egyptian power. After the fall of Jerusalem, rebellious Judeans forced Jeremiah to go with them to Egypt.

Issue: Bad things happen to good people even when God's leader tries to stop them. Babylon's government could not stop the Judeans from capturing and deporting Jeremiah. What bad things do you see happening to God's people? How can you help those people? Do you think God wants to help those people?

Tahpenes *Person* 1 Kings 11

Tahpenes was the name of or title of the queen mother in Egypt who aided the Edomite royalty during David's wars. Her sister married David's strongest Edomite enemy.

Issue: Royal women may exercise true power and have decision-making authority, or they may be political puppets whom kings use to gain political and military advantage through marriage. Where do you see women with true power, and where do you see women as pawns of masculine power struggles? Do such power struggles occur in your church? What role are you and your family playing in the struggle?

Tamar *Person* Gen. 38:6–24; Ruth 4:12; 1 Chron. 2:4; Matt. 1:3

Tamar was the wife of Judah's oldest son Er. After Er died, his brother Onan married her in fulfillment of the laws of levirate marriage but refused to get Tamar pregnant. For breaking the law, God disposed of Onan. After a time, when no one fulfilled the levirate law, Tamar posed as a harlot and lay with Judah. She became pregnant but was able to show the father was Judah, and thus sanctioned, escaped the death penalty.

Issue: Assumptions can be wrong. Judah, the guilty party, assumed his widowed daughter-in-law had become promiscuous. In what ways or with whom do you hold false assumptions? What do you assume about other people without finding all the facts?

Tamar *Person* 2 Sam. 13:1–32; 1 Chron. 3:9

David's daughter Tamar was raped by her half brother Ammon, whom her full brother Absalom then had killed in revenge.

Issue: Family discipline is a strong element in biblical teaching. David apparently refused to discipline or control his children and suffered great consequences for not doing so. How does your family handle discipline? Are you consistent? Do children know the results of bad behavior? Do you as parents work in tandem so that a child cannot play one parent off another?

Tammuz *Thing* Ezek. 8:14

Tammuz is the Hebrew transliteration of the Sumerian goddess Dumuzi, who functioned as the lover of Inanna or Ishtar, the goddess of sex, war, and vegetation. Dumuzi played important roles in rituals of sacred marriage. She was a dying and rising god who reflected agricultural cycles. Ezekiel saw Hebrew women weeping at the temple because Tammuz had died, which the people believed was to blame for a lack of food for their families.

Issue: Does your family tradition include superstitious teaching? Are some things done the same way every time for fear of bringing back luck to the family? What is the difference between modern superstitions and ancient fertility worship? What do we do to ensure the economic well-being of our family?

Tarshish   *Place*   1 Kings 10:22; 22:48; 2 Chron. 9:21; 20:36–37; Pss. 48:7; 72:10; Isa. 2:16; 23:1, 6, 10, 14; 60:9; 66:19; Jer. 10:9; Ezek. 27:12, 25; 38:13; Jonah 1:3; 4:2

Tarshish was a major seaport in the western part of the Mediterranean, perhaps southern Spain or Tarsus in Cilicia, known for its manufacture of seagoing vessels. Jonah boarded a ship headed to Tarshish rather than follow God's orders to go east to Nineveh and was punished by being eaten by a fish. Solomon gained wealth by using ships built in Tarshish and trading with the city.

Issue: Civilizations come and civilizations go. Tarshish was a major seaport envied by most other nations. Today we cannot locate it. Are you connected in an enterprise that will put you in the history books forever? Those records soon grow old and forget you. Are you inscribed in God's Book of Life?

Tarsus   *Place*   Acts 9:11, 30; 11:25; 21:39; 22:3

Saul of Tarsus became known as Paul, the Christian missionary. Tarsus was the capital of the Roman province of Cilicia, an important place of international commerce and culture. Jews enjoyed many freedoms and privileges there.

Issue: God gave the great commissions of Matthew 28 and of Acts 1:8 to a Jewish community centered in Jerusalem, but He started His major mission work through a Diaspora Jew born in another Roman province to a prospering Jewish community laden with opportunities for international contacts. Why do you think God started His major mission campaigns with Paul and not with a person who had witnessed the earthly ministry of Jesus? Do you have anything that would prohibit you from being God's missionary today? Where are you willing to go when God calls?

Tartan   *Person*   2 Kings 18:17; Isa. 20:1

Tartan was the title of the chief official under the Assyrian king.

Issue: The Bible often refers to people, especially foreign leaders, by titles rather than by names. This lets individual fame and feats slip into forgetfulness. Do you have intentions to hold well-known, authoritative positions in your culture and nation? What will you have accomplished in the long run, in light of eternal realities?

| Tel-abib (aviv) | *Place* | Ezek. 3:15 |

Tel-abib was the community in Babylon whose name meant "mound of the flood" or "Fat River," where Ezekiel and other Jewish exiles lived during the exile. It lay on the Chebar Canal near the city of Nippur. See Nippur.

Issue: Life in a foreign country with no idea of when, if ever, you might go home brings a flood of feelings. A feeling of separation and loss may overwhelm you. Have you had to spend an extended period of time away from home turf? What feelings did you have? How far away from home do you have to be to have those feelings? Does your church need to start a ministry to people in your community suffering such separation and loss?

| Tema | *Place* | Gen. 25:15; 1 Chron. 1:30; Job 6:19; Isa. 21:14; Jer. 25:23 |

Tema was an Arabian desert oasis 250 miles southeast of Aqaba and 200 miles southeast of Medina. A desert caravan stop, it faced threats from Israel's prophets and domination by Assyrian and Babylonian armies.

Issue: Isolation does not insure security against other nations or protection from God. The resources of the Arabian desert and beyond were deemed to have sufficient value that nations sent caravans deep into the desert to trade for such assets. Have you ever experienced isolation from everything and everyone who seemed important to you? Have you traveled long distances to obtain something you perceived as valuable?

Temple Tax *Thing* Ex. 30:13–16; 38:26; Neh. 10:32–33; Matt. 17:24

Israelite men had to pay one-half shekel a year as a temple tax to meet temple expenses. Jesus explained that the tax did not apply to the king's family but only to foreigners. Since Jesus and His disciples formed God's family, they were in reality not responsible to pay the tax. Still Jesus provided a miraculous way for Peter to pay the tax so that he did not stir up too much trouble over something that was a secondary issue.

Issue: Taxation has always been a burning issue in almost every nation. What taxation issues have become important in your town or country? In what ways should the government become involved in issues of church taxation such as church property tax, senior medical insurance, pastoral housing allowance, etc.?

Terah *Person* Gen. 11:24–32; Josh. 24:2; 1 Chron. 1:26; Luke 3:34

The father of Abraham, Terah began the pilgrimage from Ur of the Chaldeans to Canaan, but settled down in Haran before completing the journey.

Issue: The Bible takes seriously the accomplishments and value of the older generation. Terah began the move to Canaan that Abraham finished. Do you show members of the previous generation(s) your appreciation for what they have accomplished and the start they have given you? Do you know of a new project you could involve them in?

Teraphim *Thing* Gen. 31:19, 34–35; Judg. 17:5; 18:14–20; 1 Sam. 15:23; 19:13, 16; 2 Kings 23:24; Ezek. 21:21; Hos. 3:4; Zech. 10:2

Teraphim present a puzzle for biblical scholars. They are small in Genesis but large in Samuel. They are used by God's people to divine the will of the deity, a forbidden act. They represent household gods a woman can steal. An untrained person could make one and use it in a private home cult. It is possible that the teraphim represent a minor cultic item that was used in divinatory rites and could be created in different sizes.

Issue: Do you have objects in your church that everyone sees as essential for your worship and fellowship? Perhaps it is the place you sit every week, or a musical instrument with a church life longer than any of the members. Perhaps it is a prayer room furnished and decorated by a Bible study class. What would happen if someone tried to change these traditional objects? Too quickly and too often, special gifts to the church become essential objects for the church. Will you try changing some of your habits this week to avoid worshiping objects and not God?

Teresh *Person* Est. 2:21; 6:2

Teresh was a Persian official in the security guard for king Ahasuerus who decided to assassinate the king. Esther's uncle Mordecai foiled the plot.

Issue: Do you ever change your allegiance to a church leader or political leader? What kind of action do such shifts initiate? What causes a church to split and rise up against leadership? How can the church prevent this kind of action?

Tertius *Person* Rom. 16:22

Paul's amanuensis, or secretary, Tertius took dictation from Paul as he wrote Romans. He sent his own personal greetings to the church at Rome.

Issue: How much freedom did one of the people who actually copied down Paul's thoughts have in shaping the materials? In what way does biblical inspiration include the work of mostly unknown, educated, dedicated scribes who wrote down and preserved the work of their leaders?

Tertullus *Person* Acts 24:1–9

Tertullus was the lawyer who represented the Jewish party before governor Felix when they brought charges against Paul. He failed to make his case against Paul, and Paul was released.

Issue: How do we deal with biblical failures, those who stand on the wrong side with the false arguments? How does God deal with failures like you and me who at one point or another in life stand against God like Tertullus and Job?

Thaddeus *Person* Matt. 10:3; Mark 3:18

One of original twelve disciples, Thaddeus's name appears to mean "breast" or "nipple." Some Greek textual evidence names him Lebbaeus. It is possible he was named Judas, son of James, and then nicknamed Thaddeus in Aramaic and Lebbaeus in Hebrew.

Issue: Here is one of the twelve that we know virtually nothing about. Do you ever feel that no one knows you? How do you react? Does your faith bring any hope and strength to the situation?

Thebes *Place* Jer. 46:25; Ezek. 30:14–16; Nah. 3:8

Thebes was an Egyptian city (modern Luxor) 350 miles south of Memphis, against whom the prophets sounded oracles of judgment. At times, it served as the capital of all Egypt and became known as the richest city in the world with marvelous statuary and architecture. The Assyrian army eventually conquered it.

Issue: Thebes was the world's richest city, but that title proved ephemeral. Write down a list of your accomplishments without being overly modest. Which of these accomplishments has lasting, even eternal value? What will happen to the other accomplishments?

Thebez *Place* Judg. 9:50–57; 2 Sam. 11:21

Thebez was a town near Shechem. Abimelech the Judge put down a rebellion in the city, but then a woman of the city threw a millstone down on his head, causing his death.

Issue: Overconfidence and self-glory cannot secure an army's or an individual's position. Continued success may develop a sense of invulnerability in you, but God always knows your vulnerable spot and how to reach it. Relate your own experiences of overconfidence or self-glory. What changed your attitude then? Do your children need examples like that of Abimelech, who became proud of his accomplishments shortly before he lost them all?

Theophilus *Person* Luke 1:3; Acts 1:1

Theophilus was a Greek-speaking man whose name means "lover of God" or "beloved of God." He was interested in the gospel and supported its spread across the world. Luke dedicated both his gospel and Acts to this otherwise unknown man.

Issue: Do you know of someone needing help in completing a worthwhile project? How can you help in completing the project? Do you need someone to work with you in an extensive explanation of the gospel so that you may believe and accept the gospel? Are you ready to explain the gospel and its early growth to someone else who is beset with curiosity and questions?

Theudas *Person* Acts 5:36

Theudas was a Jewish loyalist who led the rebellion against Rome in either AD 6 or AD 44. He attempted to stage a crossing of the Jordan River like Elijah, Elisha, and Joshua had; however, Rome saw him as a threat and killed him, much as they killed Jesus.

Issue: Rome and its officials considered both Theudas and Jesus sufficient threats to the government that they executed them. How would you compare the threats each of the two men posed to Rome? What role does the example of Theudas play in the biblical narrative?

Thomas *Person* Matt. 10:3; Mark 3:18; Luke 6:15; John 11:16; 14:5; 20:24–28; 21:2; Acts 1:13

Thomas was a disciple of Jesus whose name is transliterated into Greek from the Hebrew or Aramaic and means the "twin." The Greek term for twin is Didymus. He is known for audacious statements and uncertain questions, and for calling the disciples to go and die with Jesus. He asks Jesus to explain what He meant by saying He is going from this world and then refuses to believe until he sees the nail prints in Jesus' hands. Having seen Jesus, he then proclaims Him Lord and God.

Issue: Thomas had the inquiring mind that refused to believe without strong reason to do so. He also had the inner determination to act swiftly and decisively when his questions received answers. Do you, at times, share the questioning spirit of Thomas? How does God respond to your doubts and questions? Do you also share Thomas's bent to decisive action? What have you done strictly out of faith?

Three Taverns   *Place*   Acts 28:15

Three Taverns was a resting station on the Appian Way thirty miles south of Rome. People from the Three Taverns came to welcome Paul as he arrived in Italy.

Issue: Believers came to welcome their renowned missionary leader; at the same time, they visited a prisoner about to enter a Roman prison. How do we treat famous preachers and missionaries? Why? Do we visit people in prison and encourage them and their families?

Thunder, Sons of

See Boanerges.

Thyatira   *Place*   Acts 16:14; Rev. 1:11; 2:18, 24

Thyatira was a city Paul visited on his missionary journey and was the recipient of a letter in Revelation. It stands fifty miles northeast of ancient Smyrna, forty miles east-northeast of Pergamum, and about forty miles from the Aegean Sea. It was an important transportation and trade center where guilds had great influence. Lydia of Thyatira, a purple merchant there, was among Paul's first converts in Europe. John, the author of Revelation, strongly attacked a group there for following Jezebel.

Issue: Life in a successful, culturally cosmopolitan center brings contact with and temptation to follow a multitude of religious groups. What religious groups or beliefs attract people in your city? Why do you remain faithful to your church in light of the attractive possibilities of other politically and commercially prosperous and powerful groups? Do you have a strategy to share your faith as did Paul?

Tiglath-pileser III *Person* 2 Kings 15:19, 29; 16:7, 10; 1 Chron. 5:26; 2 Chron. 28:20

King Tiglath-pileser III of Assyria (745–727 BC) defeated the Israelite army and prepared the way for Assyria's destruction of Israel. He restored the power of Assyria over small kingdoms east and west, including Babylon.

Issue: Israel attacked Assyria with a newly formed coalition, while Judah paid tribute to Tiglath-pileser. How can nations trying to worship the same God and coming from the same traditions behave so radically differently? How does your church handle radical differences among its leaders on national and international political issues?

Timnath-heres (-serah) *Place* Josh. 19:50; 24:30; Judg. 2:9

Timnath-heres was the area that Joshua asked for and received as an inheritance. The original name of Timnath-heres, "portion of the sun," was changed to Timnath-serah to avoid any opportunity to promote sun worship. Timnath-serah means "portion remaining."

Issue: Israel changed names of people and places to disassociate them from the worship of foreign gods. Do we pay attention to names of people and places in our generation to ensure we are not degrading our worship tradition and values? Or are we promoting anti-Christian beliefs by our lyrics, our clothing, our language, our body language, etc.?

Timon *Person* Acts 6:5

Timon was one of seven Greek-speaking men called by the church to minister to the Greek-speaking widows to avoid conflict between cultural and linguistic groups.

Issue: Do we best serve Christ and our witness to the world by separating cultural and linguistic groups or by attempting to maintain unity in all ministries and worship services? Which option best serves Christ and the community? See Stephen.

Tiphsah   *Place*   1 Kings 4:24

Tiphsah was a city on the west bank of the Euphrates River seventy-five miles southeast of Carchemish, which represented the northeastern border of Solomon's kingdom.

Issue: How do you measure success? Were large land holdings the greatest mark of Solomon's success? Or was it wealth, wives, wisdom, and writing skill? What criteria do you use to determine this? What do you use to measure success in your own life? Do you refer to material elements? To psychological health? To faith that spurs actions? What are you teaching the next generation?

Tirhakah   *Person*   2 Kings 19:8–9; Isa. 37:9

Egyptian Pharaoh Tirhakah from Ethiopia (690–664 BC) staved off the Assyrian invasion in support of Hezekiah under Sennacherib (704–681 BC). Later, in 671 BC, Esarhaddon successfully invaded Egypt.

Issue: Secular historians may deconstruct history and ignore deity, but faith follows the Scriptures and confesses that it is God who controls all historical events. God is sovereign, not the pharaoh of Egypt, the king of Assyria, or the emperors of Rome. How do you view history? Do you see God in charge of all events?

Tirshatha   *Thing*   Ezra 2:63; Neh. 7:65, 70; 8:9; 10:1

Tirshatha was a title of honor or office under the Persian government, which may mean either "Your Excellency" or "governor." Nehemiah held the title at one time.

Issue: How do you handle titles of respect? Do you give titles to everyone? Do you envy such people and avoid using titles whenever possible? Do you simply follow cultural precedent and use titles as culture dictates? How did Jesus react and relate to titles? What title do you most desire being called?

Tirzah *Person*

See Hoglah.

Tob *Place* Judg. 11:3, 5; 2 Sam. 10:6, 8

Tob was the city in southern Syria, east of the Sea of Galilee, to which the Judge Jephthah fled to escape his brothers' fury. Tob joined in an unsuccessful coalition against David.

Issue: How do you relate to your siblings? Have you ever tried to escape them? Why? What are the benefits you receive from siblings? What is the price you pay for having siblings?

Tobiah *Person* Ezra 2:60; Neh. 2:10, 19; 4:3, 7; 6:1–19; 7:62; 13:4–8

Nehemiah's nemesis Tobiah sought to prevent Nehemiah from rebuilding Jerusalem, even though he had a residence in the temple quarters. He had a special relationship with the Persian government that could be weakened by the rebuilding of the temple. He is referred to as an Ammonite because his family apparently escaped there when Babylon destroyed Jerusalem.

Issue: How do you react when someone else has a position you want and think you deserve? Or when you fear the person in power will depose you from your office and authority? What is the proper way to act when the opposition holds power?

Tola *Person* Judg. 10:1

Tola was a "minor" judge of Israel, from the tribe of Issachar, who judged in Israel for twenty-three years. None of his accomplishments are reported.

Issue: What separates major judges from minor judges in the book of Judges? Since the major stories in Judges relate to warfare and fighting, would it be good or bad if the author listed no accomplishments in telling your story?

Tophet(h)   *Place*   2 Kings 23:10; Jer. 7:31–32; 19:6, 11–14

Tophet was a place in the southwest corner of Jerusalem's old city. It was originally named "fireplace" but changed to "place of shame" by tradition. In the Hinnom Valley outside Jerusalem, it became a place where Jews sacrificed children in times of great lamentation.

Issue: God did not want children sacrificed to Him, yet He sacrificed His own Son for us. What distinguishes human child sacrifice from God's sacrifice of His Son on the cross? How does Christ's call to pick up a cross and follow Him fit into the sacrifice picture?

Trachonitis   *Place*   Luke 3:1

Trachonitis was an area south of Damascus and east of the Jordan River, called Bashan in the Hebrew Bible. It corresponds to modern Hauran in southern Syria. At the time of John the Baptist, Herod Philip, the brother of Herod Antipas, ruled Trachonitis. The area was known for sheep and goats and as refuge for criminals and groups seeking to overthrow the government.

Issue: How does a government deal with a wasteland where lawless people hang out? Can you think of a modern equivalent? Does the church have any way to minister to people who have fled from society to live in barren areas outside the arm of the law?

Trophimus   *Person*   Acts 20:4; 21:29; 2 Tim. 4:20

Paul's companion was named Trophimus on his return to Jerusalem. He represented the churches of Asia and brought the collection they had taken for the poor in Jerusalem. Seen in Jerusalem with Paul, he became embroiled in controversy as the evidence that Paul had taken Gentiles into the temple.

Issue: What kind of evidence do you need to accuse a person of breaking church tradition or of acting unchristian in the church? What troubles have you experienced in church because people charged other believers with very little if any evidence?

Tryphaena and Tryphosa *Persons* Rom. 16:12

Tryphaena and Tryphosa, perhaps twin sisters, were named "dainty" and "delicate." Paul sent them greetings in his letter to the Romans, calling them hard workers for the Lord.

Issue: The work women do in the church is hard and important. What recurring ways are there of acknowledging and expressing appreciation for the work women do?

Tubal-cain *Person* Gen. 4:22

Tubal-cain was a man in primeval history whose name means "maker-smith." He introduced metal work and blacksmithing to civilization.

Issue: Genesis 4 introduces the basic elements of culture. In what way is cultural progress beneficial for us, and in what way is it harmful? Does our control and use of technology represent human progress or human venture and risk? What is the relationship between God and cultural progress?

Tychicus *Person* Acts 20:4; Eph. 6:21; Col. 4:7; 2 Tim. 4:12; Titus 3:12

Paul's trusted companion Tychicus hailed from the province of Asia. Paul promised the churches at Ephesus and Colosse that Tychicus would give them a full report of Paul's ministry, and Tychicus was probably responsible for delivering Paul's letters to those churches. Paul trusted him enough to promise to send him or Artemas to help Titus.

Issue: A good minister trains and trusts young ministers to broaden the elder worker's ministry. How many of Paul's young helpers can you name? Is your church working to train young people as ministers? Are you gradually giving each of the young ministers more responsibility and a broader arena of service?

Tyrannus, Hall of | *Thing* | Acts 19:8–9

Forced to abandon the Ephesian synagogue, Paul made arrangements to teach in the hall of Tyrannus, a school building. The building was named after its owner or a prominent teacher.

Issue: Education was important to Paul. He had received the best Jewish education possible and wanted his young ministers to be as well-trained as possible. He even rented a secular school to accommodate his students and expand their horizons. How important does your church hold the education of its members to be? How much of the Bible do they understand? How much of the Bible can they teach to others? In what areas do your members have the greatest need for training? How can you provide that for them?

Unforgivable Sin | *Thing* | Matt. 12:32; Mark 3:29; 12:10; Heb. 6:4–6; 1 John 5:16–17

The unforgivable sin involves refusal to confess that God is working in Jesus Christ and the attribution of the work of the Holy Spirit to combat demonic powers. Only people who have explicitly and conclusively refused to accept Jesus as their personal savior can commit such a sin.

Issue: Do you live with a quiet fear in the back of your mind that you have committed the unforgivable, unpardonable sin? People with hearts hardened enough to commit this sin will never worry about it. Can you find ways to assure people in your Bible study group that their life of faith shows they have not committed this horrid sin?

Ur | *Place* | Gen. 11:28, 31; 15:7; 1 Chron. 11:35; Neh. 9:7

The city Ur in which Abraham was born and from which Abraham's father set out for Canaan dates back to about 4500 BC. A major trade center, it lay on the southern Euphrates River with access to the Persian Gulf, 220 miles southeast of Baghdad. One of the richest and most powerful city-states, it produced the first law codes. Ultimately the invasion of semi-nomadic Amorites and the renewal of the Elamite Empire brought Ur down in about 2003 BC. Ur remained a center of worship for the moon god, but saw political and military power shift to the north.

Issue: Historical greatness and power eventually come to an end. Living on past accomplishments leads to devotion to scrapbooks without anything to accomplish today. Are you prone to let history boost your ego while tomorrow bids hopelessness and nothing to do? Will you, like Abraham and his family, reach out on new promises and go to new places where God leads?

Urbanus   *Person*   Rom. 16:9

Urbanus was a fellow Christian in Rome to whom Paul sent greetings as a co-worker in Christ.

Issue: Paul habitually sent greetings to people and affirmed them and the work they did in Christ's service. Do you have a note-writing ministry to affirm others? In what ways do you acknowledge and show appreciation for the work other members of your church and beyond are doing in the name of Jesus? Christianity is never a one-person show. We always have a team approach with large numbers of believers on the team. Find a way to show appreciation to some of your team members today.

Uriah   *Person*   2 Sam. 11:3–26; 12:9–10; 23:39; 1 Kings 15:5; 1 Chron. 11:41; Matt. 1:6

Uriah was an elite, loyal warrior in David's army. David deceived him and slept with his wife, Bathsheba, while Uriah was out in battle. David's cover-up plan eventually called for Uriah's death. Uriah remained steadfast to his military commitment to the day he died on the front line of battle.

Issue: Adultery and planned murder can never be justified, even by the most important person among God's people. What actions do you try to justify even when you know you are guilty? What have you done for which you need to ask forgiveness from God and from other people?

Urim and Thummim | *Things* | Ex. 28:30; Lev. 8:8; Num. 27:21; Deut. 33:8; 1 Sam. 14:41; 28:6; Ezra 2:63; Neh. 7:65

The Urim and Thummim were divining tools that God gave Israel, especially the priesthood, to determine God's will in a matter. They apparently operated like dice indicating a yes or no, this one or that one answer. Israel looked forward to the coming of a new priest who had Urim and Thummim.

Issue: What ways has God given us as believers in Christ to know His will in our lives? How often do you seek God's will for a matter or condition in your life? Do you truly expect to find an answer from God?

Uz | *Place* | Job 1:1

Uz was the home of Job in the east, probably in Edom.

Issue: Central issues come from Job. You can deal with several of them: Why does God allow the righteous to suffer? How much freedom does God give a person to express anger and frustration in language that might otherwise appear blasphemous?

Uzzah | *Person* | 2 Sam. 6:3

Uzzah was the driver in charge of the cart carrying the ark of the covenant back to Jerusalem for David. When the ark slipped, Uzzah reached out to steady the ark and was killed for touching the holy object.

Issue: What do you recognize and respect as holy, representing the holy presence of God? What lends holiness to your worship? What disturbs and evacuates holiness from your worship? How does your church teach its people to have holy reverence in God's presence?

Vashti *Person* Est. 1–2

Vashti was the wife of King Xerxes of Persia who refused his order to enter and show off her beauty to the gathering of Persian nobles. With advice from his officials, he put her to death, lest all women of the empire follow her example and have contempt for their husbands.

Issue: What rights do men and women share? What rights does each have personally? And what rights does one partner have in regards to the other? Should we condemn Vashti or praise her? In what ways are her views of the rights of women shared by the Bible as a whole? What evidence do you have to back your answer?

Widow of Zarephath *Person* 1 Kings 17

The widow of Zarephath was a poverty-stricken Phoenician who fed and housed Elijah during the drought he had predicted. He ensured that she did not run out of food and eventually restored her son to life.

Issue: The sovereign God shows His healing and death-defying power in the Hebrew Bible as well as in the life of Jesus and in the New Testament. We learn from the Hebrew Bible in its own context as well as in the New Testament context. How do you interpret the Hebrew Bible? Do you expect miracles like those of the Bible to happen in our day?

Wise Woman of Abel-Beth-Maacah *Person* 2 Sam. 20

The wise woman of Abel-Beth-Maacah prevented a war and a city's destruction by reasoning with Joab, David's commander.

Issue: Listening to the intent of the other may prevent fighting. Can you think of an example of this in your church? In what recent disagreement have you consciously stopped talking to listen to the other party's side?

Woman Anointing Jesus   *Person*   Matt. 26:6–13; Mark 14:3–9

This woman spent a great sum of money for ointment, which she poured over Jesus as one would pour perfume over a dead body to stop it from stinking, in direct opposition to the disciples. Jesus accepted the woman's insight and promised her act would always be part of the Christian proclamation.

Issue: Timing and perception are two important elements of the Christian life. A good act can be done at the wrong time in the wrong environment, while an extravagant act or "wrong" timing can be uniquely appropriate. Have you ever participated in or witnessed an act like the woman's, an act that seemed totally out of place but proved to be precisely appropriate?

Woman with Hemorrhage   *Person*   Matt. 9:20–22; Mark 5:24b–34; Luke 8:42b–48

The woman with a hemorrhage's story is told in the middle of the story of a synagogue leader seeking for Jesus to heal the leader's daughter before she dies. Jesus heals the woman who interrupts His journey and then goes to raise the daughter from death.

Issue: Jesus has power over all illnesses that plague humanity, yet He remains sovereign in the use of His power. He gives us no criteria to meet before He meets our needs. Can you relate narratives about God helping you in His way and at His chosen moment? What does this teach you about your relationship with God?

Xerxes   *Person*   Ezra 4:6; Esther

Xerxes was a Persian king (486–465 BC) who quit funding construction and maintenance of local temples. He centralized authority and suppressed revolts in Egypt and Babylon but lost battles in which he sought to master Greece. He was the king featured in the book of Esther. In 465 BC, he was assassinated.

Issue: Give your opinion of the character of Xerxes. Would you want him to control your country and master your army? Would you have joined the assassination plot?

YHWH (Yah[weh]) *God*

See Jehovah.

Zabad *Person* 2 Kings 12:21; 2 Chron. 24:26

See Jehozabad.

Zacchaeus *Person* Luke 19:2–9

Zacchaeus was a short, corrupt tax collector who climbed a tree to see Jesus. Jesus then invited the widely hated public official to eat with Him. Jesus led him to faith, which led Zacchaeus to promise to return the money he had taken to the people he had cheated.

Issue: Faith brings a complete change in a person so that a person of faith seeks to restore hurts caused previously. Has your faith led you to any type of drastic action taken with people you have previously hurt in any way?

Zaphenath-paneah *Person* Gen. 41:45

Zaphenath-paneah is the Egyptian name that Pharaoh gave to Joseph when elevating him to second in charge in the country.

Issue: Why do people change their names? In what way does a change of name signify an increase in responsibility and authority?

Zaphon *Place* Josh. 13:27; Judg. 12:1; Job 26:7; Isa. 14:13

Zaphon, a mountain whose name means "North," was regarded as the home of the Canaanite gods with Baal enthroned among the other gods.

Issue: The Bible allows only one God to have true existence. Others are powerless images with no power to respond to their people. Can you name any false gods worhipped knowingly or unknowingly in our culture?

Zelophehad	*Person*	Num. 26:33; 27:1, 7; 36:2, 6, 10–11; Josh. 17:3; 1 Chron. 7:15

Zelophehad was a father who wandered in the desert with Moses. He had seven daughters but no sons. Going against patriarchal premises, he gained permission for his daughters to have the portion of his inheritance that would have normally gone to a son.

Issue: Israel was not so patriarchic that no flexibility was allowed. This case shows the flexibility of applying Israel's law in specific cases. Have you ever benefited from a point of flexibility in our law? Did the case come out fair for all? Did you have to surrender any rights or privileges to make it fair for another party?

Zipporah	*Person*	

See Circumcision.

Zoar	*Place*	Gen. 13:10; 14:2, 8; 19:22–23, 30; Deut 34:3; Isa. 15:5; Jer. 48:34

Zoar, a place whose name means "small," was where Abraham won a battle. Lot fled there and then fled even higher into the mountain above. The mountain seems to have belonged to Moab.

Issue: God's people have to find ways to defend themselves from encroaching enemies. What happens to a nation that decides to boycott all war perpetually?

Zophar	*Person*	Job 2:11; 11:1; 20:1; 42:9

Zophar was one of Job's three friends who came to see him in the midst of his suffering. Zophar tried to convince Job to repent of some sin.

Issue: If you met Job in all his sorrow and self-pity, what would you have said? What did Job need?

Zorah *Place*   Josh. 15:33; 19:41; Judg. 13:2–25; 16:31; 18:2, 8, 11; 2 Chron. 11:10; Neh. 11:29

Zorah was Samson's birthplace, thirteen miles west of Jerusalem on the border of Dan and Judah. Samson, the judge, seems to have forgotten his obligations and fought all his battles individually without gathering an army of any kind.

Issue: How much of your work for the church becomes a solo effort with no one but you invited to participate? Do you see Samson obeying or disobeying God as he battles as an army of one with no army support?

INDEX

A

B

C

F

G

H

K

L

M

Q

R

S

T